Family Feuds

Family Feuds

*Wollstonecraft, Burke, and Rousseau
on the Transformation of the Family*

Eileen Hunt Botting

State University of New York Press

Published by
State University of New York Press, Albany

For information, address State University of New York Press,
194 Washington Avenue, Suite 305, Albany NY 12210-2384

Production by Kelli Williams
Marketing by Susan M. Petrie

Library of Congress Cataloging-in-Publication Data

Botting, Eileen Hunt, 1971–
  Family feuds : Wollstonecraft, Burke, and Rousseau on the transformation of the
family / Eileen Hunt Botting.
    p. cm.
  Includes bibliographical references and index.
  ISBN 0-7914-6705-8 (hardcover : alk. paper)
  1. Wollstonecraft, Mary, 1759–1797–Political and social views. 2. Rousseau,
Jean-Jacques, 1712–1778–Political and social views. 3. Burke, Edmund,
1729–1797–Political and social views. 4. Family–Philosophy. 5. Feminist
theory. I. Title.

HQ728.B718 2006
306.85'094'09033—dc22

                                                                          2005014026

                        10 9 8 7 6 5 4 3 2 1

Contents

Acknowledgments

Yale University and the University of Notre Dame have been my homes during the time I wrote this book, and I thank them for providing the financial support necessary to complete it. My advisor at Yale, Steven B. Smith, along with the other members of my dissertation committee, David Bromwich and Norma Thompson, offered excellent commentary on this book when it was a dissertation. Steven has been the most kind and generous mentor and has ensured my safe progress through the Ph.D. and beyond. Paul Franco, who introduced me to the study of political theory at Bowdoin College, has likewise been an invaluable source of guidance. Wendy Gunther-Canada and Elizabeth Wingrove—who graciously served, and identified themselves, as the external reviewers—supplied insightful advice for the revision and improvement of the manuscript, especially the comparative dimension of the analysis. Michael Rinella, the political science acquisitions editor at the State University of New York Press, has been tremendously professional and efficient throughout the review, revision, and publication process. I am indebted to Kelli Williams and Susan Petrie for their friendliness and attention to detail in the production and marketing of this book. For the cover art, the Beinecke Rare Book and Manuscript Library at Yale University gave me permission to use a digital copy of the 1761 engraving "*La force paternelle*" (Paternal force) from Rousseau's *Julie, or the New Heloise*. My research assistants Christine Carey, Sarah Houser, Jonathan MacFarlane, and Sarah Spengeman also deserve much credit for assisting me with various projects that enabled the completion of this book. An earlier version of chapter four of this book, "The Family as Cave, Platoon, and Prison: The Three Stages of Wollstonecraft's Philosophy of the Family," appeared in the Winter 2002 issue of *The Review of Politics*.

I thank Virginia Sapiro and the other, anonymous reviewers for their support for this article, and the *ROP* for permitting me to publish an expanded version here.

I am indebted to my graduate school colleague John Lee, who gave me the idea for the title *Family Feuds*. My friendships with Sarah Dembinski and her late son Tad and husband Jan gave me inspiration to complete my dissertation when I contemplated not finishing it. In addition, my friends and colleagues at Notre Dame, particularly those on the fourth floor of Decio Hall, have been invaluable allies in the process of seeing this book through to publication. A book about the family must begin with thanks for one's family—especially my parents, Patrick and Rose Ann, my late brother Kevin, my brother Daniel, my sister-in-law Melissa, and, most of all, my husband Victor, to whom this book is lovingly dedicated.

INTRODUCTION

This book is the first sustained comparative study of the place of the
family in the political thought of Jean-Jacques Rousseau, Edmund
Burke, and Mary Wollstonecraft. Wollstonecraft (1759–1797) desired
the transformation of the family into a new, more egalitarian form.[1]
Alongside her contemporaries Rousseau (1712–1778) and Burke
(1729–1797), Wollstonecraft understood that the egalitarian transformation of the family would represent a "revolution in female manners."[2]
While Rousseau and Burke feared the detrimental effects of such a social revolution, and the subsequent loss of the patriarchal family with
sex-role differentiation, Wollstonecraft hoped that the egalitarian transformation of the family would eliminate unjust hierarchies and abuses
of power between husbands and wives, parents and children, and brothers and sisters.[3] She believed that the republican political revolutions in
America in 1776 and France in 1789 would only be complete once a social revolution in the family spurred the development of a more egalitarian culture throughout society and government.

As a vastly influential political theorist whose ideas took on a life
of their own in the hands of his readers, Rousseau definitively shaped the
public discourse about the family that his fellow philosophers Burke and
Wollstonecraft later joined in full force. Although his novels *Julie, or the
New Heloise* (1761) and *Emile, or on Education* (1762) advanced a paradoxical ideal of the family that blended certain patriarchal and egalitarian practices, Rousseau helped advance the ideal of the egalitarian family
through the widespread reception and interpretation of his ideas on childhood education and the social empowerment of women through motherhood. Burke, as a Member of Parliament and the Whig Party in Great

1

Britain from 1765 to 1794 and a political theorist of immense fame in Europe and America, publicly challenged what he perceived as the subversion of the hierarchical structure of the family by condemning some of the attempted or successful reforms of laws restricting clandestine marriage and divorce in the late eighteenth century in England and France. Wollstonecraft recognized both Rousseau and Burke's leading stature in late eighteenth-century debates about the family, critically identified them as philosophical and political partners in the defense of the patriarchal structure of the family, and used the quasi-egalitarian import of Rousseau's theories of childhood education and maternal empowerment as a theoretical foundation for her own egalitarian vision of the family.

Some historians have contended that the European family evolved from a patriarchal to a more egalitarian form during the sixteenth, seventeenth, and eighteenth centuries, as a result of changes in the laws regulating marriage, divorce, and inheritance, changes in the practices of child rearing, childhood education, and the treatment of servants, and the emergence of new conceptions of the social and civic roles of women.[4] Other historians have argued that there is little evidence of the deterioration of the patriarchal structure of the family, or the genesis of a more egalitarian family form, during the sixteenth, seventeenth, and eighteenth centuries in Europe.[5] Despite their different conclusions, both of these schools of thought agree that the family never could be said to be fully worthy of the descriptive term "egalitarian"—in terms of its human relationships, its structures and divisions of labor, or its intersections with broader class-based, sex-based, and political hierarchies—at any point during the eighteenth century.

While the debate continues among social historians about the structure and experience of European family life during the Renaissance and the Enlightenment, there has been less scholarly attention to the ways the family was theoretically conceptualized in late eighteenth-century European political thought. Literary texts have traditionally garnered more attention than philosophical works on the question of the family in this era. For example, novels by writers such as Richardson, Rousseau, Sade, Laclos, Burney, Radcliffe, and Wollstonecraft have been mined by scholars for the literary imaginings of women, the family, and sexuality that were dominant at the time. While the works of Hobbes, Filmer, Locke, and Rousseau have been carefully analyzed for their defenses of patriarchalism in its various forms, historians of political thought have generally not delved as deeply into the systematic or comparative interpretation of some of the most important political and philosophical texts from the late Enlightenment concerned with defining the structure and the social and political function of the family.[6] Though it has been fruitfully studied for its relevance to modern debates about the origins of modern liberalism, the possibilities of democratic participation, and the legacy of empire and colonialism, late eighteenth-century European political thought is equally pivotal for an understanding of the evolution of the idea of the modern egalitarian family.[7] As the historical work of Linda Kerber (1980), Carol Blum (1986), Lynn Hunt (1992), and Joan Landes (1988, 2001) has shown, the examination of this time period helps scholars understand how the unfolding of new philosophical conceptions or artistic representations of womanhood and family life was integral to the psychological and political force of revolutionary republicanism in the United States and France, as well as the reactionary discourse against these political upheavals.[8] By looking back to the writings of Rousseau, Burke, and Wollstonecraft, we are reminded that, at the very least, the *idea* of the egalitarian family was passionately theorized and hotly criticized during the most volatile period of the Enlightenment.

Although Rousseau, Burke, and Wollstonecraft have been the subject of many magisterial studies of their general significance to modern moral and political thought, the place of the family within their political theories is a topic that has enjoyed less attention. There are some notable exceptions to this trend, however. Several scholars—Virginia Sapiro (1992), Gary Kelly (1992), David Bromwich (1995), Wendy Gunther-Canada (2001), and Barbara Taylor (2003)—have discussed Wollstonecraft's critiques of Burke and Rousseau, and have addressed her potent critique of their defenses of the patriarchal structure of the family.[9] A handful of eighteenth-century experts—James Boulton (1963), Steven Blakemore (1988), and Linda Zerilli (1994)—have studied Burke's use of the concept of the family, especially in familial metaphors, within the larger system of his political thought.[10] An even wider range of literary and political theorists—Jean Starobinski (1959), Judith Shklar (1969), Allan Bloom (1979), Susan Okin (1979), Joel Schwartz (1984), Penny Weiss (1993), Mira Morgenstern (1996), Nicole Fermon (1997), Lori Jo Marso (1999), and Elizabeth Wingrove (2000)—have provided vivid interpretations of the contested place of women, sexuality, and the family within Rousseau's corpus of literary and philosophical writings.[11]

Despite the abundance of quality scholarship on Rousseau, Burke, and Wollstonecraft, it is puzzling that there has not been an extended comparative study of the place of the family in their broader systems of political thought. This gap in the scholarship is more surprising when one considers the prominence of the family in their moral and political theories, the historical and philosophical significance of their views on the family, and their fascinating intellectual relationships with one another. Rousseau was the most significant theorist of the family in the eighteenth century, and both Burke and Wollstonecraft were readers and critics of each other's and Rousseau's views on women and the family.[12] While Wollstonecraft both critiqued and built upon their ideas, she surpasses her rivals in terms of the enduring relevance of her philosophy of the family. Through her critical engagement of Rousseau and Burke's philosophies of the family, Wollstonecraft shed the residual patriarchalism that infused much of eighteenth-century thinking on the family.[13]

Although none of them believed that the family had discarded its patriarchal structure during their time, Rousseau, Burke, and Wollstonecraft authored competing philosophical responses to what they perceived as a practical, ideological, and incomplete shift toward the future generation of a *more* egalitarian family form. All three political theorists identified and interpreted certain changes in the structure and practice of family life as signs that the family would become increasingly egalitarian. These signs included the movement of women from the domestic to the public realm, in intellectual salons, theatrical events, or political protests, the attempts to reform the laws regulating divorce and clandestine marriage in late eighteenth-century England, and the legalization of divorce for men and women in France in 1792.[14]

While they created theoretical models of the family that partly responded to the practice of family life during their time, Rousseau, Burke, and Wollstonecraft moved beyond the simple description of their historical milieu by offering normative and imaginative models of family life that aimed to influence the way in which people theoretically conceived and practically experienced the family, not only in their time, but in future generations. To accomplish this goal, they joined the public debate about the proper structure and functions of the family that gradually arose during the seventeenth and eighteenth centuries in Europe. A flurry of treatises on child rearing, early childhood education, the relationship between men and women, and the role of women and girls in the home appeared on the scene from the late seventeenth century onward. Wollstonecraft, Burke, and Rousseau read a number of these works, and were familiar with the terms they set for the Enlightenment's philosophical feud about whether, and, if so, how, the family should be transformed.[15] Some of these works—such as Chétardie's *Instruction pour une jeune princesse* (1685), Fleury's *Traité du choix et de la méthode des études* (1686), Fénelon's *Traité de l'éducation des filles* (1687), Bruyère's *Les Charactères* (1688), Halifax's *The Lady's New Year Gift* (1688), Crousaz's *Traité de l'éducation des ènfants* (1722), Gregory's *A Father's Legacy to his Daughters* (1774), Fordyce's *Sermons to Young Women* (1785), and More's *Strictures on the Modern System of Female Education* (1798)—took a more fearful view of the transformation of the family and childhood education, and sought to protect their patriarchal and hierarchical structure. Other works—such as Barre's *De l'egalité des deux sexes* (1673) and *De l'excellence des hommes* (1675), Lambert's *Avis d'une mère à sa fille* (1698), Locke's *Second Treatise of Government* (1690) and *Some Thoughts Concerning Education* (1693), Astell's *A Serious Proposal to the Ladies* (1701), Buffier's *Examen des préjugez vulgaires* (1704), Montesquieu's *Lettres Persanes* (1721), Sophia's *Woman Not Inferior to Man* (1739) and *Women's Superior Excellence to Man* (1740), Burgh's *The Dignity of Human Nature* (1767), Macaulay's *Letters on Education* (1790), and Gouges's *Declaration des droits de la femme et de la citoyenne* (1791)—explicitly or implicitly questioned the value of the hierarchical and patriarchal structure of the family and offered a more hopeful view of the possibility of the transformation of the family and childhood education toward a more egalitarian model.[16]

Rousseau, Burke, and Wollstonecraft loomed large in this philosophical feud about what the structure and function of the family ought to be. Rousseau's wildly popular philosophical novel about love, marriage, and family life, *Julie,* and his authoritative philosophical novel on childhood education, courtship, and marriage, *Emile,* established him as the pivotal player in the debates about the family during the Enlightenment. Many historians have recounted the tremendous impact that Rousseau's novels had in promoting the rise of the practice of maternal breast-feeding instead of hiring wet nurses, a new understanding of women's social and political empowerment through motherhood, a greater emphasis on the upbringing and health care of young children, and the production of the modern view of childhood as a distinct time of innocence and play.[17] The popularity and influence of these works meant that Rousseau even eclipsed Locke, whose *Some Thoughts Concerning Education* had inspired many of his own ideas, as the most famous Enlightenment theorist of childhood education, marriage, parenthood, and family life.

Rousseau pinpointed the family as the cause of much of the corruption of modern European civilization. Yet he also identified the family as the potential springboard for the positive moral, cultural, and political transformation of society and the state. While Rousseau desired the demise of the family in its late eighteenth-century aristocratic and bourgeois forms, he feared the destruction of the patriarchal structure of the family. Although the first half of his novel *Julie* criticized the hierarchies of the aristocratic class system and its invidious repercussions for genuine familial and romantic love, the latter half of the novel, along with his novel *Emile*, presented a model of the family that was still patriarchal and sex-roled. Rousseau believed that the family, by maintaining a patriarchal structure and sex-role differentiation, could partly protect itself against the corrosive cultural forces of modern life, and sublimate the inevitable sexual and competitive tension between men and women into the practice of the moral, social and civic virtues. As a consequence of his defense of the patriarchal family and sex-role differentiation, Rousseau issued scathing attacks of what he perceived as growing "mixed" social relations between men and women, especially in matters of courtship and women's activities in the public sphere, in works such as *Letter to the Republic of Geneva* (1755), *Letter to d'Alembert on the Theatre* (1758), as well as *Julie* and *Emile*.

Chapter one argues that Rousseau's paradoxical status as both a champion and a critic of the transformation of the family is reflected in his account of the proper relationship between the family and the state. When five key political works—the revolutionary trio of *Julie, Emile,* and *Of the Social Contract* (1762), and his unpublished, fragmentary yet tantalizing pieces *Emile and Sophie, or Solitary Beings* and *Constitutional Project for Corsica*—are interpreted as substantively interrelated and overlapping texts, they provide an overarching model of how the rural family serves as the moral foundation of Rousseau's ideal republic. Rousseau wanted the rural family to act as a "small fatherland" in which the natural affections between family members would inspire the practice of the *moeurs*, or moral codes, necessary for the smooth functioning of an authentic republic grounded on popular sovereignty.[18]

The private, agriculturally self-sufficient, and provincial space of the rural family, as well as its reliance on patriarchal, hierarchical, and sex-differentiated roles, make it a perfect place for the formation of the denizens and citizens of Rousseau's largely rural, ideal republic. Free from the sexual and cultural corruption that Rousseau castigated in the European cities of his time, the rural republican family can habituate and educate people to care not only for their families, but also to extend their sympathies outward toward the greater good of the republican community. The private will of the individual is not lost, as in the ancient republics of the past, but instead exists alongside the general will of the greater political community.

Rousseau, however, recognizes that the patriarchal, sex-roled structure of his ideal rural family stands in conflict with the nascent culture of modern "enlightened" civilization, and illustrates this fact with the tragic endings of *Julie* and *Emile and Sophie*. He also consistently addresses, throughout the *Social Contract* and *Corsica*, the geographic, demographic, cultural, and economic challenges to implementing his ideal of rural republicanism. Through an examination of the tension between theory and practice in his account of the proper relationship between the family and the state, Rousseau emerges not as a self-defeating utopian thinker, but rather as a political theorist who combined philosophical idealism with historical realism, and expounded his familial-political ideal, despite the practical obstacles he saw to its full realization, through the near simultaneous composition and publication of the momentous and controversial works *Julie*, *Emile*, and the *Social Contract.*

Like Rousseau, Burke feared the destruction of the patriarchal structure of the family. Both philosophers agreed that the loss of the patriarchal structure of the family would pose a threat to its primordial role as the inculcator of morality and manners. In his *Reflections on the Revolution in France* (1790), Burke coined the term "little platoon" to describe the small communities, such as the family, to which we belong in society: "To be attached to the subdivision, to love the little platoon we belong to in society, is the first principle (the germ as it were) of public affections. It is the first link in the series by which we proceed toward a love of our country and to mankind."[19] For Burke as well as Rousseau, the hierarchical, patriarchal family is the most important little platoon that kindles the social bonds of sympathy, civility, and patriotism. As Burke writes in the *Reflections*, "We begin our public affections in our families. No cold relation is a zealous citizen."[20] It is within the family that the natural affection for kin transforms into public affection for neighbors, fellow citizens, and the state itself.

Chapter two unfolds the previously unwritten story of Burke's fascination with the possibility of the transformation of the family during his public career as a statesman and political theorist. Throughout his speeches and writings on the politics of England, France, India, and his native Ireland, Burke revealed his deep-seated fear that the family would cease to serve as a little platoon once it lost its hierarchical structure because it would no longer reflect and reaffirm the natural order of the universe. For Burke, the hierarchical family is the foundation of society and the state insofar as its patriarchal and class hierarchies channel and direct the natural affections for kindred into the constitution of the stabilizing social bonds of sympathy, civility, and patriotism.

Chapter three presents a critical analysis of Burke's philosophical defense of the hierarchical, patriarchal family within the framework of his natural law principles and his aesthetic theory. Recent studies of Burke's political thought have emphasized how his theory of the "sublime," as set forth in his aesthetic treatise *A Philosophical Enquiry into the Origin of our Ideas of the Sublime and the Beautiful* (1757), animates much of his thinking on politics, especially his dark reflections on the cultural and political dangers of the revolution in France.[21] Moving beyond the recent focus on Burke's preoccupation with, and use of, the "sublime," or the awe-inspiring, in his political thought, this book aims to show how the "beautiful," or those qualities that attract us and inspire us to pursue domestic, social, and cooperative ends, is an equally important facet of his thinking on the aesthetic dimensions of social and political motivation and organization. Even though it is structured around a male patriarchal authority who has the capacity to command a kind of sublime respect from his wife and children, Burke's ideal of the family mainly belongs to the realm of the beautiful because it is the primary world of girls and women, and encourages the flourishing of a feminine space within society in which people (and men in particular) are drawn toward more sociable, peaceable pastimes and outlooks than the often sublime realms of civil society and the state allow. Wollstonecraft's protofeminist critique of the premises and conclusions of Burke's aesthetic theory, however, reveals the normative problems associated with his attempt to frame his defense of the patriarchal family and other social hierarchies within his feminized conception of the "beautiful"—especially in the wake of emerging egalitarian conceptions of women's capacities and rights to contribute to society beyond the family.

Rousseau's dominating stature in the eighteenth-century debates about the family compelled both Burke and Wollstonecraft to define their own distinct positions in contrast to their common predecessor.

Burke blamed Rousseau's novel *Julie* for the moral degeneration of French society from the level of the family to that of the state. Wollstonecraft condemned Rousseau's *Emile* for upholding a patriarchal ideal of feminine beauty and feminine manners that deteriorated the moral fiber of the family and society as a whole. Wollstonecraft largely devoted her two great treatises of political theory—*A Vindication of the Rights of Men* (1790) and *A Vindication of the Rights of Woman* (1792)—to an attack of Rousseau and Burke's views of the family, female education, and the aesthetics of feminine beauty. The publication of the *Rights of Woman* rendered her the most famous—and infamous—protofeminist of her time. Past scholarship has often underscored the contention between these three eighteenth-century political philosophers and upheld them as archenemies.[22] Yet the careful comparative study of the works of Rousseau, Burke, and Wollstonecraft reveals that they share more in common than any of them probably would have openly admitted, even if they had ever met or corresponded with one another.

All three political theorists share a similar view of the function of the family as the primary venue for the inculcation of moral, social, and political virtues. Yet Wollstonecraft vehemently disagrees with Rousseau and Burke's assertion that only a family with a patriarchal structure can fulfill this role. Wollstonecraft argues that the egalitarian family—marked by moral, social, and political equality between spouses and siblings and parental respect for the dignity of children—can more effectively serve as a foundation for a modern republican society and state than its predecessor. The egalitarian family alleviates the struggles for power that traditional hierarchies incite between relatives and classes; consequently, it allows for the proper fashioning of the social bonds of sympathy, civility, and patriotism.

Wollstonecraft advanced a number of practical proposals for the egalitarian transformation of the family. She advocated reform of the divorce laws in her native England, in order that women could enjoy the same right as men to leave an abusive or adulterous spouse. She proposed the abolition of primogeniture, so that family property would be more equitably distributed among sons and daughters. She defended a new understanding of child rearing, inspired largely by Rousseau's *Emile*, that promoted the practice of maternal breast-feeding and encouraged plenty of physical exercise for infants and young children. Extending Rousseau's educational philosophy for boys to both sexes, she sought to establish a system of national public coeducational day schools that would foster the moral, intellectual, and physical autonomy of girls and boys. She desired girls and boys to be treated the same in the classroom and on the playing fields, so that they would learn to see each other as equals, not only as students, but also as future partners in marriage, business, and politics.

Chapter four traces the changes in Wollstonecraft's theological views, and their impression on the evolution of her theory of the proper relationship between family, society, and government, through a close reading of her corpus of original writings. Contemporary secular feminist labels do not capture the complexity of Wollstonecraft's philosophy of the family, since various strands of Christianity deeply shaped the development of Wollstonecraft's protofeminism. While twentieth-century feminist scholarship tended to marginalize the significance of theology in Wollstonecraft's political thought, this book contributes to the budding interest in the religious dimensions of her life and writings led by the recent work of Barbara Taylor (2002, 2003).[23] Wollstonecraft was a traditional trinitarian Anglican in her early writings, a rationalistic unitarian Christian Dissenter in her middle writings, and a Romantic deist, skeptic, and possible atheist in her late writings. The early Wollstonecraft, beholden by a bleak, Anglican-Augustinian view of human nature, views the patriarchal family as a cave that traps humanity in a morass of corruption with no hope of escape except in the next life. The middle Wollstonecraft, infused with hope that the republican political goals of the French Revolution represent the culmination of God's rational plan for humankind, believes that the egalitarian transformation of the family will enable it to serve its function as a little platoon that instills the moral, social and political virtues in new generations of republican citizens. The late Wollstonecraft, chastened by her firsthand witness of the Terror in 1793 in Paris, loses faith in the efficacy of radical social and political reform as well as the rationality, benevolence, and very existence of God's providence, and fears that the patriarchal family is a prison from which women have little hope of escape, either in this life or through passage to the next. While losing hope in the power of radical politics or religious faith to transform or transcend the current, corrupt experience of family life, the late Wollstonecraft sustains some hope that successive generations of good parenting might open the prison of the patriarchal family in the future.

Chapter five challenges the prevailing notion—in part created by Burke and Wollstonecraft's fierce, yet often polemical, disparagement of each other and Rousseau—that the trio should be understood as philosophical adversaries with little or nothing in common. Instead, Rousseau, Burke, and Wollstonecraft's theories of the family can be seen as siblings who are similar yet often in conflict; any comparative analysis of their fascinating similarities entails contrast of their equally vital differences. By contrasting their views on the question of the proper structure of the family, this book casts new light on the unexpected, underlying similarities between their respective understandings of the moral, social, and political functions of the family. Rousseau, Burke, and Wollstonecraft each use their common conception of the family as the basis of affective-social formation to undergird their particular visions of the ideal state. All three were similarly concerned with how the family could serve as either a corrupting or a regenerative basis for the state, yet each theorized the family in the service of sustaining different political ends. Rousseau imagined the rural, patriarchal family as the fundamental forum for the moral formation, civic education, and political participation of the people of his ideal, legitimate, independent republic. Burke envisioned the hierarchical family as the first, close-knit social unit in which common trials test and shape the characters of its members, and prepare them for the legally defined rights and duties of subjecthood or citizenship within a stable state whose optimal regime type is determined by its particular culture and history. Wollstonecraft dreamed of an a new, egalitarian family whose recognition of the basic equality of the souls of its members would provide the moral and tutelary basis for a republican state in which the natural rights of all human beings, regardless of sex, race, or class, would be protected by law.

Wollstonecraft persuasively argues that Rousseau and Burke's patriarchal conceptions of the family hinder, rather than foster, the affections that inspire the social virtues, and that her model of the egalitarian family provides a more practical and ethical foundation for affective-social formation, especially in the rising democratic culture of the late Enlightenment. Wollstonecraft casts away the structure of the patriarchal family while retaining the philosophical core of Burke and Rousseau's view of the moral, social, and political function of the family. She transplants their vision of the family as a schoolhouse for the moral and civic virtues into an egalitarian framework that we have in large part inherited today. Wollstonecraft's political theory had a profound impact on the most prominent European and American women's rights advocates of the nineteenth and early twentieth centuries, whose arguments in turn have aided the gradual, and continuing, political incorporation of women into democracies worldwide.[24] Wollstonecraft's ideal of the egalitarian family as the moral foundation of the democratic state has proven to be one of the most important, yet least appreciated, legacies of the Enlightenment for the theory and practice of liberal democracy.

Armed with their shared view of the family's primary role in moral, social, and political conditioning, Rousseau, Burke, and Wollstonecraft took a radical stand against the Hobbesian rationalism and individualism that gained philosophical currency over the course of the Enlightenment. Each of these political theorists recognized that affection for other people motivates human beings at least as much as—and sometimes more than—self-interest or self-preservation. They also argued that the stability, independence, and ethical quality of any political society depended on the cultivation and direction of the affections toward the social formation of future subjects or citizens. By examining Rousseau, Burke, and Wollstonecraft through a comparative lens, we can better understand the way that their writings complicate and deepen our understanding of the Enlightenment. Often individually lauded as a "father" or a "mother" of Romanticism, Rousseau, Burke, and Wollstonecraft can also be conceived as political theorists commonly engaged in immanent critiques of certain aspects of the Enlightenment, who nonetheless contribute to the development of a complex and compelling dimension of Enlightenment moral and political thought in the late eighteenth century. Attentive to the politics of particularity—or how familial bonds and affections, geographical spaces and places, and cultures and histories shape our individual and collective identities—all three thinkers complicate the much decried "universalism" of the so-called age of reason, and reveal what Sankar Muthu (2003) has celebrated as the "plurality" of Enlightenment modes of thought.[25] Rousseau denounced the ostensible "progress" of the arts and sciences, but he also stands as the architect of the purest philosophical model of popular sovereignty in the Enlightenment. Burke assailed the theorists and leaders of the French Revolution, but he was also respected by many of the radicals of his time as one of the most powerful critics of economic exploitation and political tyranny around the globe, especially in the colonies of the British Empire. Wollstonecraft used theological arguments to condemn the patriarchalism of the most prominent thinkers of her age, but she also understood herself as broadening the arguments of Locke and Rousseau to create a more egalitarian republicanism for the modern world. Neither entirely anti-Enlightenment, nor wholesale defenders of their supposed "age of light," Rousseau, Burke, and Wollstonecraft each contribute in their own way to a rich, multitoned blending of the concerns of morality and politics, reason and faith, universality and particularity, nature and culture, and autonomy and community in late eighteenth-century political thought. A comparative look at their respective familial-political ideals offers us the opportunity to reassess the meaning of the Enlightenment, then and now.

A Postscript about Interpretation

The intricacy of Rousseau, Burke, and Wollstonecraft's writings and their relationship to one another's thought demands a kind of fluidity in interpretive approach. To attend to the broad range of moral and political concerns, rhetorical styles, and genres found across their works, the integration of philosophical, theological, historical, literary, normative, and feminist analysis seems desirable, if not necessary. Sensitive to text and context, *Family Feuds* aims to bridge a number of interpretive standpoints and methods to provide an in-depth, yet accessible, comparative study of Rousseau, Burke, and Wollstonecraft's conceptions of the family as the emotional and ethical core of politics and their enduring relevance to modernity.

1

ROUSSEAU

Champion and Critic of the
Transformation of the Family

Two Paradoxes in Rousseau's
Philosophy of the Family

Both Burke and Wollstonecraft remarked on the paradoxical character of Rousseau's thought and its power to amuse, captivate, and even corrupt its audience. In 1787, Wollstonecraft read Rousseau with such avid pleasure that she exclaimed in a letter to her sister Everina that she was "now reading Rousseau's *Emile*, and love his paradoxes."[1] Later, she confessed to Gilbert Imlay that she had always been "half in love" with Rousseau, despite her vehement disagreement with his patriarchal principles concerning sex roles.[2] While admitting that Rousseau is "sometimes moral, and moral in a very sublime strain," Burke warned that one should not be "more than transiently amused with (Rousseau's) paradoxical morality" because "the *general spirit and tendency* of his works is mischievous; and the more mischievous for this mixture." Burke concluded that Rousseau, and his followers, "make even virtue a pander to vice" with their impish manipulation of paradox to convolute our received understandings of morality.[3]

That both Burke and Wollstonecraft responded to Rousseau's use of paradox with paradoxical declarations of their simultaneous attraction to, and revulsion from, his writings and their power to alter the minds and characters of his readers is in itself a tribute to the "method" in his rhetorical "madness." To the present day, readers of Rousseau have continued to acknowledge the way that he used paradox to cleverly, and seductively, advance his arguments. As commentators as divergent as Mira Morgenstern (1996) and Arthur Melzer (1990) note, Rousseau uses paradox to advance seemingly contradictory proposals or viewpoints both within and across texts that he then reveals to be more apparent than real, either through a gradual series of qualifications to his initial, often extreme and conflicting statements, or by indicating the substantive overlap between his ostensibly disconnected pieces of writing.[4] This method of argument renders Rousseau notoriously difficult to interpret, but it also makes him one of the most playful thinkers—in both the creative and the destructive sense—in the Western tradition. Rousseau uses paradox to build competing cases, tear them down, and then lead the reader, through the rubble as it were, to an entirely unexpected conclusion.

Rousseau's philosophy of the family, the place of women and men within it, and its relationship to the state, are some of the most notoriously paradoxical aspects of his social and political thought, and have yielded some equally famous criticisms of his work. Burke wryly noted that the "fate" of Rousseau's "paradoxes" concerning the family and the state was self-destruction: although Burke partly blamed Rousseau's novel *Julie* and its celebration of romantic love outside marriage for the familial and social upheaval that propelled France into its revolution in 1789, he also pointed out that such "philosophic gallantry" could not provide a stable foundation for the new republic and family forms that it had helped usher into existence.[5] Wollstonecraft forcefully argued that Rousseau often let "truth" give way "to a favorite paradox," as when he defended the "absurdity" that female infants and toddlers were naturally predisposed to certain supposedly feminine traits such as vanity and coquetry "even before an improper education" deformed their characters and limited their potential contributions to the family, society, and the state at large.[6]

In this way, Burke highlighted the apparent tension between Rousseau's theory of the family and his theory of republican government, and Wollstonecraft indicated the problematic, differential treatment of girls and women in his broader, and seemingly enlightened and egalitarian, educational and political philosophy. Two central paradoxes in Rousseau's philosophy of the family and the state, which echo Burke and Wollstonecraft's critical concerns, continue to puzzle his readers to the present day. First, why does Rousseau defend an ideal of the family in works such as *Julie* and *Emile* that seems to stand at the margins of political society, while he constructs a robust theory of popular sovereignty in his vision of the ideal modern republic in the *Social Contract*? Second, why does Rousseau advocate certain dramatic changes in the practice of family life, especially regarding children's health and education and women's understanding of their social and political influence, while he fears other changes in family life that might threaten the maintenance of its sex roles and its patriarchal structure?

Rousseau's Philosophical Puzzle

The answer to these questions lies in the systematic interpretation of Rousseau's major political works that were published or composed between 1755 and 1765.[7] The *Discourse on the Origin of Inequality*, the *Letter to the Republic of Geneva*, the *Discourse on Political Economy*, the *Letter to d'Alembert on the Theatre*, *Julie*, *Emile*, the *Social Contract*, the unpublished and fragmentary sequel to *Emile*, *Emile and Sophie, or Solitary Beings*, and the unpublished and incomplete *Constitutional Project for Corsica* should be seen as interlocking pieces of a philosophical puzzle.[8] During the composition of these substantively overlapping works, Rousseau struggled most directly with the problem of what the proper relationship between the family and the state should be. A brief look at the context of the composition of these works sets the stage for understanding their philosophical interconnection.

In 1755, Rousseau published his most philosophically important work to date, the *Discourse on the Origin of Inequality*, which came to be known as the *Second Discourse*. He inserted the *Letter to the Republic of Geneva* at the beginning of it, as a kind of preface to the longer treatise. The same year, he published his *Discourse on Political Economy* in Diderot's *Encyclopedia*; it was one of his last acts of cooperation with the Parisian *philosophes*—led by Voltaire—who mocked the apparent "primitivism" of his *Second Discourse* as a rejection of their more "enlightened" conception of civilization and its progress. Partly in response to his estrangement from the *philosophes*, Rousseau composed and published *Julie*, *Emile* and the *Social Contract* almost simultaneously during his retreat from Parisian city life at the Hermitage, in the woods of Montmorency, France, between 1756 and 1762.[9] In the midst of the runaway popular success of his romantic novel *Julie* across mainland Europe and Great Britain, Rousseau was faced with the "banning or confiscation" of *Emile* and the *Social Contract* in Paris, the burning of these works in his native Geneva, and the beginning of nearly two decades of both state-sanctioned and self-imposed exile, in which he ran from enemies who

were both real and imagined.[10] In this personal and political crucible of
1762–1763, Rousseau composed *Emile and Sophie*; he considered it one
of his favorite writings and retrieved it from his publisher in 1768 to continue work on it, although he neither finished the fragment nor returned
it for publication.[11] Through its tragic yet realistic account of the dissolution of its protagonists' marriage and family life, the fragment answers
many questions left untouched at the end of *Emile*, and renders the tale
of Emile and Sophie parallel to its companion love stories, the ill-fated
romance of Julie and St. Preux, and the less than perfect marriage of
Julie and Wolmar. In the midst of his enduring persecution for his writings, and at the behest of a Corsican soldier, Rousseau began to compose
the *Constitutional Project for Corsica* in 1765 to advise this nation on
how to implement his theory of republicanism, yet he ultimately abandoned the project as a result of the failure of the island's republican revolution, and his own itinerant life in exile.[12]

The four major political works published between 1755 and 1758—
the *Letter to the Republic of Geneva*, the *Second Discourse*, the *Discourse
on Political Economy*, and *Letter to d'Alembert*—together function as a
kind of prolegomena that provides the philosophical foundation for the
five major political works published or composed between 1761 and
1765, *Julie*, *Emile*, the *Social Contract*, *Emile and Sophie*, and *Corsica*.
The latter five works contain three tales—the tragic romance of Julie and
her circle of lovers, family, and friends in the rural Vaud region of Switzerland during the 1730s and 1740s, the story of the education, courtship,
marriage, and eventual separation of Emile and Sophie in mid-eighteenth
century provincial France and urban Paris, and a philosophical and pragmatic account of how a republic, or a legitimate state founded on the
sovereignty of the people, might come into existence in the modern
world—that might at first seem unrelated, but at closer examination can
be read as a philosophical trilogy. *Julie* ends with a reference to the educational philosophy of *Emile*, and *Emile* ends with a reference to the political philosophy of the *Social Contract*. *Emile and Sophie* likewise
begins where *Emile* ended, with a discussion of the marriage of its protagonists.[13] The *Social Contract*, in turn, establishes Rousseau's theory of
republicanism and provocatively names Corsica as the nation in mid-eighteenth century Europe best suited for its implementation, paving the way
for his actual constitutional proposal for this country. Structurally, these
works line up like links in a chain: *Julie* leads to *Emile*, *Emile* leads both
to the *Social Contract* and *Emile and Sophie*, and the *Social Contract*
leads to *Corsica*.

The First Paradox

The first aforementioned paradox reveals itself most prominently in his major political works from the early 1760s. Rousseau seems to construct ideal families, in *Julie* and *Emile*, which conspicuously occupy a place on the margins of society, in the rural countryside, far from the corruption of cities and seemingly dislocated from the business of politics. In *Emile and Sophie*, he appears to reinforce the incompatibility of his ideal family with city life by showing the destruction of Emile and Sophie's marriage and family when they move from the isolation of the country to the urban environs of Paris. On the other hand, Rousseau constructs an ideal republic in the *Social Contract* that carves a space for political activity that seems distant from, and even opposed to, the demands of the family, requires direct political participation on the part of the (adult male) citizens, who serve as legislators in the state's popular assembly and as members of the state's militia rather than relying on the services of legislative representatives and a standing army, and keeps women and children at home, in roles different from the adult male world of formal citizenship. In response to the apparent conflict between these texts, scholars have either argued that Rousseau believed the family and the state had irreconcilable purposes, or that his theory of the relationship between the family and the state is internally inconsistent.

In the first school of interpretation, Judith Shklar (1969) argues that there is an irreconcilable opposition between Rousseau's utopian ideal of the family and his utopian ideal of the republican state, and Allan Bloom (1979) and Arthur Melzer (1990) suggest that Rousseau's ideal of the family is meant to be a moral retreat from the corruption of modern governments that probably never will put his republican theory into practice.[14] In the second school of interpretation, critics such as Susan Okin (1979) and Carole Pateman (1988, 1989) argue that Rousseau's defense of the patriarchal family and women's exclusion from formal citizenship contradicts the remainder of his egalitarian political theory, especially as found in the *Social Contract*'s theory of popular sovereignty.[15]

Scholarship by Joel Schwartz (1984), Penny Weiss (1993), Mira Morgenstern (1996), Nicole Fermon (1997), Lori Jo Marso (1999), and Elizabeth Rose Wingrove (2000) has sought to close the divide that many interpreters have drawn between the family and the state in Rousseau's political theory.[16] Schwartz and Weiss each argue, in distinctive ways, that Rousseau's theory of the family is not inconsistent with, or opposed to, his theory of the state; rather, the family plays an important tutelary role in the formation of good (male) citizens insofar as women, the empresses of the domestic realm, teach men how to channel their selfish (and often sexual) passions toward the service of the common good.[17] Fermon builds on this view, and adds that Rousseau envisions his ideal of a rural, self-sufficient agricultural family as the basis of his vision of the ideal republican state. Wingrove emphasizes, on the other hand, how culturally constructed rituals or "performances" of sexuality and its dynamic of domination and submission serve to reinforce the paradoxical relationship between citizen and subject, ruler and ruled in Rousseau's ideal republic. In yet another line of argument, Morgenstern and Marso argue that, for Rousseau, the family, and especially the "subversive" women within it, should ideally be the agents for the transformation of society and politics into arenas for the realization of human authenticity, or at least reveal a path toward this goal.

Continuing in this vein, I argue that Rousseau understands his theory of the ideal family and his theory of the ideal state to be interrelated, not discontinuous. Yet this chapter places special emphasis on the significance of the textual and philosophical intersections between *Julie*, *Emile*, the *Social Contract*, *Emile and Sophie*, and *Corsica* for Rousseau's theory of the relationship between the rural family and the republican state, a topic neglected by previous scholars.[18] When they are interpreted as substantively interrelated and overlapping texts, these five works provide an overarching model of how the rural family (if properly ordered) serves as the first and fundamental venue for moral, social, and political formation—the most open, expansive, and even vital kind of political participation for the vast majority of the people—within Rousseau's ideal republic. Nevertheless, these works together contribute to the realistic concession that this ideal is difficult to implement and maintain.

Rural Republicanism

I use the term "rural republicanism" to capture the underlying synthesis between Rousseau's ideals of the rural family and the republican state. The term is broad enough to signify the complex, and interdependent, bundle of geographic, demographic, economic, structural, and cultural qualities that Rousseau understands as constitutive of his ideal state and the predominantly non-urban, agricultural or fishing families that would compose it at the grassroots level. Building on the theories set forth in the *Social Contract*, Rousseau himself used the term "rural system" (*le système rustique*) to describe the optimal set of features for founding an independent democratic republic on the island of Corsica.[19] Thus, although Rousseau himself did not use the term "rural republicanism" to describe his theory of the proper relationship between the rural family and the republican state, it clearly resonates with his own philosophical vocabulary, and conveys the important connection between rural ways of life and republicanism in his political thought.

In the *Social Contract*, Rousseau argues that only a state with a specific set of rural characteristics can possess, practice, and preserve a legitimate, or republican, government in the modern world.[20] By a state with a legitimate or republican government he means a state founded on a sovereign popular legislative assembly that then establishes by law a particular form of government (monarchical, aristocratic, democratic, or mixed) that consists of magistrates drawn from the body of the people who, in this role, can only administer and propose, but not make, the laws. The adult men of his ideal republic would be both citizens (lawmakers) and subjects (law-abiders), and thus practitioners of an authentic form of political self-governance, which stands in stark contrast to the mere subjecthood of the people who inhabit the illegitimate states of Europe.

After dramatically redefining the meaning, and relationship between, popular sovereignty and government, and subjecthood and citizenship, for his ideal of modern republicanism, Rousseau cites Corsica as the "one country left in Europe" capable of receiving the "legislation" necessary to build a state with a legitimate government.[21] While some readers have simply taken this suggestion as preposterous, and evidence of Rousseau's self-defeating utopianism, the surprising example of the small island of Corsica is better understood as Rousseau's attempt to jolt his readers into concretizing the lofty theory of popular sovereignty outlined in Book I of the *Social Contract*, and push them into consideration of the harder, pragmatic question of how and where his theory might be put into practice. Moreover, it is important to note that Rousseau only says that Corsica, at the time he is writing, is the last candidate "in Europe" for the legislation necessary for authentic republicanism, not that late eighteenth-century Corsica is the only nation in the world suited for legitimate government. He never excludes the possibility that other candidates might exist in other parts of the world or might emerge in the future in Europe or elsewhere. Indeed, the bulk of the *Social Contract* (Books II, III, and IV) is devoted to outlining the particular geographic, demographic, economic, structural, and cultural qualities that are necessary for establishing and executing an enduring republic. Rousseau's consistent attention to the question of how to implement his "rural system" (as in his 1765 *Constitutional Project for Corsica*) makes clear that he believes that his ideal state is worthy, and capable, of establishment—but only in extremely limited, and difficult to secure, circumstances.

As for the best possible geographic locations for his ideal state, Rousseau outlines two possibilities: on a remote, protected shoreline, or on a mountainous territory with "rich plains and fertile slopes."[22] In either of these locations, his ideal state would have a population that is neither too small nor too large to support an economically self-sufficient society, proportional to the available land, and evenly distributed as much as possible through villages and towns, rather than condensed in urban areas. On a remote and protected shoreline, his ideal state would have a self-sufficient fishing economy without the need, temptation, or ambition to engage in international commerce on the seas. In a mountainous territory, his ideal state would have a self-sufficient agricultural economy based on the cultivation of its limited fertile land and the gathering of the "natural produce" of its woods and pastures; it, too, would avoid unnecessary international commercial activity that would bring corrosive luxuries into its small communities and families.[23] Out of these two possibilities, Rousseau leans toward the mountainous state as more preferable. He worries that a fishing community would eventually veer toward the corruption of a naval empire. Even in the case of the island of Corsica, he proposes that it develop a self-sufficient agricultural economy, rather than depend on commerce via the sea.[24]

Building on the philosophy of history contained in the *Second Discourse*, Rousseau consistently steers a course between the extremes of savagery and civilization in his portraits of the ideal state and the families that should compose it. He neither wants to settle for the survivalist stance of the savage, nor accept the decadent luxury of the bourgeois. Instead, he supports a moderate form of human society, which is close to nature yet not subjugated by it, and community-oriented yet not enslaved to the trappings of the arts, sciences, and unnecessary commerce. Rural mountainous peoples enjoy the conditions best suited for this moderate form of human society. In the *Social Contract*, he advises mountainous peoples to build on their strengths to preserve their happy and virtuous way of life: "Devote all your efforts to agriculture, which increases the population, and drive out the arts which would only depopulate the country completely by concentrating in just a few points of its territory the few inhabitants it does have."[25] It is in such mountainous regions—like the Alps in his homeland of Switzerland—that Rousseau believes the circumstances are most ripe for implementing his theory of rural republicanism, but not without a set of obstacles to achieving this end. As he acknowledges in the *Social Contract*, "It is true that it is difficult to find all of these conditions together. This is one reason why one sees so few well-constituted States."[26] Furthermore, at the end of *Corsica*, Rousseau admits that a healthy, rural state will eventually destroy itself through an overgrowth of its population: "When a country becomes overpopulated, it will be necessary to employ the excess population in industry and the arts in order to draw from abroad those things that so numerous a people requires for its subsistence. Then, little by little, the vices inseparable from these establishments will also arise and, gradually corrupting the nation in its tastes and principles, will alter and at last destroy the government."[27] Ironically, the measure of a state's well-being—its population—is ultimately the cause of its demise. Once a republic loses its rural character, it loses everything.

For these reasons, Rousseau's ideal republican state is best understood as a "rural republic" that may contain a relatively small city or a geographically dispersed set of small cities like his home, the republican city-state of Geneva, or Corsica's centrally located, austere, and mountainous Corte, but should mainly, or entirely, consist of small, rural villages and towns like the ones found in the Valais and Vaud regions of Switzerland that he celebrates on the pages of *Julie*.[28] There will be many families who occupy the rural villages at the geographic margins of Rousseau's ideal political society, yet fulfill the most central social and political role. Rousseau's fundamental distinction between the functions of the sovereign popular assembly of adult male citizens and the elected or lawfully appointed magistrates of the government enables social and political formation within the family to be understood as the first and fundamental form of political participation. The sovereign assembly will meet infrequently to make political, civil, and criminal law if *moeurs* or moral codes—the most important form of law that is fostered largely by the family—are strong. In the meantime, the elected or lawfully appointed magistrates who constitute the government will do the daily business of administering the extant laws, leaving the door open for the remainder of the people to focus on the governance of their families and the inculcation of *moeurs* within them. Since the necessity of law-making by the assembly is rare if the nation's *moeurs* are healthy and robust, since the magistrates orchestrate the daily governance of the republic, and since women and children do not engage in the activities of formal citizenship and government administration, everyday political participation for the majority of the population does not revolve around administering or making the law. The rural family, and the roles that men, women, and children play within it, offer a fresh avenue for political participation in Rousseau's new vision of republicanism. Rousseau imagines his ideal, rural, agricultural family as the primary training-ground for the development and practice of the moral codes, and the attendant moral, social, and civic virtues, necessary for the smooth and stable operation of his ideal, independent, rural republic.

The male heads of these rural families, though citizen-legislators and members of the militia, may not be intimately involved in the daily administration of the republic like their magistrates, but they play a vital political role as the leaders of the "small fatherlands," or families, that cultivate the moral, social, and civic virtues in new generations of citizens.[29] The wives and mothers who govern the daily activities of the rural household, and take primary responsibility for the upbringing and education of the children, do not participate in the politics of the republic through membership in the legislative assembly or the militia, but they likewise play a vital political role through the cultivation and preservation of the moral, social, and civic virtues of both their husbands and the next generation.

While he pragmatically concedes that urban families may exist in a republic with a small capital city, or a dispersed set of small cities, Rousseau prefers republics primarily or exclusively populated by rural families. Rural families are ultimately more apt than urban families at the moral education of republican citizens because they stand apart from the artistic, commercial, and industrial excesses of civilization. Moreover, these rural family havens better preserve their moral purity through their distance from the unnatural diversions of city life, such as the theaters, salons, and other mixed social gatherings (and opportunities for adultery) that Rousseau denounces in *Julie* and *Emile and Sophie*, as well as in his earlier works *Letter to the Republic of Geneva* and *Letter to d'Alembert*. The vigor of Rousseau's ideal republic depends largely on the warmth, strength, and vitality of rural families that respect the power of nature, yet achieve a modest form of economic and social independence amid it. Urban families, on the other hand, are more prone to corruption and thus are potentially detrimental to the health of the state if they are not properly structured.

Rousseau argues that his ideal republican family, both rural and urban, must imitate its ancient models in Sparta and Rome with a patriarchal structure and a strict system of sex-role differentiation. By maintaining a division between the social roles of men and women as much as possible, the urban republican family can withstand the vices endemic to city life—such as the sexual corruption and competition fostered by social gatherings attended by both sexes—that the rural family largely sidesteps as a result of its countryside isolation. Yet the rural republican family must also be vigilant in its maintenance of a patriarchal structure and sex-role differentiation because moral corruption and conflict between the sexes are not endemic to cities alone for Rousseau, but to all human communities, no matter how big or small, since our collective fall from grace when humanity passed into civilization.

The Second Paradox

The problem of moral corrosion and sexual corruption within marriage and the family, and his attempt to address it through the defense of a strict, patriarchal system of sex-role differentiation for urban and rural families alike, points to the second paradox of Rousseau's philosophy of the family. Why is Rousseau a defender of a sex-roled, patriarchal structure for the family, yet an advocate for dramatic changes in family life that empowered women and children within it? The explanation for this apparent contradiction lies in the assessment of the pivotal intersections between theory and practice in Rousseau's writings on the family. Rousseau defined his ideal of the republican family in critical dialogue with the bourgeois and aristocratic families of his time, and actually changed the way the family was conceived and practiced through the publication of his influential books *Emile* and *Julie*.

Rousseau's contemporaries, including Burke and Wollstonecraft, recognized him as the most creative and provocative theorist of the family and its role in moral and political life. Rousseau's *Julie* and *Emile* are philosophical treatises on family organization and childhood education as much as they are novels. These works exercised incalculable influence on both the theory and the practice of family life in the eighteenth century. Historians generally acknowledge that Rousseau's ideas inspired, throughout Europe and America from the late eighteenth century onward, the spread of breast-feeding among mothers, the valorization of mothers as the educators of citizens, the increased attention to the health, exercise, and early education of children, and the rise of the ideal of childhood as a precious time of freedom, innocence, and play that paved the way for the development of independent yet virtuous adults.[30]

Both a visionary and a traditionalist, Rousseau was highly critical of a number of other changes he perceived in family life during his time. From early on in his writing career, Rousseau expressed fear about the destruction of the patriarchal, sex-roled structure of the family in his homeland, Geneva. Rousseau believed that the husband ought to be the legally and socially recognized head of the family, as was general practice at the time. He moreover affirmed that men, not women, should be citizens. Like his philosophical predecessor John Locke, however, Rousseau questioned the validity of Robert Filmer's defense of patriarchy and argued that a husband should not exercise tyrannical force over his wife or children.[31] Although he viewed absolute patriarchal power as illegitimate, Rousseau still argued that the family should practice a system of sex-role differentiation, so that males and females engaged in distinct occupations based on the socially useful and stabilizing qualities and abilities of their respective sexes. He contended that men should bridge the realms of family, civil society and the state, while women should remain within the bounds of the family as much as possible, where they enjoyed a distinct form of power as the "empresses" of the domestic realm.[32]

Rousseau's ideal of the republican family defined itself against the bourgeois and aristocratic families of the time, especially with regard to women's role in the moral and civic education of children.[33] Rousseau desired the destruction of the family in its late eighteenth-century aristocratic and bourgeois forms, since they promoted devotion to self-interest rather than the common good. The aristocratic family pitted its members against one another in a selfish quest to acquire a piece of the family estate, and, to this end, often sacrificed its daughters on the altar of arranged marriage. Rather than offering a sound alternative to the aristocratic family, the bourgeois family enslaved its members to domestic materialism and consumer culture and blinded them to the duties of politics. In contrast to these existing historical models, Rousseau wanted the family to serve as a kind of schoolhouse for virtuous men and women who would be willing to sacrifice their own interests for the sake of the good of the whole community. Rousseau promoted an alternative vision of family life that served as the moral and social basis of his new vision of republican politics. For Rousseau, the family is the educational space that turns selfish children into virtuous male citizens and female educators of citizens. According to Rousseau, love of family is the first step toward the transcendence of self-love and the realization of love of neighbor, fellow citizen, and the republic itself, for men and women alike.

Following the lead of Wollstonecraft, contemporary feminist critics such as Susan Okin (1979) and Carole Pateman (1988) have argued that Rousseau's view of the proper social roles of women contradicts the remainder of his egalitarian political theory, especially as found in the *Social Contract*'s conception of popular sovereignty.[34] Rousseau's defense of the patriarchal, sex-roled family is certainly not consistent with the egalitarian goals of modern democracy that emerged as a result of the American and French Revolutions. Yet it is important to understand Rousseau's apology for the patriarchal, sex-roled family within the philosophical framework of his own unique philosophy of history contained in the *Second Discourse*.[35] Perhaps his most important premise is the human propensity toward competition and conflict (especially between the sexes and for the attention of the opposite sex) once they have passed from the state of nature into civilization. Rousseau argues that human beings, once they enter society, are pitted against one another in a competition for the attention of the opposite sex, or in a selfish quest to control their love interests once they capture them. He concludes that the resultant battle of the sexes—in which women, due to their insatiable sexuality, have the upper hand—can only be pacified by the maintenance of a patriarchal, sex-roled structure for the family and society at large. Rousseau's philosophical premises in the *Second Discourse* are subject to all kinds of criticism, moral and empirical, but they nonetheless serve as the foundation of his logically consistent (though morally and politically questionable) theoretical defense of a family with sex-role differentiation and a patriarchal structure. Like Wollstonecraft and her students, I question the validity of Rousseau's loaded assumption that a transition from a state of nature to human society has rendered a war between the sexes an inevitable part of human experience that can only be tempered by the maintenance of patriarchy and sex-role differentiation. This chapter's main task, however, is to provide an accurate reading of Rousseau's own understanding of the ideal relationship between the family and the republican state, which lays the foundation for the comparative study of his thought with Burke and Wollstonecraft, and the normative assessment of the value of his theories in the light of their perceptive criticisms of him.

Theory and Practice

The tragic outcomes of the love stories of *Julie* and *Emile and Sophie,* and the realistic concession of the difficulty of establishing and preserving rural republicanism found in the *Social Contract* and *Corsica,* reveal Rousseau's preoccupation with the severe difficulty of putting his ideal family and state into proper practice. He is especially concerned with the corruption of the rural family, the moral foundation of his ideal state, due to its fundamental incompatibility with, and exposure to, the burgeoning culture of the Enlightenment, or the eventual inevitability of population overgrowth and the rise of a wealthy, landowning class. In *Letter to the Republic of Geneva*, *Letter to d'Alembert*, *Julie*, and *Corsica*, he laments that the Swiss family, in both its rural and urban forms, is crumbling—or may have already been irretrievably corrupted—under the pressure of modernization. He dreads that sex-role differentiation, the purifying influence of the wilderness, the civilizing force of feminine manners, the ancient moral virtues of rural family and community life, and the respect for certain beneficial social hierarchies tempered by a belief in fundamental human equality, all face certain extinction in the face of the march of Western technology, commerce, industry, art, science, and philosophy. Rousseau fears that the families of the rural Swiss countryside, and the urban families of the republic of Geneva, will share the same fate as their classical republican counterparts in ancient Sparta and republican Rome, whose downfall he mourns as well. Yet Rousseau is not a "utopian" thinker, as Shklar (1969) claimed, who creates familial and political ideals fundamentally incompatible with each other and history itself.[36] He is better understood as a political theorist who seeks to combine philosophical idealism with historical realism by admitting the limitations he perceives for putting his philosophical ideals into social and political practice. Through the publication of the "trilogy" of *Julie*, *Emile*, and the *Social Contract*, Rousseau shared with the public his ideal model of the relationship between the rural family and the republican state that he hoped would have some impact on human moral, social, and political practice, despite its conflict with the culture of the Enlightenment and its innate tendency toward decay.

The running tension between theory and practice in Rousseau's political thought accounts for the apparent contradictions in his theory of the relationship between the ideal family and the ideal state. On a purely theoretical level, Rousseau's conceptions of the family and the state are compatible and interdependent. Yet when one considers—alongside Rousseau—the complex array of circumstances it would take to put this theory into practice in the modern world, a real tension arises between the possibility of bringing his ideal family and ideal state

together in a unified way. The difficulty of ever realizing this goal is perhaps the reason why Rousseau separated his most prominent treatments
of the family, in *Emile* and *Julie*, from his classic meditation on the
state, in the *Social Contract*. Yet by providing important textual and
philosophical links between these texts, Rousseau keeps open the door
to contemplating the moral and political desirability of reconciling the
ends of the family and the state in a symbiotic whole, no matter whether
the ideal can be fully achieved in reality.

The Role of the Family in
Rousseau's Rural Republic

By examining the bulk of Rousseau's major political writings through
the rubric of rural republicanism, one better understands his paradoxical role as both champion and critic of the transformation of the family.
Rousseau founds his ideal of the rural republic on a new vision of the
family as the primary forum for socialization, civic education, and republican political participation in the most holistic sense. Rousseau's
ideal of the republican family retains certain structural qualities of
eighteenth-century European peasant, bourgeois, and aristocratic families, such as a patriarchal structure and sex-role differentiation. Yet it
also incorporates new approaches to the practices of childcare and education, as well as a new conception of women's social and political
empowerment through their roles as the primary inculcators of manners, mores, and civic virtues in children and society at large. Rousseau
offered a new model of family life—distinct from the existing historical and philosophical models—that became wildly popular and influential in the wake of the success of his twin romantic philosophical
novels, *Julie* and *Emile*. In the core of this chapter, I reconstruct
Rousseau's overarching theory of the proper relationship between
the ideal family and the ideal republican state in his major political
works published or composed between 1755 and 1765. First, I examine
the four works from the late 1750s that together function as a kind of
philosophical prolegomena that sets forth the basic terms, concepts,
and arguments that Rousseau uses to build his conception of rural republicanism. Second, I explore the fascinating textual and philosophical intersections between the five works from the early 1760s that
together constitute, and illustrate the limitations of, Rousseau's ideal of
rural republicanism.

Public versus Domestic Education
in the *Discourse on Political Economy*

The *Discourse on Political Economy* holds the key for understanding Rousseau's paradoxical view of the relationship between the family and the state. Rousseau begins the essay by carefully distinguishing between the structure, governance, and purposes of the family and the state. Yet he ends by suggesting that the family, though distinct from the state, has a fundamental role in politics. The moral education it provides for its children serves as the surest and most practical foundation for civic virtue, especially a sense of patriotic duty, in the modern republican state. A close examination of the arguments of the treatise reveals the compatibility of these two positions that initially appear contradictory.

At the beginning of the discourse, Rousseau discusses the origins of the term "economy." He states that it was first used to describe the domestic economy of the family, and was "subsequently extended to the government of the large family which is the state."[37] In this line, Rousseau seems to be comfortable with comparing the family and the state, at least at a metaphorical level. Rousseau moves on, however, to dispute those who blur the line between the goals and the governance of the family and the state. He concludes that "since the state and the family have nothing in common but their chiefs' obligation to make each happy, the same rules of conduct could not apply to both."[38]

Although at this point it seems that Rousseau has drawn a strict divide between the family and the state, it becomes clear that he has done so more rhetorically than substantively. In the very next line, he reveals the intention behind his initial separation of the family and the state. He confides, "It seemed to me that these few lines would suffice to overthrow the odious system which Sir Filmer tried to establish in a work entitled *Patriarcha*."[39] Rousseau rejects Filmer's equation of the structure, function, and legitimacy of the patriarchal family with the patriarchal state, on the grounds that the distinct social entities of the family and the state cannot be successfully governed in the exact same way, and that absolute patriarchal power is illegitimate under any circumstances, thus its use in the family is no justification for its use in the state and vice versa. He then aligns himself with the thought of the "first book" of Aristotle's *Politics* by distinguishing between the entities of the family and the state and their forms of governance, while designating the family as the moral and economic foundation of the state.[40] By appealing to this distinction between the family and the state, Rousseau separates his work from simple patriarchalism, yet establishes the family as a discrete social entity that nonetheless serves as the moral and economic foundation for his neorepublicanism.

Rousseau's careful distinction between the private realm of the family and the public realm of the republic provides for the protection of the distinct identity of the family against the potentially overweening power of the state. The family should remain distinct from the state while serving as its moral and economic foundation. Governed by love and a moderate form of patriarchal authority, the family seeks to cultivate the natural, domestic affections and shape them, through habit and discipline, into moral and civic virtues that regulate the behavior of its members. In this vital role, the family cannot easily be replaced, especially since state-organized, or public, education is unlikely to work in the modern world as it once worked in ancient Crete.

The clear line Rousseau draws between the family and the state also provides for the protection of the distinct identity of the state against the potentially corrosive influence of the family. Governed by universal laws reflective of the general will, the republican state seeks to serve the common good of the people who act as its sovereign. If the state were governed like a family, it would fail to complete its express purpose: to serve its citizens according to the general will or common good. If it were governed by partial passions and love of particular individuals, as in family life, it would be rife with factions and unable to serve the common good. If a patriarch ruled the state, as in the family, the state would not be a republic, or a legitimate government, since Rousseau only recognizes governments ruled by a sovereign popular assembly as legitimate.

After distinguishing between the internal dynamics of the family and the state, Rousseau argues that the family and the state are nevertheless bound together in a pivotal political relationship. He contends that the health of a republic mainly depends on the education of its citizens: "The fatherland cannot endure without freedom, nor freedom without virtue, nor virtue without citizens; you will have everything if you form citizens; if you do not, you will have nothing but nasty slaves, beginning with the chiefs of the state."[41] He furthermore argues that the formation of citizens must first take place within the family, for "It is from the first moment of life that one must learn to deserve to live; and since one shares in the rights of citizens from birth, the instant of our birth ought to when we begin to exercise our duties. Since there are laws for maturity, there should be laws for childhood that teach obedience to others."[42]

Anticipating the argument of *Emile*, Rousseau defends the ideal of private, family-based education against public, state-organized education for the purpose of instilling civic virtue, especially patriotism, in future citizens. He describes the ancient practice of public education only to discard it as a formerly honorable, but presently impractical, method of educating the denizens and citizens of a modern republic. He contends that private, family-based education is more practical given the larger size of modern republics. Only three ancient peoples succeeded in practicing public education—Lacedaemonia, Crete, and Persia—because they maintained a relatively small size. Private, family-based education, on the other hand, succeeded in producing legions of virtuous citizens for the vast empire of Rome.

Moreover, public education as it was practiced by these ancient peoples supplanted the moral authority, affectionate pull, and educative role of the family, turned the state into a kind of parent, and thus violated the conceptual divide between the family and the state that he establishes at the beginning of the essay. Hence, Rousseau argues that the best way to produce patriotic and virtuous citizens is to protect and preserve the private family as the training-ground in which these virtues are fostered and taught. Like Burke, who views the family and other small social units as "little platoons" in which people are trained to channel their natural affections for other human beings into the practice of moral and civic virtues, Rousseau posits that patriotism and sympathy dissipate over space, and best develop and flourish in close quarters: "Interest and commiseration must in some way be constricted and compressed to be activated. Now since this inclination in us can be useful only to those with whom we have to live, it is good that that (the sentiment of) humanity, concentrated among fellow-citizens, acquire in them added force through the habit of seeing one another, and the common interest that unites them."[43] Rousseau concludes that the private education found within the "concentrated" space of the family is the most effective method to instill patriotism and other civic virtues, since "we readily want what the people we love want."[44]

Although he castigates ancient Rome for its excessive size, moral corruption, and abuse of patriarchal power within the family, he implies that modern republics should follow the example of Rome in one important regard. If public education in the classical style is not possible in the modern world, then the best option for modern republics is to rely heavily on private education within the home. By turning "all their homes into so many schools of citizens," the denizens and citizens of modern republics could emulate Rome and rely on the authority and discipline of family patriarchs to help instill the virtues that will foster patriotism and commitment to the common good within the state.[45]

The *Second Discourse* on the Origins of Patriarchy and Sex-Role Differentiation

To understand why Rousseau thinks the family must possess a patriarchal, sex-roled structure in order to instill virtue and prevent the spread of moral corruption, one must return to his account of the transition from the state of nature to society as set forth in the *Second Discourse*. Rousseau argues that man in the "state of nature" (or life before organized society and government) is solitary, peaceful, and minimally social. Humans are more akin to animals in Rousseau's state of nature. They are not the social animals that dwell in Locke's state of nature, or the proto-Darwinistic animals of Hobbes's state of nature, but solitary, peaceful animals who simply prefer their own company to anyone else's. Rousseau complains about thinkers like Locke who, when reasoning about the state of nature, "intrude into it ideas taken from society," including our ideas of family life:

> They always see the family gathered in one and the same dwelling, with its members maintaining among themselves a union as intimate and permanent as exists among us, where so many common interests unite them. But the fact of the matter is that in that primitive state, since nobody had houses or huts or property of any kind, each one bedded down in some random spot and often only for one night. Males and females came together fortuitously as a result of chance encounters, occasion and desire . . . (and) they left each other with the same nonchalance.[46]

Before the introduction of homes and property, the family exists in a primitive, transient manner in Rousseau's state of nature. Procreation is a random act between strangers, marriage is nonexistent, and child rearing is a solitary and short-lived endeavor undertaken solely by mothers without the aid of the undoubtedly forgotten father: "The mother at first nursed her children for her own need; then, with habit having endeared them to her, she later nourished them for their own need. Once they had the strength to look for their food, they did not hesitate to leave the mother herself. And since there was practically no other way of finding one another than not to lose sight of one another, they were soon at the point of not even recognizing one another."[47] The radical individuality of the Rousseauian state of nature is illustrated by the lack of a lasting emotional bond between mother and child. The primitive mothers of the state of nature stand diametrically opposed to their counterparts in Rousseau's ideal republican society. Rousseau's republican mothers devote their married lives to the care and education of their children in the domestic sphere of the family. On the other hand, the relationship between the primitive mother and child exists only as long as the child's survival depends on the mother—which, in Rousseau's estimation, is only as long as it takes the child to wander off into the wilderness alone to find its own food.

In Rousseau's state of nature, the difference in physical strength between the sexes is irrelevant, because humans are asocial creatures. Their independence and antisociability lend an air of equality to men and women in the state of nature because they do not interact enough to render their physical inequalities pertinent. Yet once human beings make the transition to society from the state of nature, the difference in physical strength becomes relevant. The shift from the state of nature to society takes place in several stages, all of which involve the development of closer family relationships and stronger social bonds. The instinct of pity brings primitive nomads together in loose, unorganized groups that come together only to help each other in matters of survival. The instinct of individuals to compare themselves to others and compete with one another (in Rousseau's terms, *amour-propre*) propels the invention of private property within these nomadic groups; they ultimately split into families with the introduction of private property, particularly in the form of huts and houses.

Rousseau sardonically proclaims, "The first person who, having enclosed a plot of land, took it into his head to say *this is mine* and found people simple enough to believe him, was the true founder of civil society."[48] He then explains that it is the development of huts that was the "first revolution" that "formed the distinction between families and which introduced a kind of property, whence perhaps there already arose many quarrels and fights."[49] The building of homes does not only spur conflict, but also the first stirrings of love and family life as we know it: "The first developments of the heart were the effect of a new situation that united the husbands and wives, fathers and children in one common habitation. The habit of living together gave rise to the sweetest sentiments known to men: conjugal love and paternal love. Each family became a little society all the better united because mutual attachment and liberty were its only bonds;

and it was then that the first difference was established in the lifestyle of the two sexes, which until then only had one."[50] The transition from nature to society results from the introduction of the family home, which in turn spurs the development of distinct sex roles for men and women. According to Rousseau, until the rise of the family home, there is no difference in the lifestyle of the sexes. Once the home is built, however, women tend to remain within it to tend to the care and upbringing of the children they birth and nurse, while men tend to work outdoors and seek food and other necessities for the family's health and survival.

It is fascinating to note that Rousseau believes the family as well as sex-role differentiation are not purely natural phenomena, but rather are products of social convention and, in particular, a consequence of the introduction of private property. Rousseau anticipates the feminist, Marxist, and postmodernist arguments that sex roles are largely a result of social practices and economic relations. He differs from these contemporary schools of thought, however, insofar as he regards these sex roles as necessary for the stability of human political society, and insofar as he regard certain sex-roled activities and practices as preferable because they are, in his view, closer to nature than others. While Rousseau acknowledges that all aspects of nature are shaped by society once humans leave the state of nature, he continues to make distinctions between different levels of naturalness and unnaturalness within society. He deems certain activities—such as maternal breast-feeding, parental care and education of children beyond their infancy, paternal rule of the home, masculine outdoor and agricultural labors, and children's freedom to play in the outdoors—as natural within the context of society, more natural than their alternatives in society, and moral antidotes to certain malaises endemic to modern culture.

Why does Rousseau believe that sex-role differentiation plays an irreplaceable role in the creation of a stable society and state? The key to understanding this aspect of Rousseau's conjectural history of humanity in the *Second Discourse* is his assertion that human beings can never return to the state of nature once they have left it behind. The social passions of love and *amour-propre* irrevocably shape the human experience, and human nature itself, from this point forward. Humans in society, driven by *amour-propre*, compete with one another and strive to dominate each other.

According to Rousseau, women's physical weakness in relation to men, exaggerated by the trappings of society and civilization, requires them to be dependent on men or to be dominated by them.[51] To escape physical and sexual domination by the stronger sex, women must manipulate men to depend on them as well. Rousseau distinguishes between the "moral" and the "physical" aspects of love, arguing that the physical aspect of love simply "inclines one sex to unite with the other," while the moral aspect of love "determines this desire and fixes it exclusively on one single object."[52] Furthermore, the moral aspect of love—the basis for all romantic ideals of love, monogamy, and marriage—is a social and cultural phenomenon controlled and perpetuated largely by women: "Now it is easy to see that the moral aspect of love is an artificial sentiment born of social custom, and extolled by women with so much skill and care in order to establish their hegemony and make dominant the sex that ought to obey."[53] Rousseau believes that women, once they have entered society, use their distinctive feminine charms to seduce men into committing to the long-term emotional and moral bonds of marriage and family that protect them from brutal exploitation by the physically stronger sex.

Achieving a delicate balance of power between the sexes depends on their assumption of different but complementary and interdependent roles: women depend on men, as husbands, citizens, and soldiers, to protect them and defend their interests in the public sphere, and men depend on women, as wives and mothers, to raise their children and provide a good moral example for the family as a whole. Both sexes depend on each other to satisfy each other's sexual desires within the constraints of the marital bond. Men can no longer conquer women solely on the basis of physical strength; romantic love and monogamy replace the savage practices of rape and polygamy as the means of sexual gratification.

Sex-role differentiation entails that women remain in the domestic realm as wives and mothers, while men bridge the domestic and public realms. For this reason, he upholds women as the empresses of the domestic realm, while defending the role of men as the patriarchs who oversee the conduct of family life as their wives manage the details. Both exert power over each other and keep the other in check. Rousseau's ideal family is patriarchal insofar as the husband is the legal head and the only citizen (except for any other adult males), but the wife plays an equally powerful role as the conductress of the family's moral and emotional life as well as the primary educator of future male citizens and female tutors of citizens.

Writing Home: Rousseau's Public Letters
to, and about, Geneva

In his public letters to the city-state of Geneva, Rousseau inscribes this Swiss republic as both a paradigm of patriarchal, sex-roled family life, and a sign of its demise. By writing to his homeland, Rousseau literally writes his home—and his hopes and fears for its future—into his thinking on the ideal structure for the family. In the *Letter to the Republic of Geneva*, which was attached to the beginning of the *Second Discourse*, Rousseau praises the republic of Geneva for its long-standing practice of sex-role differentiation, in the tradition of the exemplary ancient republics like Sparta:

> Could I forget that precious half of the republic which produces the happiness of the other and whose gentleness and wisdom maintain peace and good *moeurs*? Amiable and virtuous women citizens, it will always be the fate of your sex to govern ours. Happy is it when your chaste power exercised only within the conjugal union, makes itself felt only for the glory of the state and the public happiness! Thus it was that in Sparta women were in command, and thus it is that you deserve to be in command in Geneva. . . . It is for you to maintain always, by your amiable and innocent dominion and by your insinuating wit, the love of laws in the state and concord among the citizens.[54]

Like its ancient model Sparta, the modern republic of Geneva enables its women to exert a vital role in the governance of the state through their "chaste power" over men in the realm of the family. Women set the moral codes for the republic through their example of modesty, self-control, and selfless care of their husbands and children. The wives of Geneva, by keeping their husbands' (and their own) sexual passions restrained within the marital bond and happily accepting their roles in the realm of the family, prevent the primitive, unstable forces of sexual attraction from causing chaos and disorder in both the private and public spheres.

In *Letter to d'Alembert*, Rousseau continues in this vein, praising the Genevan republic for its historic practice of sex-role differentiation, and warning its current citizens that the introduction of the theater (and the mixed audiences who would attend it) would destroy the careful balance of power between the sexes that has been maintained in the city for generations. Rousseau goes so far as to say that if the boundary between the family and the public sphere breaks down entirely, women will become like men and men will become like women. He broods that the process has already begun, for "On my last trip to Geneva, I already saw several of these young ladies in jerkins, with white teeth, plump hands, piping voices, and pretty green parasols, rather maladroitly counterfeiting men."[55] The infiltration and influence of women and their manners on the public sphere eventually even effeminize men. He upholds Paris as an ominous example, where social clubs, salons, and public gatherings are mixed: "Every woman in Paris gathers into her apartment a harem of men more womanish than she."[56]

Rousseau defends sex-role differentiation on the grounds that the proximity of the sexes to each other in society, and the corrosive influence of *amour-propre*, sparks the sexual passions between men and women to flare dangerously high. Rousseau is particularly afraid of the unfathomable depths of female sexual desire.[57] The segregation of the sexes into different educational tracks and social roles helps to encourage the practice of modesty, control women's dangerous sex drives, and maintain civility, order, and a balance of power between the sexes. For Rousseau, the power struggle between the sexes is an inescapable facet of human society that can be sublimated (into marital love, for example) but never eliminated.

Since even the city of Geneva—which in Rousseau's wistful eyes is the last great bastion of moral and civic virtue, and the last great republican city-state in the tradition of the ancient world—veers on the brink of succumbing to the temptations of Parisian life, Rousseau suggests that the rural republican families of the Swiss frontier might be the last hope for the preservation of the system of patriarchy and sex-role differentiation that ensures moral and civic virtue. He paints a rosy portrait of the patriarchal rural Swiss family in *Letter to d'Alembert*: "Each, warmly closed up with his big family in his pretty and clean wooden house, which he has himself built, busies himself with enjoyable labors."[58] Building on the historical example of the families of his native Geneva and rural Switzerland, Rousseau's vision of the ideal republican family employs a patriarchal structure and sex-role differentiation as checks against its corruption.

Julie, or the Rural Family Reimagined

Manifesting the longing for the rustic life expressed in the *Letter to d'Alembert*, Rousseau's *Julie* offers his first extensive—and most extravagant—theoretical meditation on the optimal structural and emotional contours for the rural family. *Julie* was one of the most popular novels in eighteenth-century Europe.[59] Groups of people cried in the city streets of Paris as they read copies of the romance that they rented by the hour or the day from local bookshops.[60] Consequently, the novel exerted vast influence on popular views of courtship, marriage, and family life. Perhaps what seduced the public most was the novel's clever pretense that it was not a novel at all. Rousseau pretends that real people from the Vaud region of Switzerland have written the letters that constitute his novel *Julie*, and that he is merely the editor of the volume.

In his preface to the second edition of *Julie*, Rousseau explains the moral and educative purpose behind his supposed "collection" of these letters for the public:

> I like to picture a husband and wife reading this collection together, finding in it a source of renewed courage to bear their common labors, and perhaps new perspectives to make them useful. How could they behold the tableau of this happy couple without wanting to imitate such an attractive model? How will they be stirred by the charm of conjugal union, even in the absence of love's charm, without their own union being reconfirmed and strengthened? When they are through reading, they will be neither saddened by their estate nor repelled by their chores. . . . They will fulfill the same functions, but they will fulfill them with a changed soul, and will do as genuine patriarchs what they had been doing as peasants.[61]

Rousseau claims that the book would be best enjoyed by a very specific audience: married "peasant" couples in the provinces of rural Europe, likely akin to some of the Swiss families described in the volume's letters. Rousseau does not intend the book for the corrupt Parisian elite. He quips, "When one aspires to glory, it is essential to be read in Paris; when one wants to be useful, it is essential to be read in the provinces."[62] He cynically comments that corrupt city dwellers pretend to understand and even emulate virtue by reading about the noble, moral deeds of fictional heroes and heroines in novels, yet these literary exemplars only provide a vicarious taste of what they will never truly enjoy themselves. He sorrowfully concedes that young maidens who have read romantic novels are already corrupt before they turn a page of his collection of letters. Yet he maintains that his book will not contribute to the further decay of their characters. Rather, he asserts that the novel's marital model of Julie and Wolmar ought to inspire provincial people to cherish the bonds of marriage, even if passionate love is no longer present.

Yet Rousseau's declaration of his "editorial" intent reveals itself to be as spurious as the premise that his book is in fact a collection of real letters. While *Julie* certainly celebrates the ideal of rural family life with the Wolmar home, it ultimately presents the eternal, romantic love of Julie and St. Preux as far more desirable, compelling, and sincere than the cold marital union of the Wolmars.

Rousseau understood the socially subversive quality of celebrating a passionate ideal of romantic love that challenges extant social codes concerning marriage and thus engages in a kind of pragmatic self-censorship when defining the intended audience for the work in the second preface. He no doubt anticipated his critics, such as Burke and Wollstonecraft, who argued that the racy story of Julie and St. Preux would corrupt young men and women with its brash celebration of love, secret courtship, and sexual passion outside the bonds of marriage.[63] To derail this criticism, or at least distract his readers from immediately leaping to it, Rousseau identifies the Arcadian audience of provincial, peasant, married couples as the best recipient, practically speaking, for his theoretical construction of the rural family in *Julie*. Perhaps these provincial folk, already united in the bonds of love and marriage, and far removed from the corrupt cultural and marital expectations of the aristocratic class and the decadent trends of city life, would be more likely to preserve the patriarchal, sex-roled structure of the family and incorporate more egalitarian practices (such as respect for the fundamental dignity of all family members, the empowerment of mothers as the educators of citizens, practicing maternal breast-feeding rather than hiring wetnurses, a system of childhood education that heralds physical freedom and moral autonomy above all else, and even the notion of marriage as ideally grounded on love and free choice, rather than familial and classbased arrangements) only insofar as they support the moral and political stability of the state.

Rousseau's novel falls into two parts, separated by a tragic choice. The first half of the novel recounts the illicit courtship of two young Swiss lovers, Julie d'Étange, the daughter of an aristocrat, the Baron d'Étange, and St. Preux, her lowly tutor, between 1733 and 1745.[64] Julie must choose between rejecting the wishes of her father, and remaining with her first true love, or following her father's wishes and marrying the nobleman Monsieur de Wolmar. Julie's choice is between submission to the old, patriarchal, aristocratic order and its heartless system of arranged marriage, or the newly emerging model of companionate marriage that became more prominent, especially in English aristocratic circles, in the eighteenth century.[65] Keeping with his authorial intent to blur the line between fiction and fact in this "collection of letters," Rousseau has Lord Bomston, an English aristocrat and friend of St. Preux, offer to Julie and St. Preux "sanctuary" on his estate in England, where they can be married and live together as husband and wife—an offer that Julie ultimately refuses on the grounds that she must be loyal to her Swiss aristocratic family's wish that she marry Wolmar or risk driving her father to join her mother in death as a consequence of her scandalous behavior.

The second half of the novel recounts the consequences of her choice to submit to her father's will and marry Wolmar, with whom she builds a seemingly idyllic family home in the small town of Clarens in the Vaud country. The Wolmar family is Rousseau's first attempt to theoretically construct a family and a system of household management that could provide the moral backbone of his ideal rural republican state. It is not perfect, however, and Rousseau intends it to be flawed. With the model of the rural family at Clarens, Rousseau explores the difficulties of implementing this ideal in the current cultural climate of late eighteenth-century Europe, especially amid the literary and philosophical development of more radical notions of women's capacity for, and right to, autonomy and the expression of their own freedom of will, independent of traditional notions of patriarchal authority.[66]

When Julie marries Wolmar, she vows to God, "I will love the husband thou hast given me. I will be faithful, because that is the first duty which binds the family and all of society. I will be chaste, because that is the first virtue which nurtures all the others."[67] Julie does not feel the same passion for Wolmar as she felt for her first, true love St. Preux, but she concludes, after a sudden (and suspiciously self-justifying) religious conversion at the nuptial altar, that romantic love and conjugal love serve different ends: "One does not marry in order to think solely about each other, but in order to fulfill conjointly the duties of civil life, govern the household prudently, raise one's children well."[68] Julie subsequently celebrates marriage and family life as the wellsprings of emotional connections and moral commitments to the wider social and political community, yet, because of her own tragic choice, she construes these social institutions as incompatible with the selfish, romantic, and sexual desires of the individual. A real tension persists between these two basic human aspirations that culminates in the tragic ending of the work, in which the sincerity of Julie's love for, and marriage to, Wolmar is called into question by her deathbed profession of her enduring love for St. Preux.

And yet Julie stubbornly strives to create a family with Wolmar that is akin to the one she would have liked to enjoy with her first love. Like the rural republican families of the Swiss Valais that St. Preux celebrates in his early love letters to Julie at the beginning of the novel, the Wolmars create a sex-roled household in which the husband rules as the patriarch but the wife is the manager of all the domestic affairs. In his letters from a Valaisan village, St. Preux described the dynamics of the rural families on which the Wolmars later model their own family life: "Among themselves they behave in the same straightforward way; children of the age of reason are their father's equals, domestics eat at the same table with their masters; the same freedom reigns in homes as in the republic, and the family is the image of the state."[69] St. Preux draws a direct parallel between the republican freedom of the Valaisan family and the republican freedom of the Valaisan republic. A republican spirit of equality, freedom, and fraternal affection infuses the homes of these rural families of the Swiss Valais, so that "the family is the image of the state." Children of the age of reason and even servants sit with the patriarch at the dinner table. A number of hierarchies are maintained and respected, however: the father rules the house; the underage children must respect the will of their parents, and their difference in stature manifests itself in their separate eating arrangements; the distinction between master and servant, though absent at the dinner table, remains at all other times.

Sex-role differentiation plays an important part in the organization of the rural republican families of the Swiss Valais. St. Preux notes that "even at the homes of magistrates, the wife and daughters of the house stand behind my chair, and wait at table like domestics."[70] The women are happy to serve the men in this manner; although they stand behind them during the meal, this stance celebrates and symbolizes their essential role as the empresses of the domestic realm. The women direct the course of the family while serving its needs, and express their feminine power and virtue through their submissiveness. The servile, yet statuesque, posture of the women in the Valaisan family captures the paradox of Rousseau's theory of moral and political freedom—namely, that we are truly free, or self-governing, when we submit our wills to moral duty or the common good.[71] St. Preux's romantic portrait of the patriarchal, sex-roled, rural Valaisan family becomes the model for the family life of the Wolmars at Clarens, although it ultimately fails to be fully implemented, and authentically experienced, in its new location. With her former lover's letters fresh in her mind, Julie futilely strives to create with her husband the rural family life that she once dreamed of sharing with St. Preux, but it is missing the sincere affection, and the distance from corrupt aristocratic norms of marriage and family life, that it needs for its long-term endurance.

Wolmar is much like the tutor of *Emile*; he appears all-knowing and all-controlling in his rule of his family at Clarens. Julie even compares her husband Wolmar to God Himself: "The order he has brought into his house is the image of the one that prevails in his heart, and seems to imitate in a small household the order established in the governance of the earth."[72] The well-ordered state of the Wolmar household reflects the well-ordered state of the patriarch's own soul. He governs his "small household" as God governs the earth. The microcosm of the Wolmar family seems to replicate the hierarchies of the natural order of the universe on a small scale. Yet there is something disturbingly inauthentic about Wolmar's God-like stature at Clarens. He demands absolute honesty and sincerity from all who dwell in his estate at Clarens, so that supposedly no secrets are kept among its members. Julie's former lover, St. Preux, is eventually invited to live with them as a member of their extended family at Clarens in order to facilitate his, and Julie's, "recovery" from their love for one another. Wolmar's only condition for St. Preux's residence in the Wolmar home is that he and Julie do not hide anything from him. Yet this promise is not kept by either—for they both harbor their old passions deep within their hearts, despite their outward protests and rationalizations to the contrary—and the ostensibly omniscient Wolmar is shown to be impotent in his quest to "cure" his wife and her lover of the supposed disease of their youthful love.

Structurally, economically, and geographically, however, the Wolmar family maintains the outward appearance of the families of the rural Swiss countryside it occupies. Like the rural republican families of the Valais, the Wolmar family locates itself in an isolated countryside location: Clarens is an actual small town on the north side of Lake Geneva in the Vaud country. As in the second preface of the work, Rousseau intentionally blurs the distinction between fiction and fact by giving the Wolmar family a real point on the map. Like the Valaisan families, the Wolmar family organizes itself around hierarchies based on birth, rank, class, and sex. Although their family supports the recognition of natural and social hierarchies between husbands and wives, parents and children, and masters and servants, the Wolmars strive to infuse their home with a spirit of freedom, equality, and affection like the rural republican families of the Valais. The Wolmars recognize the fundamental, natural equality of all human beings beneath the differences in age, sex, class, and rank that determine their social roles. They create traditions, like the family dinner of the Valaisan villagers, that celebrate the fundamental equality of all the people in their household, alongside their distinct and indispensable social roles. They host dances and festivals that bring together the servants, vineyard and farm workers, and the members of their immediate and extended family. Yet they carefully maintain strict patterns of sex-role differentiation in their daily household activities. Male and female servants cannot mix together, and even Julie and Wolmar separate after their breakfast in the morning to take care of their respective household duties. Julie devotes most of her time to the care and education of her children, while Wolmar oversees the work of the servants in the vineyard and the farm. Agricultural self-sufficiency is the modest, and moderate, economic goal of the Wolmar family, which ensures its independence from the corrupt excesses of bourgeois commerce.[73] Yet Julie's sparse yet ritualistic use of coffee purchased from outside the Wolmar estate signals that while she seems to submit to the moral goals of Wolmar's agriculturally self-sufficient regime, she quietly subverts the economic independence of their rural family with this small self-indulgence. Under the guise of self-denial, Julie indulges her love for coffee just as she indulges her love for St. Preux, whose company she continues to enjoy, under the careful watch of her husband, when he is incorporated into the Wolmar household as a "friend" and future tutor for her children. While the practice of agricultural self-sufficiency, patriarchy, and sex-role differentiation is intended to maintain order within the Wolmar family and its community of servants, Julie's desires, capacity for love, and freedom of will—with all their unpredictable passion—bubble underneath the surface and threaten to disturb its appearance of placidity.

However apparently well-organized in the structural or economic sense, the Wolmar family does not seem to have any connection to the aristocratic government of the Vaud country within which it exists. Puzzlingly, the men who inhabit the Wolmar family at Clarens—Wolmar, St. Preux and his English friend Lord Bomston, and, from time to time, Julie's father, the Baron d'Étange—do not spend much, if any, time engaged in conventional political or military commitments. Lord Bomston is the lone exception; as a loyal member of the British House of Lords who idolizes Britain as a republic devoted to the service of the common good, he balances his political duties and his military duties alongside his commitment to build a home next door to his friends at Clarens. It is implied that the Baron d'Étange and St. Preux, as male natives, and Wolmar, through his marriage to Julie and inheritance of her family's estate at Clarens, are at least subjects, if not citizens, of the Vaud country (which was under the patrician administration of the canton of Berne at the time, and possessed a mix of aristocratic and democratic political institutions) but their primary activities do not revolve around this status. Judith Shklar (1969) interpreted the virtual political inactivity of these three characters as a sign that Rousseau's twin utopias—the idyllic family represented by Clarens and the idyllic republic represented by Sparta—are irreconcilable ideals that entail a tragic choice between domestic bliss or political unity.[74] Alternatively, Rousseau's *Julie* can be understood as developing and moving toward an ideal of a rural republic that places rare demands on its male citizens to engage in politics as it is often narrowly and formally construed, and instead encourages the men to focus their energies on a more fundamental political duty: participation in the governance of the family, the moral foundation for the state, through their roles as fathers, husbands, tutors, friends, and farmers.

Subtly reinforcing this point, Rousseau's novel romanticizes Geneva as a model for understanding the symbiotic relationship between the patriarchal, sex-roled family and the ideal republican state. Near the end of the novel, Julie's cousin and closest confidante, Claire, visits the independent republican city-state of Geneva. Echoing the ideas of *Letter to the Republic of Geneva* and *Letter to d'Alembert*, Claire favorably compares Geneva's system of sex-role differentiation within the family and the greater society to the system implemented by Julie and Wolmar at Clarens: "Here you find obliging husbands and wives who are almost Julies. Your system is very well confirmed here."[75] Through her favorable review of the interrelationship of familial and political life in Geneva, Claire suggests that the Wolmar family household might be seen as a microcosm of the city-state of Geneva, with its rural location in the Vaud country better suited than the city for the cultivation of good *moeurs*.

Near the end of the novel, Julie and Wolmar discuss with St. Preux their intention to have him serve as the tutor for their children. They outline an alternative form of education, which replicates the main precepts of *Emile*, for St. Preux to implement when he starts work as the tutor of the Wolmar family's young boys. Julie also refers to the separate system of education reserved for Claire's daughter, which anticipates the education of Sophie.[76] The reader, however, never witnesses the education of the Wolmar children by St. Preux in this Emilean fashion. Julie dies, in a quasisuicidal fashion, after saving her son from drowning, and the novel ends with letters to St. Preux from Wolmar, Julie, and Claire that reveal the emotional breakdown of the Wolmar household. Yet there is no letter from St. Preux responding to either Julie's startling deathbed revelation that she always loved him despite her marriage to Wolmar, or Wolmar and Claire's request that he return to Clarens and fulfill his earlier promise to educate Julie's children.

St. Preux's silence is less puzzling if we understand *Emile* as the philosophical sequel to *Julie*. *Emile* reveals to its readers how Julie's children ought to have been educated, if her family had not fallen apart after her death, and how this education might have provided a more stable and happy family life for the next generation of Wolmars. *Emile* also shows us how Rousseau ideally envisions a boy and a girl could be raised with the hope of marrying for love, and building a happy rural family life together in the modern world, without the class-based, cultural and familial obstacles that Julie and St. Preux faced to making this dream happen for themselves. The aporetic ending of *Julie* makes clear that the model of rural family life at Clarens is not the end-goal of Rousseau's thinking on the subject. To the contrary, the abrupt, and ultimately unsatisfying, conclusion of the novel suggests that Rousseau intended the questions it raises to be more fully answered in its sequel, *Emile*. Clarens—with all its flaws, especially a true love unjustly denied the happy outlet of marriage and family life, and a woman's freedom unfairly limited to an austere, and insincere, regimen of self-denial—is but a shadow of the Valasian families it sought to emulate, and a shadow of what it could have been under proper circumstances. Instead, it serves as a deliberately flawed prelude to Rousseau's second model of the rural family, wherein the ideal—and thus difficult to secure—circumstances for creating a rural family suitable to serve as the moral foundation of a republic are explored.

Emile as Family Man, Subject, and Potential Citizen

Rousseau's *Emile* offers his second major theoretical model of the rural family. *Emile* is perhaps best understood as the philosophical bridge between the theory of the family set forth in *Julie* and the neorepublican doctrine of the *Social Contract*. *Emile* offers some corrections to the flaws in the model of rural family life upheld in *Julie*, and builds toward Rousseau's most thorough and definitive discussion of republicanism in the *Social Contract*. *Julie* ends with a reference to the educational philosophy of *Emile*, when *Emile* likewise ends with reference to the ideas of the *Social Contract*, when the tutor introduces Emile to the study of republican politics as a preparation for his marriage to Sophie.[77] Read as interlocking texts, *Julie*, *Emile*, and the *Social Contract* offer a cohesive theory of the proper relationship between the rural family and the republican state.

Emile has puzzled generations of scholars because its system of childhood education seems impossible to fully realize under any normal social and familial circumstances. *Emile* is the story of an orphan boy who is raised by a tutor from infancy to adulthood, and then introduced to a young woman, Sophie, who will become his wife. The narrator of the book, Rousseau, creates the fictional identity of the tutor for himself. He then creates the fictional characters of Emile and Sophie so he can explore, in theory, the possibilities for raising a child and arranging a marriage as close as possible to the dictates of nature (as they exist in society), rather than conforming to the corrupt constraints of society alone.

The tutor exerts a totalitarian power over his young charge, controlling him like a marionette in more than twenty years of highly orchestrated tutelary episodes. The tutor keeps Emile in the country, far from civilization, the city, and even most people. Emile only meets a handful of people during his childhood and adolescence, and all of these encounters are arranged by the tutor to fulfill some sort of educational mission. The only real freedom Emile enjoys is playing outdoors in nature, but even then the tutor is always watching from afar. Emile does not experience any normal form of family life—he has no mother, no father, no siblings, but only the tutor to guide him and provide for his care and upbringing. Why did Rousseau write a treatise on childhood education that initially rejects conventional family life and seems impossible to practice under any normal social circumstances?

The question of whether boys could or should really be educated in the manner of Emile is moot for Rousseau. Obviously, many of his prescriptions for childhood education were meant to be practical and practiced—such as his strident call for mothers to breast-feed their own children, for infants to be freed from swaddling clothes, and for children to freely play outdoors, so that their growth and health would not be impeded—and these tenets became popular and influential in actual child-rearing practices in late eighteenth-century Europe.[78] On a symbolic level, however, Rousseau intends the education of Emile and Sophie, culminating in their courtship and marriage, to be an allegory for his

philosophy of history and human nature.[79] Emile and Sophie's education, courtship, and marriage symbolize Rousseau's attempt to reconcile
the conflicting forces of nature and society within the rural family.

To understand how Rousseau's *Emile* fits into his broader theory
of the relationship between the rural family and the republican state, one
must look to the conclusion of the book. The end-goal of Emile's solitary education is his marriage to Sophie and the beginning of their life
within a rural family and its vital contribution to the country of their
birth. The radically different educations of Emile and Sophie anticipate
the patriarchal structure and sex-role differentiation of their marriage
and family life. The tutor raises Emile close to nature, so that he will
preserve as much of the strength and freedom of the natural man within
him as possible when he enters marriage, society, and subjecthood
and/or citizenship. Ideally, Emile would be born into, or would have the
chance to become a member of, an authentic republic wherein he would
be both a subject (a law-abider) and a citizen (a law-maker). The historical realist in Rousseau, however, places Emile in mid-eighteenth-century France, under its corrupt monarchy, to show how a man can still be
educated for the rights and duties of authentic subjecthood and citizenship, and preparing future generations for such an end, even if he initially is only faced with accepting the duties of subjecthood to laws he
has not made himself.

In Rousseau's *Emile*, physical education is an essential part of
moral and civic education because it is the first way in which masculinity and femininity are defined. In Rousseau's system of physical
education, masculinity is defined as strength, and femininity is defined
as attractiveness. The male and female bodies are trained for different
ends that have radical implications for the body politic. Within her own
family, Sophie is trained to be an attractive woman, a good wife and
mother, and the ruler of the empire of the domestic realm. With the
tutor, Emile is trained to be a "man of nature" in the first twenty years
of his life, so that he will become strong, self-reliant, self-controlled,
and at one with nature.

Yet Emile must ultimately become a subject and/or citizen. For
Rousseau, men are trained to be subjects and/or citizens by women—by
their mothers and their lovers—in the feminine empire of the family.
Emile lacks a mother because Rousseau wanted to imagine a man who
is raised apart from the corruption of the bourgeois and aristocratic families of his time. Emile is much like the natural man of the *Second Discourse* who encounters family life only once he is introduced to

marriage. In the absence of his mother, Sophie inherits the role of "civilizing" Emile for the roles of husband, father, subject, and/or citizen. Rousseau proposes a tricky balance to be struck: on the one hand, men must maintain their raw masculinity through hard exercise, manual labor, and outdoor adventures; on the other hand, they must be civilized and "feminized" to some degree by their mothers and lovers so that they can become subjects and/or citizens as well as men. Emile must be made subject to the power of the feminine empire of the family, but he must not be made effeminate—otherwise he will not be a man, subject, or citizen, but rather only a weak bourgeois slave.

Rousseau claims that Sophie is the sovereign of an "empire." On a small scale, it is the realm of women, children, home, and family. On a large scale, it includes the realm of civil society that inhabits the space between the family and the state. Rousseau writes, "Women possess their empire not because men wanted it that way, but because nature wants it that way."[80] The empire of women is a design of nature (as it exists in society), not a result of the oppression of women by men. It is in Sophie's domestic empire that Rousseau's men of nature learn how to be social and political animals. Rousseau's influential contribution to conceptions of women's social empowerment is his elevation of the domestic sphere to the level of an empire. He gave the "domestic woman" the power and status she never enjoyed before.[81] As a result, the domestic realm was widely celebrated as a sphere of power for women over men in the late eighteenth and early nineteenth centuries. Although women in postrevolutionary France and America did not share the same civil or political rights as men, they often understood themselves as shaping the body politic through their role as republican mothers, the educators of patriots and citizens.

Yet there is a tension between Rousseau's sex-roled theory of physical education and his theory of civic education in *Emile*. In Book III, the tutor introduces Emile to outdoor manual labor as the next step in his physical education. Emile wants to work outdoors because "every sedentary and indoor profession which effeminates and softens the body neither pleases nor suits him."[82] Rousseau condemns the indoor world, the world of women, as contrary to the purpose of masculine physical education. Rousseau considers the sedentary life suitable for only women, eunuchs, and weak bourgeois slaves. Men who dwell in the feminine empire of the family without periodically escaping to revive their manhood through outdoor work and exercise become completely effeminized and emasculated. The ultimate purpose of Emile's physical education is to develop the strength to withstand the effeminizing power of Sophie's empire while learning to become a subject/citizen. He must sit at Sophie's knee to learn how to be a good husband, father, and subject/citizen, all the while longing to roam free in the countryside. He must learn to be a subject/citizen without forgetting to be a man.

Rousseau argues that the main problem with modern education is that it produces neither men nor citizens, but rather petty bourgeois slaves and tyrants. These men are slaves to *amour-propre*, or the narcissistic impulse to compare themselves to others. They are also tyrants in their selfish quest to dominate their competition. Modern education unfortunately produces these pathetic bourgeois men because it foolishly attempts to educate both a man and a citizen at the same time: "Always in contradiction with himself, always floating between his inclinations and his duties, he will never be either man or citizen. He will be good neither for himself nor for others. He will be one of these men of our days: a Frenchman, an Englishman, a bourgeois. He will be nothing."[83] Rousseau contemplates whether an educator must choose between making a "man or citizen." Education cannot combat and control the conflicting impulses and influences of nature and society simultaneously. This does not mean, however, that Emile can be either, or neither, a man or a citizen. Rather, it means that education must first serve the ends of nature and subsequently the ends of society. First, the education of nature produces a man; second, this man is introduced to the education of society within the rural family, forging the perfect hybrid of man and citizen, or a man who is capable of accepting and performing the duties of subjecthood in any corrupt regime, and the rights and duties of republican citizenship and subjecthood if he is so lucky to inhabit a legitimate state.

It is "domestic education" or the "education of nature" that begets the man-citizen, not public education. Public education, as it is found in Plato's *Republic*, only forms citizens of the type represented by the Lacedaemonian man and the Spartan woman: "The Lacedaemonian Pedaretus runs for the council of three hundred. He is defeated. He goes home delighted that there were three hundred men worthier than he to be found in Sparta. I take this display to be sincere, and there is no reason to believe that it was. This is the citizen."[84] Rousseau's Spartan woman is similarly single-minded: "A Spartan woman had five sons in the army and was awaiting news of the battle. A Helot arrives; trembling, she asks him for news. 'Your five sons were killed.' 'Base slave, did I ask you that?' 'We won the victory.' The mother runs to the temple and gives thanks to the gods. This is the female citizen."[85] For Rousseau, the perfect male citizen and the perfect female citizen are deeply admirable, but deeply warped. They live only for the state, not for themselves or their families. This is why he explicitly rejects public education of the kind found in ancient Lacedaemonia and Sparta and described in Plato's *Republic,* in both his *Discourse on Political Economy* and *Emile.*

Domestic education or the education of nature, in contrast, can bring about the perfect balance between man and citizen. It is a "natural" education insofar as it follows the dictates of nature (as they exist in human society), and it is a "domestic" education insofar as mothers and wives direct it within the feminine empire of the family. Moreover, this education is both "natural" and "domestic" insofar as it establishes love, sexuality, and marriage as the basis for a broader understanding of subjecthood, citizenship, and political participation. It is through his entrance into the main institutions of Sophie's empire—marriage and family—that the man Emile becomes a father, a subject, and an educator of future subjects and, ideally, future subject-citizens.

At the end of Book V of *Emile,* the tutor asks his student, "When you become the head of a family, you are going to be a member of the state, and do you know what it is to be a member of the state?"[86] Until this late point in his education, and at the verge of his marriage to Sophie, Emile has not been exposed to the world of politics. After the tutor takes him on a tour of mostly small countries and rural areas in Europe and teaches him the neorepublican doctrine of the *Social Contract,* Emile returns to establish a "patriarchal and rustic" family life with his new wife Sophie that seems distant from the demands of republican citizenship as conventionally understood in the classical and Renaissance traditions.[87] Moreover, as the tutor taught him, the current governments of France and the other nations of Europe are far from legitimate in Rousseau's republican sense of the term. Yet Emile has been raised to be a good father and citizen, to love his country and fulfill his duties to the state, even if "the social contract has not been observed."[88] The tutor points out that the "Romans went from the plough to the consulate," and so shall Emile.[89] If his country calls him to perform civic or military service, he will happily comply. While citizenship in a republic would occasionally demand him to participate in the popular assembly to make law and reaffirm the appointment of the current government, or to defend the state from within the citizen militia, subjecthood under the French monarchy means that Emile will not "be sought out to serve the state."[90] He will be ruled from afar, and denied a role in political self-governance. Emile has been raised to find authentic self-governance in his own heart and in his own family, even if he cannot also find it within his state.

While Emile and Sophie's rural family life may be a "simple retreat" from the corruption of cities, it is not a "simple retreat" from the corruption of modern governments, as Bloom (1979) concluded.[91] Rousseau (as the tutor) envisions that the newly married Emile and Sophie, after settling down near her parents' home, will help to revitalize rural, agricultural family life, and its attendant *moeurs* and virtues, in their provincial part of France:

> I am moved by contemplating how many benefactions Emile and Sophie can spread around them from their simple retreat, and how much they can vivify the country and reanimate the extinguished zeal of the unfortunate village folk. I believe I see the people multiplying, the fields being fertilized, the earth taking on a new adornment. The crowd and the abundance transform work into festivals, and cries of joy and benedictions arise from the midst of the games which center on the lovable couple who brought them back to life. . . . It seems to be already reborn around Sophie's dwelling. You will do no more than complete together what her worthy parents have begun.[92]

Emile and Sophie, by imitating her parents with their loving marriage and their virtuous, agricultural, and domestic labors, will reanimate rural life in their region with new zest and great success. They will experience in an authentic way what the Wolmars attempted to create at Clarens with the festivals and dances staged for their farm and vineyard workers. By reforming and revitalizing rural life around them through their own sincere example, Emile and Sophie will not simply "retreat" from the corruption of their government, but will rather engage in "grassroots" political reform of the purest kind. Emile and Sophie's rural family, and the waves of renewal it spreads throughout their region, is a necessary, organic, intergenerational step toward the creation of a society in which authentic republicanism might be established. Their own rural family may not inhabit a republic, but it will help to create a culture in which future rural families will be able to serve as the moral foundation of a state with popular sovereignty. The significant textual link between Rousseau's major treatise on education, marriage, and family life, and his foremost work theorizing the possibility of establishing republican government in the modern world, illustrates the direction with which Rousseau wants Emile (and the rest of humanity) to move—toward the *Social Contract*.

Linking the Rural Family to the State:
The *Social Contract*

The key to understanding why Emile becomes a "member of the state" when he becomes the head of a remote, rural family lies in the teaching of the *Social Contract*. After all, the transformation of Emile from a man to a husband, father, and citizen takes place after he learns the teaching of Rousseau's neorepublican political theory. Ideally, Emile would have been born into a republic, not a corrupt monarchy—but at the very least he has been educated to understand his roles as husband, father, and subject or citizen to be interconnected, no matter what kind of state he finds himself as a "member." In the *Social Contract*, Rousseau opens a space for a more expansive understanding of political participation, deviating from the traditional republican understanding of political participation as voting, law-making, political office, and military service by male citizens. It is in Rousseau's ideal republic that Emile would have been best able to fluidly synthesize his identities as a man of nature, a family man, subject or law-abider, *and* citizen or law-maker.

It is clear that Rousseau upholds republicanism as the best form of government in his major political works, from his abstract theory of popular sovereignty in the *Social Contract*, to his actual prescriptions for republican constitutions in Corsica and Poland, to his long-standing concern with the moral and political health of his native republican city, Geneva, to his continual appeals to the historical examples of the republics of Sparta, Rome, and Venice when constructing his own theoretical proposals for the ideal state. Yet Rousseau completely reformulates the meaning of republicanism for the modern age in his revolutionary political treatise, the *Social Contract*. The *Social Contract* is primarily a study of how popular sovereignty and the various forms of legitimate government that may be founded on it can be realized.

In the *Social Contract*, Rousseau provocatively contends, "Every legitimate government is republican."[93] To understand this expansion of the traditional definition of republican government, one must examine Rousseau's careful distinction between the terms "sovereign" and "government." For Rousseau, the only legitimate sovereign is the collective body of the people united together by the "social contract"—or the voluntary decision of all to give up their natural rights in exchange for political rights and duties as defined by the whole. The popular assembly or sovereign, composed of all the (adult male) citizens, defines these rights and duties for the republic partly through its own deliberations and mostly through the appointment of a government that executes its united, indivisible, and unerring "general will" that seeks the good of all, not of any particular group or individual. The members of the popular assembly are both citizens and subjects of the republic; they are citizens insofar as they make law, and subjects insofar as they obey it.

A republican state grounded on popular sovereignty may take several forms of government. Rousseau surveys the advantages and disadvantages of the monarchical, aristocratic, and democratic forms of government. While he defends democracy as the form of government best suited for a republican state that has an evenly distributed population proportional to its small geographic size, he acknowledges that a pure democracy is the most difficult form of government to practice, because the same people would serve as the legislative power, or citizen-legislators, in the sovereign assembly, and as the executive power, or magistrates, in the government. The identity of the legislative and executive powers renders a pure democracy suitable only for "a people of Gods," or a people who have the *moeurs* to withstand the corruption that attends the possession of too much power.[94] On the other hand, monarchy—while suited for republican states with an evenly distributed population proportional to its large geographic size—is the most prone to despotism. Because the monarch literally stands alone, apart, and at a distance from the citizen-subjects of the geographically expansive state, he does not have enough checks on his executive power and thus can more easily abuse it than a group of magistrates could.

Rousseau seems most inclined to defend the elective aristocratic form of government (a small number of magistrates elected by the popular assembly) as the most stable and enduring form of government that is free from the dangers of either mob or monarchical tyranny. Such a government is best suited for a republican state that has an evenly distributed population proportional to its moderate geographic size. Economically speaking, it should display "moderation among the rich and contentment among the poor" rather than the extremes of either the "rigorous equality" of a poor state or a severe inequality of a decadent aristocratic class system.[95] In praise of elective aristocracy, Rousseau writes, (elective) Aristocracy has the advantage of choosing its members; for in popular Government all Citizens are born magistrates, whereas this Government restricts them to a small number, and they become magistrates only by being elected; a means by which probity, enlightenment, experience and all the other reasons for public preference and esteem are so many further guarantees of being well governed. Moreover, assemblies are more easily convened, business is discussed better, and dispatched in a more orderly and diligent fashion, the State's prestige is better upheld abroad by venerable senators than by an unknown or despised multitude. In a word, the best and most natural order is to have the wisest govern the multitude, so long as it is certain that they will govern it for its advantage and not for their own; institutions and procedures should not be multiplied needlessly, nor should twenty thousand men be employed to do what a hundred well chosen men can do even better.[96]

Rousseau suggests that elective aristocracy is perhaps the most successful and stable among all the fundamentally flawed forms of government, because the small number of magistrates makes everyday governance of the republic smoother and more efficient, and their offices are subject to the institutional check of election. Here, it becomes clear that while Rousseau remains a vehement critic of the cultural practices of hereditary aristocracy (such as the class system and its unjust institutionalization of arbitrary economic and social inequalities), he is not opposed to the practical value of elective aristocracy as a mode of government for a republican state. Not only do the small group of elected magistrates govern the republic more effectively than would the entire sovereign assembly, but their administrative work permits the bulk of the population to devote most of their time to other matters, such as the service of their families, the "small fatherlands" that together compose the greater republic. Although he praises elective aristocracy, Rousseau concedes that all forms of government are subject to corruption and the overreaching arm of tyranny; hence, the people, or the sovereign, must always be vigilant in its political virtue, never allowing the government to become the "master" and it to become the "slave."

The most mind-bending aspect of Rousseau's redefinition of republican government is that the sovereign popular legislative assembly is the essential quality of the state, and the form of government—whether democratic, aristocratic, monarchical, or various mixes of these types—is a second-order trait determined by the legislation of the assembly. For example, Rousseau believes it is possible to have a republic with a monarchical government, wherein the monarch is solely the administrator of the laws made by the sovereign people. For reasons mentioned earlier, however, he admits that this form of government will likely deteriorate into tyranny.

But perhaps the most crucial, and overlooked, dimension of Rousseau's thinking on republicanism is his emphasis on the relevance of a state's geographic size and population for choosing the appropriate government for it. Here, it is important to note that what matters most for Rousseau is the proportional relationship between population and land mass, and the even distribution of the population throughout the country. The population should neither be sparse, and fodder for tyranny, or dense, and ripe for moral corruption—but rather, even, moderate, and capable of sustaining a self-sufficient agricultural economy. In other words, all forms of republican government—democratic, aristocratic, monarchical, or mixed—can be best administered in states that are essentially rural or not dominated by a single city or set of cities. Rousseau has the most hope that small to medium-size states with mainly rural populations and democratic or elective aristocratic governments can found and practice enduring, genuine republics grounded on popular sovereignty. Such states have enough geographic space to support a self-sufficient agricultural economy, in which the labor of its denizens yields produce in moderate excess of its needs. Rousseau argues that in "places where the excess of produce over labor is moderate suit free peoples; those where an abundant and fertile soil yields much produce in return for little labor lend themselves to being governed monarchically."[97] For this reason, small to medium-size states with moderate agricultural production are most likely to be economically self-sufficient and least likely to fall prey to either economic dependency on foreign trade or political dependency on the rule of a despot.

Just as he expands the meaning of the term republicanism from mixed government, as it was understood in the classical and Renaissance traditions, to a range of forms of government founded on popular sovereignty, Rousseau expands the meaning of popular political participation. He portrays the rural family as the moral foundation of the republican state, even though it often stands remote from the actual daily governance of the state. The physical distance of these rural families from the governmental administration of the republics they inhabit is not a sign that Rousseau believed that the natural man and the citizen could never be reconciled, that one could choose either the natural life of the countryside or the political life of the city. Rather, the rural families of *Emile* and *Julie* attempt to illustrate how this idyllic reconciliation of nature and culture could be possible—though, like all human social institutions, they are not immune to the difficulties of implementation or the inevitable threat of corruption.

The domestic life of the rural family is not meant to be an escape from citizenship and politics; rather it represents an alternative, and essential, form of political participation for a sizeable chunk of the republic's male citizens, female caregivers and educators of future citizens, and the young denizens and future citizens of the republic. For it is within the family that the invaluable project of the moral and civic education of citizens first takes shape, and rural families, because of the protective buffer between them and the corruption of the city and even the daily administration of the republic, serve this purpose better than their urban counterparts. Rural life, domestic life, and the care and education of children take on a political hue in Rousseau's republican reveries.

While the patriarchs of these rural families serve in the militia and attend the meetings of the popular assembly described in the *Social Contract*, their most important political role is that of the paterfamilias—the ruler of the "small fatherland" that is the family, the microcosm and building-block of the state itself.[98] With an elective aristocratic form of government, the elected magistrates and their appointed assistants can manage the daily administration of the republic and execute the body of law already established by the sovereign people. Consequently, the male citizens participate in the political life of the republic mainly through the care, support, and education of their families. Indeed, Rousseau argues that the best sign of a good government is the growth of the state's population in proportion to its geographic size, an outcome that hinges on the flourishing of its families: "What is the aim of the political association? It is the preservation and prosperity of its members? And what is the surest sign that they are preserving themselves and prospering? It is their number and their population."[99] Moreover, in Book III, Chapter XIII, Rousseau suggests that when the territory of a republic is larger than a single city-state, the population should be spread evenly throughout it, and the sovereign assembly should meet periodically in different provinces, rather than in a single, set, central, urban capital. A rotating location for the popular assembly respects the integrity of the various rural communities that form the state. In other words, the sovereign assembly, alongside the government, should foster and support rural, agricultural family life, not compromise its ability to thrive. Rousseau additionally advises, "People the territory evenly, extend the same rights throughout it, spread abundance and life throughout it, that is how the State will at once have as much force and be as well governed as possible. Remember that the walls of cities are only built with the wreckage of farmhouses. For each Palace I see rise in the capital, I seem to see an entire countryside reduced to hovels."[100] In other words, the political independence and economic balance of Rousseau's ideal republic depend on the preservation of its overall rural character—and the deterrence of the development of a predominantly urban, commercial society rife with the extremes of poverty and wealth.

The mothers of these rural families, though excluded from formal citizenship, perform a political role perhaps even more important than any vote cast in the popular assembly, and equal in selflessness as that of the soldier. Rousseau glorifies women as the primary educators of future citizens and the inculcators and caretakers of manners and *moeurs* and, as such, they exert as much, or perhaps even more, influence on politics, as it is most broadly conceived, compared to their male counterparts. As the tutor preaches in *Emile*, "The good constitution of children initially depends on that of their mothers. The first education of men depends on the care of women. Men's *moeurs*, their passions, their tastes, their pleasures, their very happiness depend on women."[101] Women spend more time raising and educating the children, while the fathers spend more time supporting the family through their work both inside and outside the home. Women are responsible for legislating what Rousseau calls the most important laws of all—"*moeurs*" that are "not engraved on marble or bronze, but in the hearts of the Citizens."[102] Echoing the sentiments of his philosophical mentor Montesquieu, he argues in the *Social Contract* that *moeurs,* or moral codes, are vastly more influential and effective than civil or political laws in regulating human behavior. Because women are the chief architects of *moeurs* in the next generation, they act as the main conservators of the moral and social order of the republic. Women continue the tutelary role of the founder or legislator, celebrated in Book II of the *Social Contract*, who establishes the initial code of *moeurs* in a republic before he departs to let the people govern themselves according to these moral laws engraved "in the hearts of the Citizens."

Many women writers in the late eighteenth century upheld Rousseau as a champion of women because he praised and popularized their role as moral and civic educators. Madame de Staël, in her *Lettres sur les écrits et le caractère de J. J. Rousseau* (1788), claimed Rousseau as her hero. She praised his philosophy of the family for empowering women and celebrating them as the "empresses" of the domestic realm. His famous fictional female heroines, Julie and Sophie, provided unforgettable illustrations of the power he expected women to wield within the constraints of the patriarchal family. Rousseau's vision of women as the empresses of the home, the primary educators of future citizens, and the moral exemplars for both men and children, infused the roles of wife and mother with newfound moral, social, and political cachet. Late eighteenth-century women writers from both sides of the political spectrum—religious conservatives such as Hannah More and radical republicans such as Helen Maria Williams—embraced the Rousseauian ideal of motherhood and wifehood because it called attention to the positive moral influence that women may exercise over men, children, and future generations of citizens.

Rousseau's philosophy of the family exerted vast influence on the late eighteenth, early nineteenth-century movement in France and America that celebrated "republican motherhood," or the political role that mothers play as the primary caregivers and moral and civic educators of children.[103] Although his commitment to sex-role differentiation unjustly trapped women in the domestic realm, Rousseau's philosophy of the family recognized the tremendous moral, social, and political influence that wives and mothers can wield from within the family. Rousseau thus stands in late eighteenth-century European political thought as a paradoxical supporter of both female empowerment and male patriarchal authority. It is precisely this paradoxical character of his thinking that has captivated the imagination of his followers, and ignited the critical fires of his enemies, from his own time to the present day.

The Fall of Rousseau's Rural Republic:
Julie, Emile and Sophie, and *Corsica*

Although aspects of Rousseau's ideal of republican motherhood and his vision of childrearing enjoyed great influence on popular social practices in Europe and America, his philosophical defense of the rural republican family is problematic as a holistic social and political model because of its conflicts with modern history, economics, law, and culture. Bits and pieces of Rousseau's philosophy of the family have been profoundly relevant to modern democratic politics, but it has never been, and never could be, fully applied in the aftermath of the philosophical, political, and economic revolutions of the Enlightenment. While Okin (1979) argues that the tragic "fate of Rousseau's heroines" revealed deep internal inconsistencies in his treatment of the relationship between the family and the state, I contend that Rousseau uses the characters of Julie and Sophie to realistically explore the difficulty of putting his ideal of the rural republican family into practice.[104] Rousseau himself recognized the impracticalities of his own philosophy of the family in the wake of the revolutions of his time, and reveals the practical flaws in his own familial ideals with the tragic endings of the love stories of *Julie* and *Emile and Sophie*, and the realistic concession found in *Corsica* that the agricultural success and population overgrowth propagated by healthy rural families will eventually lead to the fall of any rural republic that manages to come into existence, even under the best of circumstances. Contrary to what Johnston (1999) argues, however, Rousseau's concern with the tragic dimensions of human society does not drive him to total pessimism about the possibility of realizing authentic republican social and political institutions in the modern world.[105] Rather, it leads him to a realistic assessment of the tension between theory and practice in republican statecraft, and the acceptance of the likelihood that any successful reform will be piecemeal and/or impermanent.

Emile and Sophie tells the sad tale of how the marriage and family of his two protagonists falls apart when they move from the rural countryside to the corrupt environs of Paris. Seduced by the mixed social gatherings in the city, Sophie commits adultery and becomes pregnant by her lover. Devastated, Emile abandons his wife and their young son for a solitary life. The story ends with Emile enslaved by a series of foreign masters, from a Barbary pirate to the governor of Algiers. As a slave and a servant, Emile rediscovers, despite his chains, the natural, internal freedom and independence of mind and spirit that the tutor had instilled in him as a boy. Emile returns to the only state of nature available to him—the oasis of his own soul and mind, where he stands free of any bonds or any betrayals.

Emile and Sophie charts the tragic fall of the rural family as found in *Emile*. In this cautionary tale, Rousseau sets forth the conditions under which he believes his ideal of the family remains vulnerable to corruption and disintegration. The dissolution of Emile and Sophie's rural family hinges on four fatal choices: their move from the moral purity of the country to the corruption of the city, their participation in mixed social gatherings instead of practicing the separation of the sexes in certain roles and activities, Sophie's failure to respect the patriarchal authority of her husband and resist the temptation to have an affair, and Emile's failure to remain selflessly committed to his wife and family despite his wife's adultery. These tragic choices represent the ways in which the ideal of the rural family as set forth in *Emile* can easily fall apart, if the proper conditions for its survival are not maintained. A prescriptive reading of *Emile and Sophie*, in light of the teaching of the *Social Contract*, reveals that the rural republican family needs a countryside location, a morally sound national culture, respect for patriarchal authority, sex-role differentiation, and the love and commitment of all its members to one another, in order to survive and thrive.

The tragic ending of *Julie* also exposes the vulnerabilities of the rural family. Like the story of *Emile and Sophie*, *Julie* ends with an infidelity. It is an infidelity of the mind, unconsummated in reality, yet it yields the same destructive consequences. Julie, who becomes gravely ill after saving one of her children from drowning, admits in a letter written on her deathbed that she always loved St. Preux more passionately than her husband Wolmar and that she looks forward to being unified in spirit with her true love in the afterlife. As she writes to St. Preux, "Nay, I leave thee not, I go to await thee. The virtue that separated us on earth shall unite us in the eternal abode. I die in this flattering expectation. Only too happy to pay with my life the right to love thee still without crime, and to tell thee so one more time."[106] Privy to the contents of her dying letter to St. Preux, Wolmar is bereaved of both his wife and the belief that she had been "cured" of her passion for St. Preux, and the family they built together is no longer the perfect haven of affection, communicative transparency, and trust that it once seemed.[107]

Like the adulterous Sophie, Julie could not conform to the prescriptions of patriarchal authority passed from her aristocratic father to her husband Wolmar. Forced into an arranged marriage by her father, Julie fooled herself into thinking that she could love a man she did not choose for herself. Yet, in her heart of hearts, she always remained free, and as a free woman she always loved St. Preux. The constraints of the aristocratic, patriarchal family cannot trap Julie into denying her own feelings. The final message of Rousseau's most romantic of novels is that true love cannot be constrained, arranged, or imposed—it must be freely chosen.

Rousseau uses the captivating characters of Julie and Sophie and the moral quandaries they encounter to explore the incongruity of his model of the rural patriarchal family with the social and political ideals of the Enlightenment. Sophie and Julie are both masterful women; they rule the homes in which they live with a kind of moral authority that even pontiffs might envy. Even when they admit to moral failure, they take a moral stand. In *Emile and Sophie*, even Emile admits that Sophie maintains her virtue and exhibits courage through the honest admission of her affair and pregnancy: "In the very depths of ignominy this strong spirit still retains all her courage; she is guilty without being base; she may have committed a crime, but not an act of cowardice."[108] By admitting their sexual passion for men other than their husbands, Sophie and Julie challenge the patriarchal order that aims to constrain their sexuality and delimit their choice of loves, and exercise their natural, primordial freedom of will that no cultural or political order can justifiably contain, especially in matters of the heart. As Marso (1999) perceptively concludes, Julie and Sophie are not typical, docile female victims trapped within the literary conventions of an eighteenth-century romance; rather, as Rousseau's fictional feminine alter egos, they subversively challenge the patriarchal and aristocratic culture of his time and even provide implicit criticisms of the patriarchal and hierarchical dimensions of his own thought.[109]

The stories of Julie and Sophie teach us that notions of female autonomy and empowerment are not, in the end, fully compatible with the patriarchal family, arranged marriage, and sex-role differentiation. Although Julie outwardly defends the patriarchal, sex-roled structure of the family she builds with Wolmar, she secretly reserves her highest hopes for her spiritual reunion with St. Preux in the afterlife, where they will abide together in the true equality of lovers who have merged together in a single identity. Sophie, likewise, resists obedience to the constraints of the patriarchal family and chooses to have an affair that satisfies her craving for sexual freedom, but destroys her family. The conflicted lives of Sophie and Julie parallel Rousseau's own paradoxical stance as a philosophical idealist and historical realist. In composing the tragic endings to his twin love stories, Rousseau acknowledged the impracticality of his familial ideals, and their conflicts with the principles and practices of the culture produced by the Enlightenment.

In Book II, Chapter X of the *Social Contract*, Rousseau boldly proclaims Corsica as the last option left in mid-eighteenth-century Europe for the implementation of his system of rural republicanism. His 1765 *Constitutional Project for Corsica* builds on this striking claim, cinching the final link in the chain of textual and philosophical interconnections among his five major political texts from the early 1760s. This text provides Rousseau's most direct, elaborate, and practical account of how the rural family ought to serve as the moral, economic, and political backbone of his ideal republic. While *Julie* and *Emile* offered appealing visions of the rural family with the Wolmar home and the fledgling marriage of Emile and Sophie, these texts focused more on describing the internal dynamics of these families, rather than their external relationship to the states in which they reside, and either implied or stated that their respective governments in the Vaud country and France were less than legitimate. In this way, Rousseau used the models of rural family life in *Julie* and *Emile* as illustrations of the imperfect steps that must be taken on the course toward the pragmatic realization of his familial-political ideal. With *Corsica*, Rousseau offers his readers a tantalizing glimpse into what he imagines his rural republican state could be, if only it had the best circumstances for implementation. Yet with the courageous taste for facing the tragic dimensions of human reality that peppers his entire oeuvre, Rousseau systematically traces the impediments to achieving and preserving his ideal synthesis of rural family life with republican government even on the near-idyllic island of Corsica.

Rousseau believes the island of Corsica is ripe for the implementation of his theory of rural republicanism because it is "incapable of growing rich in money."[110] Its location, size, topography, culture, and political history render it unlikely that Corsica will ever succeed at international commerce. Instead, Corsica can "grow rich in men" by multiplying its population so that it is proportional to, and evenly spread across, the geographic space of the island.[111] Agriculture is the economic activity by which both the "means of subsistence" and the population will grow in this balanced and moderate manner.[112] Agriculture, the defining activity of any rural community, has many benefits for a prospective republic such as Corsica. The farming life renders men and women healthier in body and temperament and hence more fertile: "Those women who are most chaste, and whose senses have been least inflamed by habits of pleasure, produce more children than others; and it is no less certain that men enervated by debauchery, the inevitable fruit of idleness, are less fit for generation than those who have been made more temperate by an industrious way of life."[113] Increased fertility and sexual health for the residents of the island is essential for it to counteract the depopulation caused by decades of war against Genoa. As Rousseau indicated in the *Social Contract*, depopulation renders a nation vulnerable to despotic rule: "The least populous countries are thus the most suited to Tyranny: wild beasts reign only in wildernesses."[114] Corsica thus should aim to strike a balance between the extremes of depopulation and overpopulation, both of which will lead to its ruin.

The self-sufficient agricultural lifestyle shapes peasants who are "much more attached to their soil than are townsmen to their cities."[115] As a consequence, the Corsican farmer possesses "that satisfaction with his own way of life which makes a man peaceful" and "that love of country which attaches him to its constitution."[116] The rural way of life, in other words, renders the men of Corsica capable of patriotic citizenship. Farm labor also "makes men patient and robust, which is what is needed to make good soldiers."[117] Echoing his emphasis on Emile's rugged, outdoor labors, Rousseau concludes, "the true education of a soldier is to work on a farm."[118] By localizing the training of soldiers within the agricultural work of the rural family, Rousseau envisions Corsica defending itself with a set of regional citizen militias, rather than compromising its republican independence by relying on the dangerous, mercenary power of a centralized, standing army. Without good citizen-soldiers, Corsica will be unable to defend its precarious position as an island republic near the mainland of Europe. By giving them economic independence and strong citizen militias, agriculture paves the way for the enduring political autonomy of the Corsicans.

One of the cultural flaws of the Corsican people is its tendency toward what Rousseau calls "family feuds" (les haines de famille).[119] He notes that Corsicans are infamous for their "ferocious temper" and their "schemes of vengeance" against each other, especially among families warring over theft and jealousy about money.[120] The restoration of an "industrious," agricultural "mode of life" will provide a buffer against such self-destructive, greed-driven conflicts between Corsican clans. Rousseau hopes that "their regular and simple occupations, by keeping them in the bosom of their own families, leave them few issues to settle between them!"[121] Indeed, the laws of the new Corsican republic ought to protect family life from such destabilizing disturbances, by "making land a necessary condition of paternity."[122] Rousseau suggests that after abolishing the system of "municipal feudalism" that exists on the island, a new, three-tiered class system, oriented around the rights and duties of citizenship, should be gradually implemented. All twenty-year-old men will swear an oath to the state and become "aspirants" to citizenship; all legally married aspirants who own property beyond their wives' dowries will become "patriots"; and all patriots, married or widowed, who have two living children, a house, and enough land for agricultural self-sufficiency, will become "citizens."[123] Rousseau argues that this class system will direct the ambitions of Corsican men toward marriage, family life, home and land ownership, agricultural self-sufficiency, and an understanding of the rights and duties of republican citizenship as contingent on these practices. Although Rousseau's proposed class system only gives full citizenship to adult men who are land and home-owning farmers with families, it aims to create a sense of economic and social equality among the nation's families that is essential for its political autonomy. Rousseau notes that even those citizens who serve as magistrates of the government "all return to the equality of private life," reinforcing his point that the rural, agricultural family should be the commonality shared among the people of Corsica.[124]

Rousseau argues that the mountainous terrain and fairly spacious geographic size of the island means that a pure democracy cannot be implemented as its form of government. A pure democracy is "suitable rather to a small town than to a nation."[125] It would be too onerous for all the Corsican citizens to travel to a single, central location for meetings of the popular assembly and the government. Instead, Rousseau suggests that a mixed government with a popular assembly that would meet in sections, rather than en masse, through the twelve regions of Corsica, and a small number of frequently elected magistrates that would be centered in the remote country-town of Corte, would better suit Corsica's geographic character. The emphasis Rousseau places on agriculture implies that the bulk of the lives of the people of Corsica will be devoted to this enterprise, generating good *moeurs* and reducing the need for frequent law-making by the assembly. The primary forum for political participation is found in the family, with its agricultural labors serving as the basis for the development of the moral and civic virtue of both present and future generations.

When France purchased Corsica from Genoa and suppressed its republican rebels in 1768, Rousseau had no further reason to complete his constitutional project for this nation.[126] Included in the final pages of the manuscript, however, is evidence that Rousseau himself foresaw that rural republicanism, even if established, could not indefinitely persist on Corsica for reasons beyond the obvious threat of colonization by an European empire. Rousseau acknowledges that the rural way of life that he hoped would continue to thrive on Corsica contains the seeds of its own self-destruction: the inevitability of the overgrowth of the state's population due to the health and fertility of its rural families, and the development of a class of land-rich farmers whose successful labors eventually make them dangerously wealthy and thus a threat to the economic equality and political independence of the state. With *Corsica,* Rousseau presents his highest hopes for the realization of his ideal of rural republicanism under the best circumstances available in the modern world, yet honestly reveals it to be a fragile ideal, worthy of pursuit, yet vulnerable to threats both external and internal to its integrated familial, economic, and political systems.

The discontinuity of Rousseau's ideal of the rural republican family with the historical circumstances of his time points to its subversive philosophical role. Rousseau is neither interested in wholly defending the patriarchal, aristocratic order nor the newly emerging democratic, bourgeois, commercial culture of the late eighteenth century. Encapsulated in his self-criticism of his ideal of the rural republican family is an equally savage critique of the perils of both the ancien régime and modern "enlightened" European civilization. For Rousseau, the rural family as imagined in *Emile, Julie,* and *Corsica* may be impractical and vulnerable to self-destruction, but it offers a moral ideal of family and community life that far exceeds any past or present historical models. Through the proliferation of this ideal via the expanding print culture of his time, and through his (albeit aborted) attempt to shape familial and constitutional policy for Corsica, Rousseau aimed to wield massive influence on the way people believed the family and the state should be best organized and interrelated—and largely succeeded due to his phenomenal popularity among revolutionary-era political thinkers and leaders in France. Despite his own recognition of their impracticalities and disjunctures with the trajectory of modern history, Rousseau's theoretical models of the rural family and the republican state nevertheless purveyed great practical impact.[127]

Shklar (1969) famously situates Rousseau's *Emile* and *Julie* within the utopian tradition of Western political thought. She contends that Rousseau constructs utopian worlds with full knowledge of their impracticability in order to use them as critical tools for understanding contemporary social and political life.[128] Yet while Rousseau the Romantic dreamer certainly never failed to acknowledge the impractical nature of his reveries, he nevertheless upheld them as ideals most expressive of the deepest longings of the human soul.[129] The rural republican family of the Swiss countryside, moreover, represents for Rousseau a historical example and a practical, albeit tenuous, fragile, and rapidly vanishing, model for the reconciliation of the age-old conflicts between men and women, nature and culture, love of family and duty to the state that arrived with our departure from the state of nature.

Rousseau is not a total pessimist; he would not have written and published *Emile* and *Julie* as novels for a popular audience if he did not hope for his ideas to make some kind of broad social impact. He is, however, a realist when it comes to assessing the limited potential for preserving the rural republican families of the Swiss and Corsican countrysides, or for propagating in the modern world this familial ideal and the ideal republican state it supports.

Burke and Wollstonecraft, standing in the wake of Rousseau's tremendous fame and influence on contemporary debates about the transformation of the family in the late eighteenth century, felt that there was a tinge of hypocrisy to his supposedly revolutionary rethinking of the family. Although she was drawn to his paradoxical style of thought, Wollstonecraft felt compelled to condemn her philosophical mentor for what she perceived as his contradictory stance on the inequality of the sexes. She devoted her magnum opus, *A Vindication of the Rights of Woman*, to a critique of his theory of sex inequality and a coeducational application of his theory of child rearing. Wollstonecraft perceived the fatal flaw in Rousseau's attempt to play both champion and critic of the transformation of the family; she understood that his philosophy of education demands the transcendence, not the preservation, of patriarchy and sex-role differentiation for it to be effectively and consistently applied within the emergent egalitarian politics of their time. Building on his ideas, she gave a more egalitarian structure to Rousseau's conception of the family as the educational site for the moral and civic virtues, and used it as a foundation for her own vision of a representative republic that would include the voices of people, formerly excluded on the basis of sex, class, or race, in its governance.

Early in his career, Burke wrote relatively positive, anonymous reviews of Rousseau's *Letter to d'Alembert* and *Emile* for the *Annual Register*. In his 1762 review of *Emile*, Burke noted the significant philosophical overlap between Rousseau's *Second Discourse*, *Julie*, and *Emile*, and especially the parallels in Rousseau's treatment of female education in his two novels. He also favorably cited the line from *Emile*, "To love a tranquil and domestic life, we ought to be well acquainted with it."[130] Like Rousseau, Burke upheld women and mothers as the moral center of family life, and family life as the moral foundation for politics. With a Rousseauian appreciation for the power of women and mothers to shape the moral tone of a society, and a Rousseauian fear of the destruction of the patriarchal family and its vital role as a little platoon, Burke embarked on his own systematic study and critique of the transformation of the family.

Yet it was Rousseau's *Confessions* (1782), and its shocking revelation that the author had abandoned all five of his children to a foundling home in the supposed spirit of Plato's *Republic*, that pushed Burke to condemn his predecessor as one of the forces behind the destruction of the patriarchal family, rather than as one of its defenders.[131] The glaring contradiction between Rousseau's romantic reimagining of the family in *Emile* and *Julie* and his heartless destruction of his own family spurred Burke to identify Rousseau's philosophy of the family with the dangerous utopianism of the *philosophes* and political radicals who had championed the Enlightenment and its most explosive political revolution in France. Despite his public defamation of his philosophical predecessor, Burke continued to share Rousseau's understanding of the patriarchal family as the emotional and moral core of the state, and its primary role in shaping *moeurs*, the most pervasive and stabilizing form of law in any political society. With an eye on the intricacy of his debt to, and his criticisms of, Rousseau, it is to Burke's reaction to the possibility of the transformation of the family that we turn in chapter two.

2

BURKE'S FEAR OF THE DESTRUCTION
OF THE HIERARCHICAL FAMILY

The Loss of a Little Platoon?

One of Edmund Burke's great fears was that the French Revolution would destroy the hierarchical family—with its ranks based on sex, class, and age—as he knew it in the eighteenth century.[1] In *Reflections on the Revolution in France*, he portrays the mob's removal of the French royal family from Versailles to Paris on 6 October 1789 as a portent for the demise of the hierarchical family not only in France, but also across European states. In his *First Letter on a Regicide Peace* (1796), he laments the legalization of divorce in France in 1792 as a sign that Christian marriage was no longer the bedrock of European civilization.

Yet his dread of the destruction of the hierarchical family predated the French Revolution. Speaking as a member of the British House of Commons in 1781, he opposed the attempted repeal of the Marriage Act of 1753 on the grounds that allowing children to marry without parental permission would undermine the perpetuation of family property and social stature. As a member of the Commons Select Committee on Indian Affairs from 1781 to 1794, he protested the exploitation, torture, and ruin of the noble and peasant families of India at the tyrannical hands of the East India Company. In each of these cases, Burke feared the destruction of sex, class, and age-based hierarchies across cultures, whether in class structures (which are partly perpetuated through families) or in the structure of families themselves.

Burke believed that the decay of the hierarchical form of the family—whether in England, France, India, or his native country, Ireland—would threaten the family's primordial role as inculcator of morality and manners, love of neighbor and love of country. In one of the

most famous passages of the *Reflections*, Burke advances his concept of
the "little platoon": "To be attached to the subdivision, to love the little
platoon we belong to in society, is the first principle (the germ as it were)
of public affections. It is the first link in the series by which we proceed
toward a love of our country and to mankind."[2] In the lines preceding this
passage, Burke lambastes those men of the Third Estate who "despise
their own order."[3] He encourages them to respect the little platoon that
is their social class, lest they risk losing their sense of connection to not
only their peers, but also their country and all of humanity. When read in
the context of his broader social theory, Burke's term "little platoon" can
be applied to a variety of social groups—whether class, family, church,
neighborhood, or profession—that define the communal identity and
relationships of an individual.

The family is, for Burke, the most important one of these little platoons that forms social identity, social relationships, and social virtues.
In his view, the family represents a more natural and fundamental kind
of little platoon than class or church. Joining the company of Rousseau,
Burke concludes that the family stands prior to, and provides the moral
foundation for, the realms of civil society and the state. While all little
platoons spring from the human social instinct, the family represents the
most natural expression and form of human sociability. Whether it is the
little platoon of the family or the little platoons of civil society, Burke
views all such social groups as fulfilling some social need that an individual cannot satisfy alone, and that the state should not satisfy lest it
overreach its legitimate scope of power.

It is not insignificant that Burke uses the metaphor of a small,
hierarchical military unit to describe the "subdivisions" in society—
including the family—that promote love for country and humanity.[4]
Like a military platoon, the Burkean family is a small community in
which people bond, develop a group identity, and learn to love and sacrifice for others as they share joys and struggles within the psychological and physical space defined by their common abode, relationships,
pursuits, rules, traditions, and hierarchical structures. As a consistent
critic of despotism in all its forms, Burke never endorses the abuse of
authority based on hierarchical or patriarchal social structures. Instead,
he defends the presence of hierarchies in the family or other institutions only insofar as they are used in a benevolently parental manner
to promote the practice of sympathy, civility, and a moderate, stabilizing form of patriotism.

For Burke, the hierarchical family fulfills its role as the moral foundation of society and the state to the extent that its structural framework creates a tutelary environment in which natural affections serve as the emotional basis of social formation. The natural affections, as understood by Burke and his contemporaries and friends David Hume and Adam Smith, are passions, such as love or sympathy, that draw us into social relationships with other human beings.[5] Burke blends the insights of these Scottish Enlightenment thinkers with the teachings of the Christian natural law tradition; he argues that these natural affections, or social passions, promote the development of social bonds that encourage moral, social, and political stability by reinforcing the natural order of the universe that God ordained. The passion of sympathy promotes moral stability by inspiring people to put their rational grasp of the natural law into action. Codes of civility promote social stability by encouraging people to respect social hierarchies that mirror the natural order of the universe. Patriotism promotes political stability by fostering respect for political hierarchies that stand symmetrical to the natural order.

Burke believes that the family itself must be modeled after the natural order of the universe in order to uphold moral, social, and political stability. He views class and patriarchal hierarchies as reflections of the natural order and understands the presence of these hierarchies in the family as conditions for social and political harmony. Burke perceived that laws regulating the inheritance of property are one of the main ways in which class and patriarchal hierarchies are preserved within societies; for this reason, he supported primogeniture, limited or no access to divorce, and legally mandated parental consent for the marriage of minors during his service as a Member of Parliament.

While Rousseau compares the family to a "small fatherland," Burke likens the state to a multigenerational family.[6] For Burke, the state is like a family writ large insofar as one's political inheritance is like a familial inheritance. Most famously, he conceptualizes the English constitution, and the liberties that it entails, as inheritances from the nation's ancestors. All the people who have died have passed onto posterity their rights and responsibilities and the political institutions that guarantee them. These political institutions, which Burke seeks to shield from the onslaught of the French Revolution, are hereditary succession in the monarchy, hereditary property and aristocracy, and the tradition of a constitutional policy. Burke's clever manipulation of familial metaphors allows him to cast law and politics as outgrowths of nature itself—distancing himself from Rousseau's stark distinction between the purity of the state of nature and the corrupting forces of society and aligning himself with the ancient thinking of Aristotle and Aquinas on the natural bases and ends of human communities.

Persisting with the metaphor of inheritance, Burke concludes that respect for the traditions, customs, and prejudices inherited from one's ancestors is the best guide for political action. The order of the state, and the actions of its leaders, should pay heed to the principle of familial inheritance that governs the natural order. Just as families pass property from one generation to the next, states and their leaders hand political wisdom and institutions from the past to the people of the present and the future. Although Burke draws a figurative parallel between the state and the family, he is careful, like Rousseau, to maintain the conceptual and practical distinction between the two realms and their social and political roles. He considers the Jacobin supporters of the French Revolution to be politically dangerous in part because they sought to replace love of family with an all-consuming patriotic loyalty to the state.

A thorough sweep through his writings exposes how Burke's preoccupation with the family pervades every level of his political argumentation. As a political theorist, he seeks to define the proper structure and function of the family and its relationship to civil society and the state. As a political rhetorician, he deploys familial metaphors and images to buttress his political arguments. As a statesman and political analyst, he is interested in how laws and public policies shape the family's historical development and trajectory across a variety of cultures and political systems. Despite its prominence as a concept, image, and policy issue in his political thought, only Boulton (1963), Blakemore (1988), and Zerilli (1994) have offered systematic treatments of the place of the family in Burke's works.[7] While Boulton helpfully identifies the family as one of the images Burke uses in his arguments against the French Revolution, his reading overlooks that Burke's fear of the loss of the hierarchical family is a real political concern, as central to his thinking as the threat of a Jacobin uprising in England in the 1790s. By examining Burke's attention to the family at both the conceptual and policy levels of his political thought, Blakemore explains that Burke is committed to the defense of patriarchal institutions from the family to the state, and Zerilli underscores Burke's fear of the destruction of these patriarchal institutions. Zerilli perceptively traces the connection Burke draws between the sabotage of traditional laws regarding marriage and inheritance and the collapse of all the patriarchal social and political institutions of the ancien régime.

Building on the work of these three scholars, this chapter analyzes Burke's familial anxieties at multiple levels of his political discourse, yet stresses that Burke's defense of the hierarchical family is not an unreflective acceptance of a traditional social institution, or an endorsement of despotic power in any form. Rather, Burke's defense of the hierarchical family is qualified by his insistence that such a family form is only legitimate and beneficial insofar as it encourages the flourishing of the natural affections and directs them toward the practice of the moral and civic virtues that foster sociability and stability throughout any given political community. Peace, in other words, is the end-goal of Burke's defense of the hierarchical family as the moral foundation of the state. For Burke, the hierarchical family, with its ranks based on class, age, sex, and social role, dispenses discipline, upholds trusted moral standards, and supports social stability more effectively than any egalitarian model could.

An array of scholars have indicated the central place of the natural affections in Burke's aesthetic, moral, and political theory, and generally mention in passing that Burke identifies the family as the main source of these natural affections.[8] What has been left unexplored is the genealogy of Burke's concern with preserving the hierarchical family as a transcultural moral foundation of stable civilizations and political regimes. In his speeches on America and Ireland, Burke suggests that unethical and imprudent economic and political policies lead to the corruption and dissolution of the natural affections that inspire sympathy, civility, and patriotism—the social bonds that hold a people together in a civilized and politically stable fashion. In his writings and speeches on England, India, and France, he focuses directly on the family as the most vital little platoon for the cultivation of such natural affections. He worries that the destruction of the patriarchal and class hierarchies that have determined the structure of families and their role in the greater social order entails the distortion and disintegration of the natural affections as well. By reconstructing, in a thematic narrative, Burke's recurring apprehensions about the destruction of the hierarchical family across a broad spectrum of his political writings, this chapter aims to help the contemporary reader understand the urgency behind his vindication of the hierarchical family, and the reasoning behind his fear of its extinction.

Burke's Fear of the Loss of the
"Great Principle of Connection" in
Ireland and America

Burke's speeches and writings on America and Ireland are engrossed with the problem of how bad economic and political policies contribute to the corruption and dissolution of the natural affections that inspire the stabilizing social bonds of sympathy, civility, and patriotism within the British Empire. Conor Cruise O'Brien (1992), Uday Mehta (1999), David Bromwich (2000), and Luke Gibbons (2003) have upheld Burke as an early and influential critic of many of the exploitative economic and political policies of the British Empire toward its colonies.[9] While he provided a powerful critique of the tendency of empires to abuse their power, especially as they greedily reached further beyond their epicenters, Burke generally, and somewhat quixotically, sought to repair and restore the "great principle of connection" that tied the varied peoples of the British Empire together, so that peace and stability might flourish among them.[10] In his majestic *Speech on Conciliation with the Colonies* (1775), he preached "peace sought in the spirit of peace, and laid in principles purely pacific" as the appropriate goal of British negotiations with the American colonies during the early stages of the revolution, and only fully supported the side of the rebels when Britain failed to give them more political and economic autonomy in exchange for a modest allegiance to the empire.[11] Although he justified the American Revolution as a cultural expression of the colonies' spirited republican political tradition, he still clung to the desirability of reconciliation even after the war's formal outbreak. Moreover, he continued to mourn the detrimental psychological and moral effects of the war on these peoples now separated by more than just an ocean.

In *A Letter to the Sheriffs of the City of Bristol* (1777), Burke describes Britain's war with colonial America as a "civil war" and condemns its destructive impact on civility among the English people and their American counterparts. As he solemnly observes, "civil wars strike deepest of all into the manners of the people."[12] Burke understands a system of manners to be the set of social rules that secures civility within a given community. He contends that civil war destroys the natural basis for the artifice of manners: the natural affections that inspire the bond of love, in its many forms, among a people. Burke draws a link between the hostility of civil war and the demise of natural affections: "by teaching us to consider our fellow-citizens in a hostile light, the whole body of our nation becomes gradually less dear to us. The very names of affection and kindred, which were the bond of charity whilst we agreed, become new incentives to hatred and rage when the communion of our country is dissolved."[13] The breakdown of the affectionate bond between relatives, neighbors, and citizens leads to the undoing of the patriotic tie to the state.

Burke questions the people of Britain who want to persist in the war with America in order to punish the colonists for revolting against the colonial taxation policy. He faults them for taking "no notice of the great principle of connection" that unites the peoples of America and Britain, and their willingness to "alienate your minds from your own kindred" for the sake of saving face even at the cost of civil war.[14] For Burke, nothing can justify the destruction of the "great principle of connection" that forges a bond between people through love and respect of kindred, fellow citizens, and country. This "great principle of connection" is founded on the natural affections—and the sympathy, civility, and patriotism they inspire—that the British civil war with the American colonies (and later, the French Revolution) threatens to disrupt.

In the *Speech at the Guildhall at Bristol* (1780), Burke reports how Catholic families in Ireland have been oppressed by the so-called popery laws or Irish penal code. Since the late seventeenth century, the Irish penal code prevented Catholics in Ireland from taking positions in the state, the church, the legal profession, or the armed services, among other penalties. Many Catholics, including Burke's father, felt compelled to publicly convert to Protestantism to gain access to these privileges.[15] Burke argues that "bad laws are the worst sort of tyranny" and that the Irish penal code is a particularly sinister example of this tyranny.[16] He describes the damaging impact that these laws had on Irish Catholic families: "In this situation, men not only shrink from the frowns of a stern magistrate, but they are obliged to fly from their very species. The seeds of destruction are sown in civil intercourse, in social habitudes. The blood of wholesome kindred is infected. Their tables and beds are surrounded with snares. All the means given by Providence to make life safe and comfortable are perverted into instruments of terror and torment."[17] Burke compares the homes of Irish Catholics to prisons or traps; it is as though their "tables and beds are surrounded with snares." Fear of informers made Irish Catholics uncomfortable and insecure even in their own homes as well as distrustful of their fellow subjects. In this way, the penal code compromised both natural affections and civic connections in the familial and political culture of Ireland.

Burke interprets the passage of a series of Catholic Relief Acts by the British Parliament in the 1770s—for which he tirelessly worked as a member of the House of Commons—as the end of the effacement of a tranquil and stable family life and civic life for Irish Catholics.[18] The passage of the Catholic Relief Acts helped push the British Empire toward "what we ought always to have been, one family, one body, one heart and one soul."[19] Burke hoped that the reclamation of peaceful family life for Irish Catholics would reinvigorate harmonious political relations within the British Empire. Catholic homes would no longer be prisons, but rather family havens; and the British Empire, no longer divided by the popery laws, would become "one family" again. He also hoped that the eventual, complete repeal of the Irish penal code, along with the end of the British civil war with America, would revive the "great principle of connection"—or the social bonds based on natural affections—between all the members of the British family. By positing the idealized image of the British Empire as an affectionate, cross-cultural family, Burke does not seek to gloss over its many abuses of power over time, but to make clear that he endorses the political ends of the empire to the extent that it works toward peace and unity, rather than despotism and disrespect of human dignity.

Burke's Fear of the Escalation of Divorce and Clandestine Marriage in England

In eighteenth-century England, a man, usually rich or aristocratic in status, had to scale a number of daunting legal hurdles in the ecclesiastical courts as well as in Parliament to acquire a divorce from his wife.[20] In 1771, the House of Lords introduced a bill intended to further detract from the desirability of divorce.[21] Some thought that the divorce rate had significantly increased as many spouses actively sought out adulterous relationships in order to set the slow wheels of the divorce process in action. The 1771 bill aimed to discourage spouses from using adultery as a means for acquiring divorce by legally barring the adulterous spouse from remarriage or the legitimization of any children born outside the original marriage. Burke fervently supported this bill in a speech given to the House of Commons on 29 April 1771.

Burke begins his speech with a stirring defense of the absolute centrality of marriage and female freedom to the civility and peace of the political order: "The foundation of all the order, harmony, tranquility and even civilization that is amongst us turns upon two things: the indissolubility of marriage and the freedom of the female sex. To these we owe every advantage that Europe has over the world—if it were not a fundamental precept of Christian religion, it ought to be made as it is a fundamental law of the State—and I have always lamented, that Parliament has thought fit to break through this law, even in cases of convicted adultery."[22] What does Burke mean by his startling declaration of the "freedom of the female sex" as a pillar of civilization? Burke views the freedom of women in a different light than Wollstonecraft; he conceives of female freedom as created and protected by the law, whereas Wollstonecraft wants to extend and advance the law so that it serves and protects the natural rights of women. For Burke, the law must protect women—the weaker sex—from physical domination and exploitation by men. In civilized societies in which marriages are stable, lasting, and revered under the law and by the church, women are free from brutal domination by barbaric tribes who seek to enslave them for their sexual services and capacity for childbearing. Marriage legally ties a woman to a single man who must respect her and care for her and their children. Fearful for the dangers divorce poses for both women and civilization itself, Burke laments that divorce is even permissible, and wishes to render it as inconvenient as possible to deter people from pursuing it and upsetting the social and political order.

In 1781, the British House of Commons proposed and successfully passed a bill to repeal the 1753 "Act for the better preventing of Clandestine Marriages" that the House of Lords later rejected. Under the 1753 Marriage Act, it was illegal for English people under the age of twenty-one to marry without parental permission. Many young people then traveled to Scotland to marry in secret, since clandestine marriage was outlawed in England.[23] The 1781 bill aimed to reform the severity of the 1753 Marriage Act. The 1781 bill suggested that men at age eighteen and women at age sixteen should be free to marry without parental consent.[24] In the *Speech on a Bill for the Repeal of the Marriage Act,* spoken before the House of Commons on 15 June 1781, Burke argued against the repeal on the following grounds.

First, Burke asks whether minors should be allowed to marry when they have not fully developed into independent adults. Emotionally, they lack maturity. Intellectually, they lack "mental discretion."[25] Financially, men lack the means to support a family during their time of apprenticeship: "Men are well qualified for propagation long before they are sufficiently qualified even by bodily strength, much less by mental prudence, and by acquired skill in trades and professions, for the maintenance of the family."[26] Burke emphasizes that men need to be independent in body, mind, and finances in order to handle the responsibilities of marriage and fatherhood; intriguingly, Wollstonecraft later applies a similar argument to women and their suitability for marriage and motherhood.

Burke decries the clandestine marriages of persons under twenty-one because they endanger not only the well-being of hapless offspring but also the stability of the broader community: "to enable and authorize any man to introduce citizens into the commonwealth, before a rational security can be given that he may provide for them and educate them as citizens ought to be provided for and educated, is totally incongruous with the whole order of society."[27]

Here Burke draws a direct link between the family and the state: it is the role of parents to "introduce," "provide for," and "educate" citizens. Parents, in short, create citizens. The harmonious ordering of society depends upon the ability of parents to fulfill their duties toward their children, since in so doing they shape the next generation of citizens who will compose, govern, and obey the state.

Burke suggests that older, established families suffer the most unjust economic consequences of irresponsible clandestine marriages. He chastises, "The improvident marriage of one man becomes a tax on the orderly and regular marriage of all the rest."[28] Young families without the means to support themselves place an undue burden on the charity of their relatives' responsible, financially independent families.

Burke contends that parents should have the power to arrange the marriages of their children, precisely because they look past the short-term interests of fleeting passion to the long-term interests of preserving family wealth and social stature. He concedes that the 1753 Marriage Act "tends to accumulate, to keep up the power of great families, and to add wealth to wealth" because it enables noble families to arrange the marriages of their children under twenty-one with the intent of augmenting the family fortune.[29] He defends the aristocratic bent of the act on the grounds that all principles of law and government, in order to be "useful to the community," must serve the advantage "of those who have the greatest stake in the country."[30] He acknowledges that the 1753 Marriage Act encourages "avarice," "ambition," and the "black train of villainies which attend that wicked passion," but accepts these vices to glean the benefits that arranged marriages among the nobility bring to the entire community. According to Burke, the main benefit is the social, and political stability that results from respect for the rank of the nobility and the emulation of their manners.

According to Burke, the 1753 Marriage Act encourages the growth of the natural affections by discouraging youths from poor marital matches that bring "a thousand misfortunes" to "embitter every part of a man's domestic life."[31] Ill-chosen marriages fail to hold families together, tearing apart "the dearest ties in human society" that in turn supply the ground for sympathy, civility, and patriotism. Against those who claim the 1753 Marriage Act invites the avarice of fathers who disregard their children's marital happiness for the sake of amalgamating the family fortune, Burke retorts: "You are afraid of the avaricious principle of fathers. But observe that the avaricious principle is here mitigated very considerably. It is avarice by proxy; it is avarice not working by itself or for itself, but through the medium of parental affection, meaning to procure good to its offspring. But the contest is not between love and avarice."[32]

In the *Rights of Men*, Wollstonecraft accuses Burke of supporting property laws (such as primogeniture) that undermine the natural affections of families by inciting avarice and ambition among their members. Burke admits that the 1753 Marriage Act permits paternal avarice to sway the arrangement of a marriage. In contrast to Wollstonecraft, however, he argues that such avarice is mitigated by the influence of parental affection, which seeks not only the good of the family but also the good of the children to be married. Thus, the "contest is not between love and avarice," but rather paternal avarice is tempered by parental love. Fathers seek to augment the family fortune as well as to marry their children securely and happily, fulfilling the long-term interests of the family as well as the individual spouses. Burke argues that the repeal of the 1753 Marriage Act would replace the "benevolent avarice" of the father with the "unmitigated" avarice of the fortune hunter. As in his 1791 critique of the secret affair between the lowly tutor and the aristocratic girl in Rousseau's *Julie*, Burke has harsh words for those who would romanticize the intentions of social climbers who seduce rich underage girls into clandestine marriage: "Do not call this by the name of the sweet and best passion, love. It is robbery—not a jot better than any other."[33]

Burke feared that the repeal of the 1753 Marriage Act would eliminate the hierarchical family, noble and common, as the moral foundation of British society. Fathers would suffer the degradation of losing their daughters and their property to fortune hunters. Daughters would suffer the moral outrage of debauchery. Sons would be tempted, or even compelled, to lead the life of the mercenary suitor. Clandestine marriages, left unchecked by law, would tear families apart both emotionally and financially. Hence Burke calls the members of the House of Commons to prevent the repeal of the Marriage Act: "Have mercy on the youth of both sexes; protect them from their ignorance and inexperience; protect one part of life by the wisdom of another; protect them by the wisdom of laws and the care of Nature."[34] Burke believes that the wisdom and experience of their parents should guide children, and that such wisdom, inspired by "the care of Nature," should remain codified in British law. His aim is not the oppression of youth, but rather the protection of youth from the dangers of libertinism and disrespect for authority.

In the *Reflections*, Burke contends that political decision-making should be based on the inherited wisdom of our forefathers. Likewise, in his 1781 speech on the proposed repeal of the 1753 Marriage Act, Burke argues that the decision to marry should be regulated so that youth are informed by the wisdom of their elders. A marriage should serve not only the short-term interests of the individual, but also the long-term interests of a family, and the greater society, in all its generations—the partnership between "those who are living, those who are dead, and those who are to be born." [35]

Burke's Defense of the Hierarchical Families of India

From 1786 to 1794, Burke devoted a large part of his work in the House of Commons to the ultimately unsuccessful attempt to impeach Warren Hastings. As head of the British East India Company and the governor-general of Bengal from 1773 to 1784, Hastings stripped the last vestiges of power from the Nawab of Bengal and fully established the sovereignty of the British Empire in Bengal.[36] In the *Speech on Mr. Fox's East India Bill* (1783), the *Speech in Opening the Impeachment of Warren Hastings* (1788), the *Speech on the Sixth Article of the Charge* (1789), and the *Speech in General Reply* (1794), Burke argues that the unjust and exploitative economic policies of the East India Company, under the leadership of Warren Hastings, have led to the devastation of both the common and noble families of India. Alongside his writings and speeches on Ireland and America, Burke's speeches during the trial of Warren Hastings illustrate the consistency of his moral outrage against all forms of colonial despotism. In the *Speech on Mr. Fox's East India Bill*, he describes the abuse of the Indian princesses and their families in a way that anticipates his famous harangue against the abuse of the queen of France and her family in the *Reflections*. He decries the cold commercial greed and the violent, tyrannical abuse of power that characterized the East India Company's business policies. He argues that these policies have brought about the ruin of the noble families of India, as a result of their utter lack of respect for the hierarchies, manners, and domestic ties that held these families together.

Burke vividly recounts the tragic circumstances under which families, both noble and common, were shattered by the corrupt economic and legal policies of the East India Company in Bengal. Under the rule of Warren Hastings, the East India Company cancelled the tax-collecting powers and the ruling authority of the zamidars, or the local large landholders in Bengal, and transferred their power and authority to the "highest bidders"—who were often the personal agents of the East India Company.[37] Burke argues that the extortionate taxes and rents imposed by the new landed political elite forced the peasant tenant-farmers who tilled their fields into desperate poverty.[38] In his *Speech in Opening the Impeachment of Warren Hastings*, Burke recounts how some peasants, in the region governed by Devi Singh, sold their own wives and children into slavery to survive: "The peasants were left little else than their families and their bodies. The families were disposed of. It is a known observation, that those who have the fewest of all other worldly enjoyments are the most tenderly attached to their children and wives. The most tender of parents sold their children at market. The most fondly jealous of husbands sold their wives. The tyranny of Mr. Hastings extinguished every sentiment of father, son, brother and husband!"[39] Here we witness a horrific example of how exploitative business practices and economic policies can extinguish the natural affections—"every sentiment of father, son, brother and husband"—and break families apart. In his *Speech in General Reply*, Burke likewise recounts how Colonel Hannay, under the command of Warren Hastings, imprisoned in cages, dungeons, and mud forts the peasants who could not pay their extortionate rent to the East India Company, compelling them to sell their children into slavery to pay their debts. Burke blames the unbearably oppressive rule of the East India Company, not the preexistent slave trade, for bringing about such desperate measures on the part of parents:

> The prisoner's counsel has attempted to prove that this had been a common practice in that country. And though some person as wicked as Colonel Hannay might have been there before at some time or other, no man ever sold his children but under the pressure of some cruel exaction. Nature calls out against it. The love that God has implanted in the heart of parents toward their children is the first

germ of that second conjunction which He has ordered to subsist
between them and the rest of mankind. It is the first formulation
and the first bond of society. It is stronger than all laws; for it is the
law of Nature, which is the law of God. Never did a man sell his
children who was able to maintain them. It is, therefore, not only
a proof of his exactions, but a decisive proof that these exactions
were intolerable.[40]

Burke asserts that God ordained as a "law of Nature" the love of parents
for their children. This natural affection of parental love is the "first
bond of society" that inspires all other social bonds. The violation of
this primal bond through the sale of children into slavery is proof for
Burke that the economic policies of the East India Company have
crushed these peasant families and the natural affections that enable sociability among them.

   Burke bewails how noble families suffered an equally devastating
fate at the hands of the tyrannical rule of Warren Hastings. The great
evil of the East India Company, according to Burke, is that it brought
about "the destruction of the most ancient families of the country, as I
believe in so short a time never was unveiled since the world began."[41]
In the *Speech on Mr. Fox's East India Bill*, Burke reports how the mother
and wife of the late Nawab of Oudh, Shuja al-Daula, the "second man in
the Mogul Empire," were ruined by the corrupt business policies of
Warren Hastings, the head of the East India Company: "The instrument
chosen by Mr. Hastings to despoil the relict of Sujah Dowlah was her
own son, the reigning Nabob of Oude. It was the pious hand of a son
that was selected to tear from his mother and grandmother the provision
of their age, the maintenance of his brethren, and of all the ancient
household of his father."[42] Hastings destroyed this noble family in the
most insidious way possible: he destroyed it from within. He taints the
"pious hand of a son" by using the reigning Nawab of Oudh as an instrument to ruin his own family. Not only does the Company show no
respect for natural domestic ties within Indian families, but it also shows
no respect for local traditions and manners: "It remains only to show,
through the conduct in this business, the spirit of the Company's government, and the respect they pay toward other prejudices, not less re-
garded in the East than those of religion: I mean the reverence paid to
the female sex in general, and particularly to women high rank and condition."[43] Anticipating his defense of chivalry in the *Reflections*, Burke
points out that in the East, women, and especially women of high rank,
are paid the same reverence as objects of religious devotion. The East

India Company respected neither the family nor the women who serve as its moral pillars. Consequently, it forced the "ancient matron," the wife of the late Shujah al-Daula, and all the women and children under her care, to leave their own home—only to be plundered of all the belongings they tried to take away with them.[44]

Burke reports that the Company also plundered the secondary palace of the late Shuja al-Daula that housed his second family of con-cubines and illegitimate children. In the *Speech in General Reply*, Burke explains that both the children and the concubines held positions of high social rank according to the customs of the country: "all these sons and daughters were considered as persons of eminent distinction, though in-ferior to the legitimate children,—assuming the rank of their father, without considering the rank which their mother held (and) these women were considered as objects of a great degree of respect, and of the greatest degree of protection."[45] Burke upbraids Hastings's men for starving and beating these women and children, disregarding both their natural frailty and their noble rank, and refusing to sympathize with their plight on the grounds that they were whores and bastards. In the same speech, Burke also reproaches Hastings's men for pillaging the seraglio of the Rajah Chait Singh and robbing these women and chil-dren of their only property and subsistence. No matter what its local idiosyncrasies are, no matter whether it occupies a palace, a hut, or a seraglio, Burke fights for the deference due to the hierarchical family in all its culturally unique manifestations. In this way, Burke follows his philosophical inspiration, Montesquieu, who offered a rather cos-mopolitan, and sometimes sympathetic, view of the practices of polygamy and concubinage in his *Lettres Persanes*. Likewise, Burke moves beyond the "enlightened" provincialism of his other mentors, David Hume and Adam Smith, who both judged the practice of polygamy in non-European cultures as barbaric and uncivilized, partic-ularly in its treatment of women.[46] Burke's somewhat surprising open-ness toward the seraglios of India is telling for his theory of the hierarchical family's cross-cultural political relevance. For Burke, what matters most is that families have a hierarchical structure that helps fos-ter the development of affection and stability throughout their particular cultural and political order. The hierarchical seraglios—whose families were as loved, and loving, as their legitimate counterparts—fulfill a vital socializing function within their own "exotic" political system—and thus should be respected as foundations, not subversions, of Indian culture. As a defender of the benevolent, parental, politically stabilizing role of patriarchal and hierarchical structures within a variety of cross-cultural family forms, Burke is less concerned with the constraints that patriarchal orders place on women and more interested in how even an Indian seraglio can provide a hospitable environment for affective-social formation within its particular political tradition. Wollstonecraft, of course, will later compare European women to the concubines in an "eastern harem," indicating the irony that she and her peers are not free of patriarchy any more than their Asiatic counterparts.[47]

In the *Speech in Opening the Impeachment of Warren Hastings,* Burke sets forth his most dramatic and arresting depiction of the destruction of the hierarchical family. He begins the speech with a detailed account of the caste system, or "family orders," of India, which the East India Company sets out to ruin: "The Gentoo people, from the oldest time, have been distributed into various orders, all of them hereditary: these family orders are called castes; these castes are the fundamental part of the constitution of the Gentoo commonwealth, both in the church and in their state."[48] Burke explains that the caste, or the collections of families under a certain social rank, is the most fundamental unit of Indian society. Brahmins occupy the highest-ranking caste; but with the social privileges that attend their caste comes a fate worse than death if they are excommunicated for dishonor: "the Brahmin . . . if he loses his caste . . . is thrown at once out of all ranks of society. . . . No honest occupation is open to him; his children are no longer his children; their parent loses that name; the conjugal bond is dissolved. Few survive this most terrible of calamities. To speak to an Indian of his caste is to speak to him of his all."[49] The loss of one's caste is the loss of rank, occupation, family, and society itself. Burke dwells on the loss of family because it has the most shattering impact on a person's capacity to identify with a broader community. The East India Company's ruthlessness dishonored many a Brahmin in order to subject them to this unparalleled indignity.

Burke describes in gruesome detail how Brahmin families were physically tortured by the East India Company as punishment for their noncompliance with its extortionate system of bribes. In these scenes of torture, sacred family bonds were coldly and perversely mocked in the most sadistic manner: parents were forced to watch their children almost scourged to death; fathers were tied face to face with their sons so that both would suffer the same whipping; virgins were raped in public with their parents in view; wives were publicly stripped so that their breasts could be brutally cut with bamboo. Physical wounds were not the only wounds of this inhumane torture; every stroke of the whip wounded and lacerated "the sentiments and affections of nature."[50] Burke drives home that this horrifying scene of torture means more than just the defeat of a particular family or families; it signifies the excision of the "sentiments and affections of nature" that hold families and society together. Burke also mourns the destruction of these noble families through their torturer's deliberate disrespect for the Brahmin code of honor. The public disgrace suffered by these innocent victims tragically entailed the loss of their caste: "All the relations of life are at once dissolved. His parents are no longer his parents; his wife is no longer his wife; his children, no longer his, are no longer to regard him as their father. It is something far worse than complete outlawry, complete attainder, and universal excommunication."[51] The loss of caste is the worst possible fate, in the eyes of both Burke and the Indians themselves, because it entails, first and foremost, the loss of one's family. Burke argues that it is the evil deeds of the East India Company, not the caste system itself, that is to blame for the Brahmins' fate: "My Lords, we are not here to commend or blame the institutions and prejudices of a whole race of people, radicated in them by a long succession of ages, on which no reason or argument, on which no vicissitudes of things, no mixtures of men, of foreign conquest, have been able to make the smallest impression."[52] Burke, with a Montesquieuian respect for the laws unique and appropriate to the ancient culture of India, casts no judgment on the moral rectitude of the caste system, but rather censures the East India Company for its flagrant manipulation of its native sanctity in order to overthrow the ruling noble families. Burke understands the caste system as a cultural institution that has thrived for centuries; for him, its longevity alone is worthy of our transcultural respect and a sign that it serves some agreeable social functions. Burke's defense of the Indian caste system shares an important component with his defense of the aristocratic family in England and France: in all three cases, he defends those hierarchical and patriarchal family structures codified in the law and culture of the society that foster the development of the natural affections and the moral and civic virtues.

Burke's Allegorical Reading of the Fate of the Royal Family of France

One of Burke's most striking analyses of the destruction of the hierarchical family, its political causes, and its moral consequences is his allegorical account of the invasion of Versailles by a hungry Parisian mob in the *Reflections*. Critics have long noted that Burke's account of the events of 6 October 1789 is neither accurate nor objective.[53] In his 1791 critique of Burke's account of the mob's expedition to Versailles, Thomas Paine dryly noted, "I can consider Mr. Burke's book in scarcely any other light than a dramatic performance; and he must, I think, have considered it in the same light himself, by the poetical liberties he has taken of omitting some facts, distorting others, and making the machinery bend to produce a stage effect."[54] Paine perceives the dramatic purpose behind Burke's hyperbolic, fantastical account of the mob's attack on the French royal family: Burke is writing a prophetic allegory, not an objective history.

Boulton (1963) argues that the family is one of the main metaphors that Burke uses to bolster his rhetorical attack against the French Revolution.[55] Yet the family functions as more than only a metaphor in the *Reflections*, for Burke intends his audience to interpret the attack on the French royal family as a portent for the storming of their own little platoons. Through his allegorical narrative of the mob's removal of the French royal family from Versailles to Paris, Burke suggests that the imprudent politics of the French Revolution will destroy not only the hierarchical structure of the family but also the system of aristocratic, chivalrous, and feminine manners that is in large part perpetuated within it. He portends that the loss of the hierarchical culture that elevates people above animal brutality paves the way for regression to a barbaric world in which both civility and stability are unknown.

Wollstonecraft, as well as many critics after her, unfairly charge Burke with a perverse fascination with Marie Antoinette.[56] Often the queen is the focus of scholarly discussion regarding Burke's account of the raid of Versailles, as though she were the only worthy topic of interest in this rich and complex part of the *Reflections*.[57] This is not so. In fact, Burke begins this section of the *Reflections* by engaging the reader's sympathy for the king of France.

Burke cynically quips, "among the revolutions in France must be reckoned a considerable revolution in their ideas of politeness."[58] It is precisely this revolution in manners that has led to the humiliation of the king. Burke argues that although the English have traditionally learned their manners from the French, he is grateful that the English "have not so far conformed to the new Parisian mode of good breeding . . . to say, to the most humiliated creature that crawls upon the earth, that great public benefits are derived from the murder of his servants, the attempted assassination of himself and his wife, and the mortification, disgrace, and degradation that he has personally suffered."[59] The revolution in manners has led to the destruction of natural ties between human beings and traditional signs of basic human decency. Natural affections and manners have been sacrificed to the moral calculus of utilitarianism; the mob justifies the murder of the king's servants, the attempted assassination of himself and his wife, and his own personal degradation, by the promise of "great public benefits." It is clear, then, that Marie Antoinette is not the only focus of sympathy in Burke's allegorical recreation of the events of 6 October 1789. The king, the queen, the children, and the servants of the royal family are all to be pitied. It is the royal family, and not Marie Antoinette alone, that is the focus of Burke's sympathy.

On one level, Burke is speaking of any ordinary family when he speaks of the royal family of France. He continually refers to the queen as the king's "wife" and the king as the queen's "husband," driving home the point that these are real people with a real marital relationship like other men and women. He brings the king and queen down from their lofty heights by continually emphasizing what makes them the same as any other couple: their manhood, womanhood, spousehood, and parenthood. His depiction of the mob's overrunning of Versailles is preceded by the domestic scene of the royal couple settling down to bed to "indulge nature in a few hours of respite and troubled, melancholy repose."[60] By helping the reader to identify with the king and queen, Burke elicits the deepest sympathy for the plight of the royal family. He wants us to see the attack on the royal family as an attack on our own little platoons.

The siege of the royal family is a bad omen for Burke, for it foretells the destruction of the hierarchical family. When Marie Antoinette runs from the mob that invades Versailles, it is to her husband the king she flees. But he is no more secure than she is, and neither are their infant children. It is not just the woman who is endangered in this "revolution in manners." The entire family—husband, wife, and children—is endangered: "The King, to say no more of him, and this queen, and their infant children (who once would have been the pride and hope of a great and generous people) were then forced to abandon the sanctuary of the most splendid palace in the world, which they left swimming in blood, polluted by massacre and strewn with scattered limbs and mutilated carcasses."[61] Here Burke paints a gory portrait of Versailles transmogrified from the ideal home and palace into the setting for a gothic novel. It was once the "sanctuary of the most splendid palace in the world" and now is "swimming in blood" and "polluted by massacre." Through the blood-ying of the home, all that is held sacred in family life has been symbol-ically defiled and the family has been symbolically destroyed.

Burke's parenthetical comment in this passage is quite signifi-cant. By claiming that the infant children of the royal family "once would have been the pride and hope of a great and generous people," Burke implies that what the French people has lost is the honorable ability to see the royal family as symbolic of their own families and the nation as a whole. This is Burke's call to Britain to maintain its claim to be a "great and generous people," to see the royal family as symbolic of their own families, and to realize that the destruction of the royal family paves the way for the destruction of the hierarchical family in general.

Burke's Vilification of Rousseau's Philosophy of the Family

In *A Letter to a Member of the National Assembly* (1791), Burke vilifies Rousseau as the founding father of the French Revolution, a title—both laudable and ignominious—that has stuck to him for more than two cen-turies. As such, he is the philosopher who provided the theory for the practice of the destruction of civilization, the state, and their foundation, the hierarchical family. Burke casts Rousseau as the man who destroyed the family both in theory and in practice: on the one hand, he provided the philosophy for the subversion of the hierarchical family in his novel *Julie*; on the other hand, he tore apart his own family by sending his five children to a foundling hospital. Burke's defamation of Rousseau re-mained the dominant view of him in England until Byron and Shelley resurrected him as a father of Romanticism.[62]

Burke begins his discussion of Rousseau in *A Letter to a Member of the National Assembly* by returning to the plight of the French royal family. This time he is concerned with 14 July 1790: the first anniversary and celebration of the fall of the Bastille. The pillorying of the king and queen during the celebration of the fall of the Bastille demonstrates, for Burke, how the natural affections of the people have been perverted by the revolution. He writes: "On this pillory they set their lawful king and queen, with an insulting figure over their heads. There they exposed these objects of pity and respect to all good minds, to the derision of an unthinking and unprincipled multitude, degenerated even from the ver-satile tenderness which marks the irregular and capricious feelings of the populace."[63] The "versatile tenderness" that used to uplift the otherwise "capricious feelings" of the populace is gone, leaving them with nothing but an "unprincipled" and "unthinking" disrespect for their king and queen. For Burke, the pillorying of the king and queen is even worse than what happened on 6 October 1789. It is precisely because the festival is a calculated act in a time of peace that makes it so morally despicable. It shows just how deep this "revolution in manners" has gone; it has rid the French of any sense of their former "tenderness" and natural affections for their royal family, for now they can calculatedly celebrate the indignities they have imposed on their former rulers. Burke's fears as expressed in the *Reflections* have been realized; he portrays the events of 14 July 1790 as the logical outcome of the events of 6 October 1789.

Burke argues that one of the main reasons why this dissolution in manners, morals, and natural affections has occurred is that the National Assembly has taken the moral teaching of Rousseau under its wing. As a result, they encourage in the young the evil dispositions of adolescent vanity rather than the Christian virtues. The National Assembly builds statues of the "moralist" Rousseau by melting down the "bells of their churches."[64] By upholding an immoral man as the moralist for a new generation of Frenchmen, they undermine the traditional Christian morality of France. No longer is it the body and blood of Christ that is held sacred by the Catholic people of France, but rather it is Rousseau's "blood" they "transfuse into their minds and into their manners" and his body they celebrate in statues built out of church bells.[65] Rousseau has become their "canon of holy writ," replacing the canon of centuries of Catholic teaching.[66] In contrast to Christianity, in which "true humility . . . is the low but deep and firm foundation of all real virtue," Rousseau's system of morals turns the "selfish, flattering, seductive, ostentatious" vice of vanity into a "ruling virtue."[67] Rousseau offers a dangerous new system of religion, morality, and education for revolutionary France.

What Burke finds especially dangerous about this new ruling virtue of vanity is that it leads to the destruction of the family. Burke concludes that just as Rousseau destroyed his own family with his vanity, the vanity of Rousseauian revolutionaries will destroy all the families of France. Rousseau's vanity is a kind of deranged adolescent egocentrism that allows him to expound to others the need for "universal benevolence" to mankind, while "his heart was incapable of harboring one spark of common parental affection."[68] Likewise, the professors of the Rousseauian philosophy preach "benevolence to the whole species" but "want of feeling for every individual with whom (they) come in contact."[69]

Rousseauian vanity turns people into egomaniacs who can only feel connection to an abstract, universal notion of humanity but not to any particular human beings. Burke wryly suggests that even "bears" are better at caring for their young than "philosophers" like Rousseau; Rousseau's vanity allows him to profess love for humanity, but he "casts away, as a sort of offal and excrement, the spawn of his disgustful amours." [70] According to Burke, Rousseau treated his children like the waste products of a vulgar sexual encounter, rather than the sacred gift of the moral bond between husband and wife and the cherished center of family life.

"Vanity," Burke points out, "finds its account in reversing the train of our natural feelings."[71] He concludes that Rousseauian vanity has led to the reversal of the natural feelings that serve as the bond that holds families and society together. Moreover, Rousseau's "ethics of vanity" brings about the destruction of families in general for the sake of establishing a revolutionary republic: "As the relation between parents and children is the first among the elements of a vulgar, natural morality, they erect statues to a wild, ferocious, low-minded, hard-hearted father, of fine general feelings; a lover of his kind, but a hater of his kindred. Your masters reject the duties of this vulgar relation, as contrary to liberty; as not founded in the social compact, and not, of course, the result of free election, never so on the side of the children, not always on the part of the parents."[72] The revolutionaries reject the natural bonds between parent and child on the grounds that it is not based on a "free election." People do not choose their parents, and often parents have not chosen to have the children they produce. Thus, Rousseauian vanity replaces the "natural morality" of family life. The social compact and the rights of man replace the family as the basis of all social bonds. Burke fears that the French people, under the sway of Rousseauian philosophy, are now committed to serving the general will, but not the wills of their own children and kindred.[73]

Next comes Burke's assault on the model of the educator set forth in Rousseau's novel *Julie*.[74] Burke draws a parallel between the character of St. Preux and Rousseau's role as an educator for the French revolutionaries. Burke interprets the revolutionaries' commemoration of Rousseau in a statue as a symbolic celebration of St. Preux as the ideal preceptor for the youth of France. Burke suggests that tutors will no longer play a parental role now that Rousseau's philosophy has rid France of all respect for parental authority. Rousseauian educators are nothing but "gallants" and "danglers at toilets."[75] These men, like St. Preux, will betray the most fundamental family trusts by debauching their female pupils in the homes of their parents. In this way, "they dispose of all the family relations of parents and children, husbands and wives."[76] The Rousseauian educators, following the lead of the Rousseauian legislators in the National Assembly, will be the moving force behind the demolition of the hierarchical structure of the family, and the natural affections, manners, and morality it cultivates. Burke predicts that Rousseauian educators will invade the home (much like the mob at Versailles) and corrupt everyone and everything in it, violating the most basic family mores.

Burke contends that the followers of Rousseau, both legislators and educators, are determined to despoil not only family bonds and natural affections but also aristocratic manners and chivalry. He laments, "Through Rousseau your masters are resolved to destroy these aristocratic prejudices."[77] Burke argues that the revolutionaries celebrate the vulgar passions and succumb to those appetites that their ancestors ennobled through the use of aristocratic manners. They also destroy the traditional conception of chivalric love, a love that is of "utmost importance to the manners and morals of every society."[78] Emulating the ideas of *Julie*, the Rousseauian educators will teach a new kind of love: "they infuse into their youth an unfashioned, indelicate, sour, gloomy, ferocious medley of pedantry and lewdness; of metaphysical speculations, blended with the coarsest sensuality. Such is the general morality of the passions to be found in their famous philosopher, in his famous work of philosophical gallantry, the *Nouvelle Eloise*."[79] The Rousseauian educators will not only destroy the natural bonds between family members, but also destroy the love that used to bind men and women together in a civilized way within the institutions of marriage and the family.

Burke contends that these immoral educators will accomplish the political goal of the National Assembly: fracture the moral framework of the hierarchical family in order to replace it with an abstract conception of the general will of a republican assembly. By seducing their students and blending into their families more successfully than St. Preux, the Rousseauian educators will break down the social barriers between the classes. Burke concludes: "In this manner, those great legislators complete their plan of leveling, and establish their rights of men on a sure foundation."[80] The Rousseauian educators will debase the hierarchical families they invade, ruining all bonds and distinctions between parent and child, husband and wife, maiden and suitor, and dislodge the hierarchical family as the moral foundation of the state.

The National Assembly aims not only to confound aristocratic manners, but also the aristocracy itself. To do so, they must "destroy, to the best of their power, all the effect of those relations which may render considerable men powerful or even safe."[81] In order to wreck these relations, they "endeavor to subvert those principles of domestic trust and fidelity which form the discipline of social life."[82] To overthrow the nobility, they must upset the relations that make the nobility powerful, and, to do that, they must weaken the hierarchical order of aristocratic families. By immortalizing Rousseau in bronze, the National Assembly upholds his hero St. Preux, the lowly tutor who betrays his aristocratic master by seducing his daughter, as the model for the infiltration of the noble family: "by the false sympathies of the *Nouvelle Eloise*, they endeavor to subvert those principles of domestic trust and fidelity, which form the discipline of social life. They propagate principles by which every servant may think it, if not his duty, at least his privilege, to betray his master. By these principles, every considerable father of a family loses the sanctuary of his house."[83] Burke speaks of how the "tranquility and security of domestic life" will be laid waste and the "asylum" and "sanctuary" of the house turned into a "gloomy prison" once domestics and servants are infused with the revolutionary philosophy of Rousseau.[84] Once a nobleman can no longer depend on the obedience of his servants, he is a prisoner in his own home, and the aristocratic order is overturned.

At the end of his diatribe against Rousseau, Burke reveals how the National Assembly uses terror to execute its policies: "Whoever opposes any of their proceedings, or is suspected of a design to oppose them, is to answer with his life, or the lives of his wife and children."[85] Subjected to the terror of the revolutionaries, all families share the same fate as the royal family. Burke fears that the National Assembly will overrun all the families, both noble and common, that stand in the way of its plan to replace the private family with the general will as the moral foundation of the republican state.

Burke's dark portrait of Rousseau and his sinister relevance to the French Revolution is stridently polemical, and thus obscures many of the commonalities between the two thinkers. Burke's insistence that *Julie* will continue to cause familial and class upheaval in France, and that the *Social Contract*'s notion of the general will has been the engine of the National Assembly's plot to reconstitute state power on the abstract concept of popular sovereignty, and sever the private family from its role in a moderate kind of civic formation, are exaggerations of two central problems in Rousseau's political thought. Rousseau himself acknowledged the potential for *Julie* to either corrupt or transform the familial mores of its audience. He also admitted in the *Social Contract* and other works that small, private, fractious and selfish societies—like the feuding families in the Corsican countryside—are a real threat to the longevity of any republican regime grounded on the ideal of submitting to the common good. Even Burke suggested in the *Reflections* that had Rousseau lived to witness the French Revolution in "one of his lucid intervals," he would have been shocked by how his ideas were purportedly implemented by his "servile imitators."[86] Burke's sympathetic thought-experiment can be fruitfully extended to further underscore the common ground between him and Rousseau: perhaps if Rousseau had lived to read *A Letter to a Member of the National Assembly* in a lucid state, he may have agreed with much of it, perhaps especially its perceptive reading of the tensions in his thought, and its critique of how his persona and ideas were used by the revolutionaries in France. Burke's paranoid rant against Rousseau and his supposed followers can also be seen as an ambivalent tribute to the rhetorical power of Rousseau's own conspiratorial writings from his later years in exile.

Burke's Condemnation of the Legalization
of Divorce in France in 1792

In the *Letters on a Regicide Peace* (1796), Burke rails against the policies of the French Republic that have exacerbated the dissolution of the hierarchical family and the natural affections it cultivates. The *Letters on a Regicide Peace* contain Burke's most incendiary writing; his rage at the destruction of familial, social, and political hierarchies in the name of revolutionary egalitarianism had never been so publicly incensed. He reserves his most vitriolic speech to condemn the legalization of divorce for men and women, for the first time in French history, by the French Legislative Assembly in 1792.[87] Burke argues that the legalization and liberalization of divorce have corrupted the social bonds of sympathy, civility, and patriotism that indissoluble marriage helped to maintain.

In the *First Letter on a Regicide Peace*, Burke notes that the French republic views the family as a rival and threat to its sovereignty, rather than as its moral foundation. He argues that revolutionary regimes must resort to tyrannical tactics to inspire patriotism, since they uproot the traditional institutions that had fostered it before. He reports that the Directory, in the first year of its rule in 1795–1796, orchestrated public displays of treason against family members to reinforce a perverse total commitment to the political cause of the French republic:

> All sorts of shows and exhibitions, calculated to inflame and viti- ate the imagination and pervert the moral sense, have been con- trived. They have sometimes brought forth five or six hundred drunken women calling at the bar of the Assembly for the blood of their own children, as being Royalists or Constitutionalists. Some- times they have got a body of wretches, calling themselves fathers, to demand the murder of their sons, boasting that Rome had but one Brutus, but that they could show five hundred. There were in- stances in which they inverted and retaliated the impiety, and pro- duced sons who called for the execution of their parents. The foundation of their republic is laid on moral paradoxes.[88]

Through these perverse public displays of familial violence, the Direc- tory denies that the natural affections of the family are the original source of patriotic love for the state. The emotional ties of the family pose a serious threat to the cultivation of the patriotic loyalty necessary to preserve their new and fragile regime; for this reason, they set out to destroy the natural bonds of family life and replace them with an unnat- ural and all-consuming patriotic devotion to the state.

Burke professes that the legalization of divorce in 1792 was the most effective and invasive way for the revolutionaries to slacken the ties, both natural and conventional, that hold families together. No longer was marriage a Christian sacrament solemnized and certified by the Church, but rather a civil contract easily dissolvable by divorce:

> Other legislators, knowing that marriage is the origin of all rela- tions, and consequently the first element of all duties, have en- deavored by every art to make it sacred. The Christian religion, by confining it to the pairs, and by rendering that relation indissoluble, has by these two things done more toward the peace, happiness, settlement and civilization of the world than by any other part in this whole scheme of Divine Wisdom. The direct contrary course has been taken in the synagogue of Antichrist—I mean in that forge and manufactory of all evil, the sect which predominated in the Constituent Assembly of 1789. Those monsters employed the same or greater industry to desecrate and degrade that state, which other legislators have used to render it holy and honorable. By a strange, un-called-for declaration, they pronounced that marriage was no better than a common civil contract.[89]

At the hands of the revolutionaries, France transmuted from a Catholic country that absolutely denied divorce to a fiercely secular country. Anyone, male or female, could obtain a divorce within three months of marriage on the grounds of nothing more than personality difference.

Burke suggests that this licentious right to divorce is the logical outcome of the principles advanced by the revolutionaries in 1789: "Proceeding in the spirit of the first authors of their Constitution, succeeding Assemblies went the full length of the principle, and gave a license to divorce at the mere pleasure of the either party, and at a month's notice."[90] Just as the state may be destroyed and replaced with another regime if the will of the people so dictates, marriage is likewise subject to the same corrosion if it is the will (capricious or not) of a single spouse. Like the state, marriage is reduced to a loose civil contract. Burke compares this degraded state of marriage to English houses of prostitution: "With them the matrimonial connection is brought into so degraded a state of concubinage, that I believe none of the wretches of London who keep warehouses of infamy would give out one of their victims to private custody on so short and insolent a tenure."[91] He suggests that French wives are legal prostitutes of the sorriest sort—unpaid for the brief, demeaning trysts that their soon-to-be ex-husbands extort from them.

One of the most radical aspects of the legalization of divorce in France was that it granted the same right to divorce to men and women alike. Such an egalitarian directive was unprecedented and heralded as a revolutionary leap toward the liberation of women. Burke expressed skepticism about the benefits of the legalization of divorce on the condition of women, however: "There was, indeed, a kind of profligate equality in giving to women the same licentious power. The reason they assigned was as infamous as the act: declaring that women had been too long under the tyranny of parents and of husbands. It is not necessary to observe upon the horrible consequences of taking one half of the human species wholly out of the guardianship and protection of the other."[92] Burke, arguing from the standpoint of the chivalric manners he defends in the *Reflections*, contends that women should not hold the right to divorce because it takes them out of the protective custody of men, endangering them rather than empowering them. Like Rousseau, he conceives the sexes as interdependent and complementary in society; each aids the other in different ways. Burke believes that men protect women from physical dominance, and women save men from their own animal brutality by civilizing them. To the claim that the right to divorce enables women to escape from abusive husbands, he retorts that the aim of the legalization and liberalization of divorce in France was not the "relief of domestic uneasiness" but rather the "total corruption of all morals, the total disconnection of social life."[93] It is to Burke's credit that he acknowledges the existence of domestic suffering within the bond of marriage. Yet he firmly believes that the intention and effect of the 1792 divorce law were not to facilitate domestic peace, but rather incite moral corruption and social disconnection.

Burke blames the legalization and liberalization of divorce for the "total disconnection of social life" in France. The French revolutionaries actively encouraged social disorder via its permissive divorce policy and took perverse pride in the chaotic freedom it inspired. Burke observes that divorces were placed first on the public register, in front of births, marriages, and deaths, as if to give them the "post of honor."[94] Prefiguring the work of sociologists and historians of the family in the twentieth century, Burke embarks on a research mission to discover and quantify the actual impact of the legalization and liberalization of divorce on the French family.[95] He reports that the number of divorces in Paris in 1793 amounted to 562, while the marriages were 1,785, concluding, "The proportion of divorces to marriages was not much less than one to three: a thing unexampled, I believe, among mankind."[96] He then inquired at the Doctor's Commons to find the number of divorces permitted in England over the course of the eighteenth century, and made the following surprising discovery: "all the divorces (which, except by a special act of Parliament, are separations, and not proper divorces) did not amount in all those courts, and in a hundred years, to much more than one fifth of those that passed in the single city of Paris in three months."[97] Shocked at the explosion in the rate of divorce in Paris, Burke concludes that it was precipitated by the legislation of the egalitarian divorce law in 1792. Burke also observes that the legalization of divorce in France wreaked "havoc" on the "all the relations of life," and in particular the relationships of the family: "With the Jacobins of France, vague intercourse is without reproach; marriage is reduced to the vilest concubinage; children are encouraged to cut the throats of their parents; mothers are taught that tenderness is no part of their character, and, to demonstrate their attachment to their party; that they ought to make no scruple to rank with their bloody hands in the bowels of those who came from their own."[98] In this passage, Burke draws a connection between the effects of the legalization of divorce and the public displays of treason against family members that the Jacobins orchestrated. Both cause the breakdown of the natural affections between spouses, parents, and children, and thus instigate the suspension of the stabilizing social bonds of sympathy, civility, and patriotism.

It is important to remember that while Burke uses the derogatory phrase "vilest concubinage" to describe the demeaned status of women within the contract of marriage in revolutionary France, he does not so callously insult the concubines of India. Burke is attentive to the cultural context in which marriage is legally defined. In India, with its Hindu and Buddhist religious traditions and its caste system, seraglios are institutionalized as additional families for noblemen, and are an integrated part of their culture's mores and political system. Burke does not challenge the moral rectitude of this practice from the perspective of his own European and Christian values, but rather accepts this exotic form of the hierarchical family as long as it seems to be benevolent toward its members. In France, however, Burke perceives the shift from a patriarchal, covenantal, Christian notion of marriage to an egalitiarian, contractual, and legalistic understanding of marriage as a betrayal of the nation's long-standing Catholic culture, and a real rupture of the social and political order.

Burke argues that along with the egalitarian right to divorce, the legal erasure of the distinction between legitimate and illegitimate children also contributed to the destruction of the patriarchal structure of the family in the French republic. Burke recalls how Jacobin legislators brought a prostitute—whom they called a "mother without being a wife"—in front of the National Assembly to appeal for the "repeal of the incapacities that in civilized states are put upon bastards."[99] Legislation inspired by her plea granted bastards the same legal footing as legitimate children in the French republic. Consequently, marriage not only lost its sanctity as a permanent bond unto death, but it also its legal status as the sole legitimate relationship for reproduction.

Burke envisions the decomposition of the whole of Europe if it follows the example of France. Atheism will trump Christianity, Jacobin radicalism will overtake political prudence, and regicide will replace respect for traditional social and political hierarchies. In the *Fourth Letter on a Regicide Peace*, Burke imagines a future celebration of the "glorious execution of Louis the Sixteenth" that witnesses

a rattling of a thousand coaches of duchesses, countesses and Lady Marys, choking the way, and overturning each other, in a struggle who should be first to pay her court to the Citoyenne, the spouse of the twenty-first husband, he the husband of the thirty-first wife, and to hail her in the rank of honorable matrons before the four days' duration of marriage is expired!—Morals, as they were, decorum, the great outguard of the sex, and the proud sentiment of honor, which makes virtue more respectable, where it is, and conceals human frailty, where virtue may not be, will be banished from this land of propriety, modesty, and reserve.[100]

This biting satire envisions a future French republic in which its leaders marry upward to thirty times, amid public aplomb, to boot. Burke's conclusion is that the three great pillars of Western civilization—Christian morality, feminine decorum, and masculine chivalry—crumble once the relationships between husband and wife and subject and state are diminished to contracts of convenience.

The Detrimental Impact of the French Revolution on the English Family

In 1790, Burke retained hope that Britain could withstand the revolutionary tide rising from France. In the *Reflections,* he concluded his account of the mob's invasion of Versailles by contending that if "the king and queen of France, and their children, were to fall into our hands by the chance of war, in the most acrimonious of hostilities . . . they would be treated with another sort of triumphal entry into London."[101] Burke felt that Britain, unlike France, had not lost its respect for royal families. As a result, it had not lost its respect for families in general. All women and children, all kings and queens, and all families—including the royal family of an enemy country—still received the sympathy and respect they deserved in Britain. Yet as early as 1791, Burke concluded that England and its hierarchical family structure had not remained impervious to the cultural assault of the French Revolution.

In *An Appeal from the New to the Old Whigs* (1791), Burke rails against the "New Whigs"—the members of the Whig party who sympathized with the revolutionary cause—for their call to end the law of primogeniture. He mocks their critique of the destructive effect of primogeniture on English families: "They have the confidence to say, that it is a law against every law of nature, and nature herself calls for its destruction. Establish family justice, and aristocracy falls. By the aristocratical law of primogenitureship, in a family of six children, five are exposed. Aristocracy has never but one child. The rest are begotten to be devoured. They are thrown to the cannibal for prey, and the natural parent prepares the unnatural repast."[102] Burke frequently uses imagery of cannibalism to illustrate the irony of how revolutionary doctrines feed on the people they should be serving. It is not the institutions of primogeniture and aristocracy that cannibalize the people, but rather those revolutionary doctrines that undermine the natural affections and set people at each other's throats like animals. Burke identifies primogeniture and aristocracy as cultural and legal practices that help maintain the hierarchical structure of the family and the stable political order that rests on it.

Burke also condemns those "New Whigs" who fail to respect their aristocratic heritage and instead uphold the Jacobin cause. In *A Letter to a Noble Lord* (1796), he singles out Francis Russell, the fifth Duke of Bedford, who fancied himself a "radical" aristocrat after the fashion of Philippe d'Egalité, the Duke of Orleans in France. These radical aristocrats, by sympathizing with the Jacobin cause, "disowned their families, betrayed the most sacred of all trusts, and by breaking to pieces a great link in society, and all the cramps and holdings of the state, brought eternal confusion and desolation on their country."[103] These men represent for Burke the ultimate traitors. If the aristocrats themselves do not respect their own rank in society, and the centuries it took to build the "prejudice of an old nobility," a "great link of society" is broken.[104] There will no longer be a class that can perpetuate the traditions and prejudices that hold society together in a socially and politically stable fashion. The security of the little platoon that is social class will be betrayed from within.

In the *Fourth Letter on a Regicide Peace*, Burke admonishes those English sympathizers with the Jacobin cause about the dangers of exposing their children to French schools. He fears that if English children return home with the ideas spawned by these "schools of atheism," both England and the Anglican Church will be swept under the revolutionary tide. He cries, "Better that this island should be sunk to the bottom of the sea than that (so far as human infirmity admits) it should not be a country of religion and morals."[105]

Burke also fears that schools established by Dissenters within the borders of England itself are promoting the Jacobin cause. In *A Letter to a Noble Lord*, he accuses the Dissenting academies of infecting the families of England with atheism and political radicalism: "But the times, the morals, the masters, the scholars have all undergone a thorough revolution. . . . I still indulge the hope that no grown Gentleman or Nobleman of our time will think of finishing at Mr. Thewall's lecture whatever may have been left incomplete at the old Universities of his country. . . . Every honest father of a family in the kingdom will rejoice at the breaking up for the holidays, and will pray that there may be a very long vacation in all such schools."[106] Burke recognizes that education is the means by which Jacobin ideas will be transmitted to England. Radical ideas will infiltrate the minds of the young students who attend lectures by Dissenters such as John Thewall, and prod them to question paternal authority within their own families. Burke makes clear that fathers need to guide their children toward the right moral education not only at home but at school as well. Consequently, Burke concludes that keeping children out of Dissenting academies is essential for maintaining order and stability both within the home and English society at large.

Burke's public preoccupation with the destruction of the hierarchical family thus extends from his early years as a Member of Parliament in the 1770s to the very end of his life, in the late 1790s. In all the speeches and writings in which he discusses the family, he consistently decries any laws, public policies, intellectual ideas, or cultural changes that threaten the class-based, age based, and sex-based hierarchies of the family, sex-role differentiation within the family and the broader society, and the hierarchical family's role as a little platoon for the cultivation of the moral, social, and civic virtues across cultures and regime types. It is to a critical evaluation of Burke's philosophical defense of the hierarchical family and its role as a little platoon to which we turn in chapter three.

3

BURKE'S PHILOSOPHICAL DEFENSE
OF THE HIERARCHICAL FAMILY

The Aesthetic Foundation of
Burke's Philosophy of the Family

I have traced the development of Burke's fear of the destruction of the hierarchical family throughout his political writings and speeches on America, Ireland, England, India, and France from the 1770s to the 1790s. But what is the philosophical reasoning behind his defense of the class, age, and sex-based hierarchies of the family? Burke conceives the hierarchical family as a "little platoon" that fosters natural affections such as love. In the *Enquiry*, Burke argues that the natural affection of love, inspired by what we perceive as "beautiful," spurs the development of the social passions of sympathy, imitation, and ambition. The aesthetic theory of the *Enquiry* provides the groundwork for Burke's moral and political philosophy and in particular his account of how hierarchical family structures help to cultivate the social bonds of sympathy, civility, and patriotism within a range of possible regime types that are attentive to a nation's particular cultural tradition.

To understand the place of Burke's aesthetic theory within the whole of his moral and political philosophy, one must unravel the multiple philosophical traditions he intertwines in his corpus of writings and speeches. Commentators have been unable to situate Burke in any one school of thought, since he marshals arguments drawn from many different, and often seemingly contradictory, philosophical sources. Alfred Cobban's *Edmund Burke and the Revolt against the Eighteenth Century* (1929) argues that Burke defended a blend of Christian natural law theory and the "sentimentalism" of Hume and Smith. Charles Parkin's *The Moral Basis of Burke's Political Thought* (1956), Peter

Stanlis's *Burke and the Natural Law* (1958), and Francis Canavan's *The Political Reason of Edmund Burke* (1960) build on Cobban's insights, yet emphasize Burke's place in the natural law tradition. Conor Cruise O'Brien (1992) paints Burke as a multifaceted and complex thinker who wove together strands of several intellectual traditions into a cohesive and consistent "melody." J.G.A. Pocock likewise argues in *Politics, Language, Time* (1971) that Burke's "unified view of reality—if he had one" derives from multiple philosophical sources, including the common law tradition, natural law theory, the philosophies of Hume and Montesquieu, and Romantic sensibility. Following the lead of O'Brien and Pocock, Stephen K. White (1994) suggests that Burke spoke "multiple languages" in his philosophical and political writings. White notes the languages of sentimentalism, classical political economy, revolutionary fear, and traditionalism in Burke's works. White recalls the insights of Cobban insofar as he points out the primacy of Burke's "sentimentalism" among these distinct vocabularies.[1]

White coins the term "aesthetic-affective" to describe Burke's moral theory. He argues, "The aesthetic, or better, aesthetic-affective, dimension was always for Burke closely intertwined with the character of the natural, divinely ordained structure of the world."[2] Reinforcing the findings of Cobban's landmark study of Burke's moral philosophy, White recognizes the substantive relationship between Burke's commitments to the Christian natural law tradition and the sentimentalism of the Scottish Enlightenment. According to Burke's synthesis of these two philosophical traditions, the natural affections spur human beings to put their rational grasp of God's natural law into action. White concludes that the originality of Burke's moral theory lies not in his secondhand use of the natural law tradition, but rather in his innovative account of how the natural affections inspire aesthetic, and, in turn, moral judgments.

Recently, Luke Gibbons (2003) has reminded scholars that Burke, although he shares the Scottish Enlightenment's concern with the role of the natural affections in moral judgment, is not a clear-cut member of this school of thought. The *Enquiry*'s conception of sympathy is crucially distinct from the Scottish school's, particularly as found in Hume and Smith, insofar as it emphasizes the way that human beings are drawn into a direct sympathetic identification with other people's pains and joys, rather than standing at a kind of impartial distance from them. It is precisely the direct, emotional experience of sympathy that renders it an *effective* affective platform for human ethical conduct. In this way, Burke is strikingly similar to Rousseau, who argues in the *Second Discourse* that sympathetic identification with another human being's pain—or pity—is one of the starting points for human society.[3]

Building on the work of White and Gibbons, I argue that Burke grounds his philosophical defense of the hierarchical family on the *Enquiry*'s theory of the relationship between affective response, aesthetic and moral judgment, socialization, and the divinely sanctioned natural order. Burke argues that the order and stability of society and the state depend on the cultivation of the social passion of sympathy for other human beings, as both equals and unequals, within the affective space of the hierarchical family. For Burke, sympathy is a social passion that develops into a social bond. The social passion of sympathy, and the social bond of the same name, is first developed within the relationships of the family. A child's instinctual sympathy for his or her parents gradually develops and extends itself into the habitual practice of sympathy toward other human beings. The social passion, or instinct, of sympathy thus leads to the spread of the social bond, or habitual moral practice, of sympathy throughout society. In the *Enquiry*, Burke argues that sympathy is the first of the three main social bonds that hold society together, for it teaches people to look beyond their own self-interest and show concern for the well-being of others.

According to the *Enquiry* (and as expounded in Burke's later writings), the three social passions—sympathy, imitation, and ambition—help to develop the other two major social bonds, civility and patriotism. For Burke, civility is the art of adhering to the feminine, chivalrous, and aristocratic systems of manners. These systems of manners are in large part perpetuated within families. Burke defines patriotism as love of country; contrary to the French revolutionaries, he insists that it should build on, rather than supersede, love of family.

Burke fears that the family will no longer be able to foster sympathy, civility, and patriotism once its age-based, sex-based, and class-based hierarchies are leveled. Without regard for the natural order of the universe as replicated in hierarchical social institutions such as the family, humans not only lose sympathy for what makes them "equal" but also sympathy for what makes them "unequal." For Burke, the social passion of sympathy should be directed not only toward egalitarian self-identification with others (such as sympathy toward one's mother as a fellow human being or family member), but also deferential recognition of what makes others either stronger or more vulnerable in comparison to us (such as sympathy toward one's mother's role as the primary caregiver or the moral authority in the family, or sympathy for one's mother's situation as a member of the physically weaker female sex). He concludes that the social bonds of sympathy, civility, and patriotism only encourage moral, social, and political stability insofar as they recognize and reinforce the natural order of the universe that God ordained.

According to Burke, the passion of sympathy promotes moral stability by inspiring people to put their rational grasp of the natural law into action. Codes of civility promote social stability by encouraging people to respect social hierarchies that mirror the natural order of the universe. Patriotism promotes political stability by fostering respect for political hierarchies that also mirror the natural order. In short, familial, social, and political hierarchies are legitimate for Burke insofar as they mirror the natural order and channel the natural affections toward the promotion of the moral, social, and political stability exemplified by God's ordering of the universe. Burke identifies the hierarchical family as the primary source and site of the basic social bonds that hold society together in a stable and civil fashion.

Beauty, Love, and the Social Passions

Burke's *Enquiry* provides the epistemological foundation for his moral and political philosophy. In the *Enquiry*, Burke investigates, in classic Enlightenment fashion, the physiological and emotional responses of the body to beautiful and sublime objects. Like Locke, he takes an empirical approach to the study of the relationship between the mind and the body. Unlike Condillac, he escapes the twin charges of atheism and materialism by acknowledging the role of the Creator in designing the way the body and mind respond to the beautiful and the sublime.

Burke explains that the human mind and body respond to objects that have the capacity to excite either pleasure or pain. Physical pain excites the passions that concern self-preservation, the most powerful passions known to humankind. A "sublime" object excites the passions of self-preservation, coupled with a feeling of "delight," for it stands at a comfortable distance from the viewer and poses no real threat to him or her. Physical pleasure excites the passions that concern (1) the "society of the sexes" (sexual relationships between men and women) and (2) "general society" (all other relationships between humans, as well as between humans and the natural world).[4] A "beautiful" object excites pleasure, and, in turn, the passions of society.

The passions of self-preservation are more intense than the passions of society because the preservation of one's life is a prerequisite for all other pursuits. Burke stoically surmises that the absence of sexual pleasure is not "attended with any considerable pain" because propagation is not meant to be our "constant business."[5] He proceeds to distinguish between the sexual drives of men and animals. Animals instinctually seek to mate with any member of the opposite sex in their species. Men, on the other hand, are "carried to the sex in general, as it is the sex, and by the common law of nature; but they are attached to particulars by personal beauty."[6] It is important to note that here, as in the remainder of the *Enquiry*, Burke speaks of men not in the universalistic sense of "humanity" but as the male half of the human species.[7] He uses the term "the sex" to describe the female half of the species to which men are drawn by the laws of nature (the instinct to procreate, in particular).

Men are generally attracted to the females of their species, but they fall in love with individual women because of their particular qualities of beauty. Throughout the *Enquiry*, Burke speaks only of the sexual attraction of men toward women, and the aesthetic judgments about female beauty that spring from the male experience of sexual attraction toward women. Burke's *Enquiry* is most accurately understood as a theory of male psychology, not human psychology.[8] In this way, the *Enquiry* reflects Burke's assumption that the patriarchal structure of society is a fundamental and beneficial reflection of the natural order of the universe.

Burke defines love as a "mixed passion," for it is both the beautiful qualities of individual women and the natural instinct to procreate that attract men to the opposite sex. He identifies beauty as a "social quality" because it draws men into relationships with those people and things they find attractive: "I call beauty a social quality; for when women and men, and not only they, but when other animals give us a sense of joy and pleasure in beholding them . . . they inspire us with sentiments of tenderness and affection toward their persons; we like to have them near us, and we enter willingly into a kind of relation with them, unless we would have strong reasons to the contrary."[9] In sum, beauty inspires the natural affection of love, which in turn leads men to form a complex web of social relationships. Beauty draws men into the pleasures of "particular society": "Good company, lively conversations, and the endearments of friendship, fill the mind with great pleasure."[10] As with Aristotle, Burke's man is a social animal. Beauty draws men into social relationships that bestow the greatest pleasures and fulfill their essentially social nature. The three main social passions inspired by beauty, other than the passion for the "society of the sexes" and the passion for "general society," are sympathy, imitation, and ambition. Imitation and ambition shape the social bonds of civility and patriotism, which, along with sympathy, help to hold society together in a moral, well-mannered, and politically stable fashion.

Yet Burke's social animal is decidedly male. The *Enquiry* takes as its epistemological perspective what many contemporary feminist critics have called "the male gaze," or an exclusively male point of view in matters of aesthetic and moral judgment.[11] Burke does not attempt to universalize his theory of aesthetic judgment for humanity as a whole; instead, he explicitly presents men as the appraisers of the beauty and sublimity of the external world, and women as part of the external world that men appraise.

According to Burke, there are sublime and beautiful virtues, just as there are sublime and beautiful objects. Beautiful virtues—such as compassion, kindness, and liberality inspire love, while sublime virtues—such as justice, fortitude, and courage—inspire admiration, or even fear. Burke identifies the beautiful virtues with the domestic realm occupied by women and the family: "Those persons who creep into the hearts of most people, who are chosen as the companions of their softer hours, and their reliefs from care and anxiety, are never persons of shining qualities nor strong virtues. It is rather the soft green of the soul on which are rest our eyes, that are fatigued with beholding more glaring objects."[12] Family life requires softer virtues than the hard public world of business and politics. Burke continues in this vein by identifying fathers with the sublime virtues, and mothers and grandfathers with the beautiful virtues: "The authority of a father, so useful to our well-being, and so justly venerable upon all accounts, hinders us from having that entire love for him that we have for our mothers, where the parental authority is almost melted down into the mother's fondness and indulgence. But we generally have a great love for our grandfathers, in whom this authority is removed a degree from us, and where the weakness of age mellows it into something of a feminine partiality."[13] This passage provides a vital portrait of how Burke envisions the aesthetic-affective moral theory of the *Enquiry* as the foundation for his philosophical justification of the hierarchical structure of the family. Burke suggests that children love and respect the authority of their mothers and grandfathers for their "beautiful" virtues of kindness and indulgence, whereas they admire and even fear the "sublime" patriarchal authority of their fathers. Burke suggests that grandfathers, because "their authority is removed a degree from us," can practice both sublime and beautiful virtues without compromising their masculine identity or their gentler practice of patriarchal authority. Fathers, whose authority must be more immediate and forceful to be effective, must practice the "sublime" virtues in order to garner respect for their supreme authority as the patriarchs of their families. Burke implies that women should aspire to practice the "beautiful" virtues to maintain their feminine and maternal allure, on which their softer, more loving, and secondary authority rests amidst the variety of age-based and sex-based hierarchies within their families

Sympathy and Its Social Role

Burke argues that there are two kinds of sympathy: "sublime" and "beautiful." The passions of self-preservation inspire a "sublime" sense of sympathy, while the passions of society inspire a "beautiful" sense of sympathy. We experience "pleasure" when we sympathize with the happiness of others, because the sight is "beautiful." Likewise, we experience "delight" when we sympathize with the pain of others, because the sight is "sublime." Burke explains the paradox of why it is natural and good that we feel delight when we sympathize with the suffering of others: "(Since) our Creator has designed that we should be united by the bond of sympathy, he has strengthened that bond by a proportional delight; and there most where our sympathy is most wanted, in the distresses of others if the passion was simply painful, we would shun with the greatest care all persons and places that could excite such a passion."[14] Delight before the pain of others is not a sadistic instinct, as de Sade portrayed it, or cathartic, as Aristotle claimed, but rather a natural physical impulse, designed by God himself, that guides humankind toward charitable behavior it would otherwise avoid. The feeling of delight brought about by sympathizing with another's pain is not unmitigated; it is accompanied by a feeling of uneasiness that "prompts us to relieve ourselves in relieving those who suffer."[15] Sympathy, whether inspired by the passions of society or of self-preservation, leads human beings to establish relationships with one another and care for each other's needs.

According to Burke, the social passion of sympathy inspires the practice of the "beautiful" virtue of compassion. The family and the feminine social milieu are the paradigmatic realms of the "beautiful" for Burke. Most people learn the virtue of compassion in the family, following the tender example of a mother or female caregiver. Burke fears

that the destruction of the hierarchical family will shut down the schoolhouse for the "beautiful" virtue of compassion; the dissolution of sex-
role differentiation, and the dismantling of patriarchal and class
hierarchies, will corrode the family's capacity to foster this vital social
bond. Without compassion, people stop caring for each other, and society slips into the reckless pursuit of self-interest.

Burke believes that sympathy can be experienced between both
equals and unequals. A striking illustration of Burke's provocative account of the psychology of sympathy can be found in the *Speech in
Opening the Impeachment of Warren Hastings*. In this speech, Burke
appeals to the sympathy of the members of the House of Lords, asking
them to aid the oppressed people of India and preserve their traditional
social order from the ravages of the East India Company:

> It is not from this district or from that parish, not from this city or
> the other province, that relief is now applied for: exiled and undone
> princes, extensive tribes, suffering nations, infinite descriptions of
> men, different in language, in manners, and in rites, men separated
> by every barrier of Nature from you, by the Providence of God are
> blended in one common cause, and are now become suppliants at
> your bar. For the honor of this nation, in vindication of this myste-
> rious Providence, let it be known that no rule formed upon munic-
> ipal maxims (if any such rule exists) will prevent the course of that
> imperial justice which you owe to the people that call you from all
> parts of a great disjointed world.[16]

To inspire compassion for a foreign people far from the view of Britain,
Burke first appeals to the moral supremacy, "mysterious Providence,"
and "imperial justice" of God. The British people, as rational creatures
bound by the universal moral laws of God, should assuage the suffering
of fellow human beings in India. Yet Burke realizes that an abstract appeal to the natural law is not enough to rouse the lords from their apathy.
Human beings need the emotional boost of sympathy to put their rational grasp of the natural law into action.

With his graphic account of the torture of Brahmin families by the
henchmen of Warren Hastings, Burke aims to engage the sympathy of
the lords, so that they take legal action to relieve both the suffering of
the Indians and the discomfort they feel in vicariously witnessing it.
Burke seeks to inspire "sublime" sympathy for the oppression of these
hierarchical Indian families, so that this source and site of sympathy and
the "beautiful" virtue of compassion might escape destruction. Hence,

he offers a disturbingly detailed account of the torture of the Indians by the East India Company. He includes a shocking description of the joint whipping of fathers and sons, the public rape of virgin daughters in front of their parents, and the mutilation of women's breasts and wombs—all violations of the most basic natural affections and family ties. As discussed in chapter two, the public torture of these Brahmin families forced the victims to lose their caste. Through these inhumane spectacles, the East India Company sought to undermine the ancient hierarchical social order of India. By inspiring "sublime" sympathy for the plight of the Indian people through his speech, Burke seeks to prevent the East India Company from destroying the Indian social hierarchy, the hierarchical families that occupy its ranks, and the "beautiful" virtue of compassion that these families have taught their children.

Andrew McCann (1999) and Claudia Johnson (1995)—who claim Burke's explicit representation of these acts of torture, as well as his portrayal of revolutionary violence against women in France, reveals a sexually "lurid" and "voyeuristic" side to his aesthetic and moral theory—have blurred Burke's critical reception in the late eighteenth century with his own philosophical intention.[17] To be sure, Burke was widely misunderstood, and even mocked, for his sympathetic identification with the victims of colonial exploitation in India and the revolutionary uprisings in France, especially in his epic quest to impeach Hastings, and in his operatic homage to Marie Antoinette in the *Reflections*. Certainly, his speeches and writings on violence—particularly violence toward women—shaped the feminized and sexualized discourse of sentimentality in Romantic and Gothic literature. Yet the examination of Burke's *Reflections* and *Speech in Opening the Impeachment of Warren Hastings* within the context of his broader moral and political philosophy reminds us that his intent in presenting these accounts of sexual violence was not to excite a "prurient curiosity" in these despicable acts of torture and aggression, but to inspire the natural affection of sympathy in the hearts of his audience, so that they might exercise the beautiful virtue of compassion and seek to aid the oppressed families of India and France as they would their own families in Britain.[18]

In his equally shocking account of the invasion of Versailles by the mob in the *Reflections*, Burke seeks to inspire "sublime" sympathy for the plight of the royal family of France. Burke not only wants the reader to identify with the royal family of France as equals, but to respect them as unequals. The members of the French royal family are our equals in two senses. First, they are our equals insofar as they are a typical family, composed of parents and children. Second, they are our equals insofar as they are human creatures. We, the readers of the *Reflections*, should sympathize with their plight because "such treatment of any human creatures must be shocking to any but those who are made for accomplishing revolution."[19] The mistreatment of the royal family is as shocking as cruelty toward "any human creatures" would be. We are to identify with the royal family, not only as fellow family, but also as fellow human beings.

Yet Burke is quick to point out that this cannot be the only ground for sympathy toward the royal family. The revolutionaries, guided by the light of Enlightenment reason, treat everyone as equals; but because they make no distinctions between people, they treat everyone as means to their utilitarian ends. Consequently, they do not find "shocking" the suffering they inflict on people, whether they are beggars or kings, in order to achieve their revolutionary goals. For this reason, Burke calls the reader to sympathize with the royal family on both levels: as "any human creature" and as creatures of distinction:

> Influenced by the inborn feelings of my nature, and not being illuminated by a single ray of this new-sprung modern light, I confess to you, Sir, that the exalted rank of the persons suffering, and particularly the sex, the beauty and the amiable qualities of the descendant of so many kings and emperors, with the tender age of royal infants, insensible only through infancy and innocence of the cruel outrages to which their parents were exposed, instead of being a subject for exultation, adds not a little to any sensibility on that most melancholy occasion.[20]

Our sympathy should be aroused by the threat to what makes them unequal to us, both in the sense of what makes them stronger and what makes them weaker. We should sympathize with them because of the loss of what makes them stronger: namely, their exalted rank and the queen's noble lineage. We should also sympathize with them because of the attack on what makes them weaker: namely, the queen's sex and beauty and the children's infancy and innocence.

Burke fears that in an egalitarian society—such as the French revolutionaries desire—disrespect for humanity itself will follow quickly behind disregard of rank and sex. Burke's weapon against this fate is his literary flair for inspiring a sense of "sublime" sympathy in his readers. By engaging their sympathy for the humiliation of the king, the queen, and their children, he enables his audience to see the attack on the royal family as an assault on the hierarchical familial, social, and political order (and the natural order it mirrors) and the humane atmosphere of compassion and civility that has reigned within their own families and European society as a whole.

In his analysis of the storming of Versailles, Burke's conception of the proper objects of human sympathy is shaped—and even broadened—by his concern with maintaining class hierarchies as integral parts of the natural order. Burke views sympathy as a social instinct and practice that paradoxically respects yet transcends social rank; in other words, the capacity for sympathy allows us to identify with and respect people who are both like us and unlike us. In contrast, Rousseau offered a more limited, yet purely egalitarian, definition of the experience and ends of pity: we are truly "moved" by others, and thus pushed to act on their behalf, when we can fully identify with their feelings and experiences, and particularly their brushes with death. In Rousseau's view, differences in social standing—such as the royal rank of a queen—do not inspire sympathy, but rather cultivate an (often insincere) respect based on artificial codes of civility. Rather, it is what humanity shares in common—particularly its pains, losses, and failures—that inspires genuine sympathy. Wollstonecraft, along with many of her counterparts in Dissenting Christian circles, took this Rousseauian insight into human affective experience and concluded that genuine sympathy for what is common among human beings may be translated into a radical egalitarian politics.

Indeed, the "radical" Burke who championed the rights of the oppressed in America, Ireland, and India was a man motivated by this same egalitarian sense of sympathy. Why then did he recoil from the egalitarian philosophy of the French revolutionaries? Burke refused to take the social bond of sympathy to its potentially radical political conclusions on account of his assumptions about the natural hierarchical order of the universe, the ranking of individuals, families, other little platoons, and states within it, and how political reform should be orchestrated in a slow, cautious fashion respectful of existing social and political institutions and traditions. Burke feared that the French Revolution would overturn the traditional social and political hierarchies that fostered civility, political stability and even the capacity for human sympathy. Hence, he is willing to sympathize with the suffering, and to enact piecemeal reforms to help them, but not to enact a total social and political revolution to alleviate their pain.

The "revolutions" Burke defends during his political career—such as the American War of Independence, the uprisings by the Indians against the East India Company, and even the aborted republican revolution of Corsica—are not true revolutions in his view, for they do not entail a total overturning of traditional moral, social, and political codes. Following the arguments of his philosophical mentor Montesquieu on the "fit" between a particular culture and its political regime, Burke actually viewed the American War of Independence as the consummation of the spirit of freedom that infused the American people and their republican culture on the colonial frontier since the mid-seventeenth century, and ultimately sprung from deeper roots in various strands of the English political tradition. Likewise, in the case of Corsica, Burke exuded a kind of Rousseauian enthusiasm for the nation's brave and independent character, which he believed was well-suited to republican government, and thus despicably violated and suppressed by its imperial conquest by France.[21] For Burke, a revolution is not a revolution unless it is both a political and a cultural revolution, for which 1789 gave the world the most "sublime" and terrible example.

Civility and Its Social Role

According to Burke, the three social passions of sympathy, imitation, and ambition work together to create the systems of aristocratic, feminine, and chivalric manners that encourage a spirit of "civility" in society. The *Enquiry* posits that the desire to imitate is akin to sympathy insofar as "sympathy makes us take a concern in whatever men feel, so this affection prompts us to copy whatever they do."[22] Burke defines imitation as "one of the strongest links in society."[23] It is a "species of mutual compliance which all men yield to each other, without constraint to themselves, and which is extremely flattering to all."[24] By copying the actions and appropriating the beliefs of one another, humans encourage social cooperation and stability.

Burke concludes that God placed the instinct for imitation within us to help us realize our social natures. Imitation, rather than precept, is the most pleasant and effective means for both intellectual and social learning. Burke points out that the arts possess a special power to inspire imitation and hence serve as an important vehicle for imparting manners and mores. By imitating other people, whether in our everyday social interactions or through exposure to the arts, we shape "our manners, our opinions, our lives."[25] Ambition, on the other hand, counteracts the conformity produced by imitation. According to Burke, God implanted the social passion of ambition within us in order to promote human improvement. Consequently, we experience pleasure by both imitating and improving on the actions and ideas of other men and women. The imitation of other people's beliefs and actions leads to the development of an established code of social conduct, or, to use Burke's term, a "system of manners." A system of manners is a set of social rules for securing "civility" within a given community. Civility is an artificial social bond that fosters cordiality and diplomacy in relationships outside of the close emotional bonds of family and friendship. Even in a city full of strangers, civil behavior is guaranteed as long as there is a shared system of manners. The social passion of ambition drives people to pay strict homage to the established systems of manners, in the hope of attaining a place in, or at least a vicarious allegiance with, a little platoon such as a social circle or class of higher rank.

As a good student of Montesquieu, Burke fairly assesses the vital role that manners play in shaping the moral contours of any political society. In the *First Letter on a Regicide Peace* (1796), Burke outlines the relationship between manners, law, and morality: "Manners are of more importance than laws. Upon them, in great measure, the laws depend. The law touches us but here and there, and now and then. Manners are what vex or soothe, corrupt or purify, exalt or debase, barbarize or refine us, by a constant, steady, uniform, insensible operation, like that of the air we breathe in. They give their whole form and color to our lives. According to their quality, they aid morals, they supply them, or they totally destroy them."[26] For Burke, manners are the foundation on which law and morality are built. Manners are "of more importance than laws" because the influence of the former shapes every aspect of personal and public life, while the latter extends only to actions relevant to the interest of the state. Manners even shape the character of morality: good manners may either support or supply a nation's moral code, while bad manners spur its destruction.

Later in the *First Letter*, Burke argues that a shared system of manners is the key to maintaining peace and civility not only within a particular nation, but also between different nations:

> Men are not tied to one another by papers and seals. They are led to associate by resemblances, by conformities, by sympathies. It is with nations as with individuals. Nothing is so strong as a tie of amity between nation and nation as correspondence in laws, customs, manners, and habits of life. They have more than the force of treaties in themselves. They are obligations written in the

> heart. . . . The secret, unseen, but irrefragable bond of habitual in-
> tercourse holds them together, even when their perverse and liti-
> gious nature sets them to equivocate, scuffle and fight about the
> terms of their written obligations.[27]

Manners, more than laws and treaties, maintain social and political stability within and between nations. Echoing both Montesquieu and
Rousseau, who respectively speak of religious principles and *moeurs* as
laws "engraved" on the heart, Burke portrays "customs, manners, and
habits of life" as "obligations written in the heart."[28] Like both of these
thinkers, Burke conceptualizes morality, manners, and customs as practically intertwined; standards of right and wrong are rationally grasped,
emotionally intuited, and put into practice within particular communities and habituated through their cultural traditions. Also following
Montesquieu and Rousseau, Burke emphasizes the central place of personal autonomy within this account of ethical formation by metaphori-
cally describing interpersonal connections and duties as inscribed on the
heart; for while a person's moral codes are inculcated within a particular community, they are ultimately experienced and put into practice
from within an individual's own psychic interior.

Building on this notion of the "secret, unseen, but irrefragable
bond" between peoples, Burke furthermore contends that even the di-
verse nations of Europe share an underlying set of manners drawn from
ancient Germanic and Roman customs and legal codes: "From all those
sources arose a system of manners and of education which was nearly
similar in all this quarter of the globe—and which softened, blended,
and harmonized the colors of the whole. . . . From this resemblance in
the modes of intercourse, and in the whole form and fashion of life, no
citizen of Europe could be altogether an exile in any part of it."[29] The
common origins of European culture gradually shaped a shared system
of manners and education that bridged the superficial differences between the nations, and even made it possible for individuals—like
Burke himself—to understand themselves as part of a transnational European identity or possessing a cosmopolitan European citizenship. Yet
while writing the *First Letter* in 1791, Burke feared that the French Revolution had fractured this common bond between European persons and
nations by proliferating a radical new egalitarian ideology that challenged the hierarchical social order and its correspondent systems of
manners. He was even moved to ask Catherine the Great, in a letter written in November 1791, to declare war on the French Republic in the

name of preserving the "ancient manners of Europe" from the "barbarism and ruin" instigated in France by the revolutionaries.[30]

Burke theorizes that manners are in large part taught and transmitted in the family; boys learn to be chivalrous and courageous by imitating their fathers, girls learn to be modest and gentle by imitating their mothers, and young aristocrats learn how to be noble and high-minded by imitating their elder relations. Hence, Burke concludes that the destruction of sex-based, age-based, and class-based familial hierarchies in France triggered a "revolution in manners" and replaced traditional codes of conduct with radical, innovative modes of social behavior. For one, Burke perceives the movement of women into the public sphere as an ominous sign of the breakdown of sex-role differentiation and the feminine manners that attend this practice. When Burke sees women acting like men in revolutionary France, he interprets it as a sign of the immanent extinction of Europe's patriarchal system of manners. Burke portrays women as the moral pillars of the codes of chivalry and feminine decorum; without their support, these systems of manners come crashing down. As Burke sets forth in the *Enquiry*, the realm of the beautiful is the realm of femininity, domesticity, and sociability. Women are the keepers of this realm; their role is to preserve and perpetuate the "beautiful," feminine, domestic, and social virtues. Burke feared that the French Revolution not only threatened to turn women into men, but also would drag men and women down to the level of animals. Thus, it is not by chance that Burke, in the *Reflections*, begins his story of the mob's storming of Versailles preoccupied with the problem of women losing their femininity.

Burke decries those women who have forsaken their feminine manners for the sake of joining the brutal revolutionary fray. He compares the mob of women and men who stormed Versailles on 6 October 1789 to a "procession of American savages."[31] Burke also recounts how the National Assembly of France worked amid the "tumultuous cries of a mixed mob of ferocious men, and of women lost to shame."[32] Later, Burke marshals even stronger language to denounce the wild behavior of the female mob as they dragged the royal family to Paris: "Their heads were stuck upon spears and led the procession, whilst the royal captives who followed the train were slowly moved along, amidst the horrid yells, and the shrilling screams, and frantic dances, and infamous contumelies, and all the unutterable abominations of the furies of hell in the abused shape of the vilest of women."[33] Leading the procession with the heads of royal servants stuck on their spears, the women have surpassed the ferocious amorality of "savages" and "animals" and transmogrified into evil "furies of hell." The procession from Versailles to Paris is a diabolical celebration of the suffering and humiliation of the royal family, Burke's great symbol for all that is civilized. Burke demonizes these women because they outright reject, rather than protect, the moral code and system of manners that distinguishes between good and evil. Moreover, these acts represent to him women's invasion of the public and political spheres and, consequently, the breakdown of the aesthetic, moral, and social categories of the *Enquiry*. If women act like men, and men and women act like animals or even demons, then society has lost the civilizing influence of femininity.

According to Burke, the code of chivalry comprises both sympathy for the weakness and beauty of the female sex and respect for their class rank. In this way, it builds on both the feminine and aristocratic systems of manners. Chivalric manners teach men to treat women differently from men, yet not indifferently. A chivalric man seeks to honor the rank of a woman, and to sympathize with her beauty and weakness, by protecting her from the "uncivil" actions of other men. Intriguingly, Burke reaches back into the medieval era to reclaim the notion of chivalry, and yet expands its meaning beyond its original usage. Chivalry, for Burke, only tangentially refers to the set of manners that swirled around the romantic longings of the unmarried in medieval court society. Instead, Burke understands chivalry as a general, centuries-old, European system of manners that stems from the culture of medieval court society, yet evolved beyond it. Chivalry in this broader sense is encouraging men to put women on a pedestal, respect their fundamental differences from them, and protect them from various threats due to their physical or social vulnerabilities.

In the *Reflections*, Burke portrays the threat of the rape of the queen as symbolic of the stripping away of the system of feminine, chivalrous, and aristocratic manners by the "enlightened" egalitarian philosophy of the revolutionaries. He dramatically describes the moment the mob supposedly broke into the queen's bedroom: "A band of cruel ruffians, reeking with his blood, rushed into the chamber of the queen and pierced with a hundred strokes of bayonets and poniards the bed, from whence this persecuted women had but just time to fly almost naked, and . . . had escaped to seek refuge at the feet of a king and husband not secure of his own life for a moment."[34] Burke casts the piercing of the bed by a "hundred strokes of bayonets and poniards" as a symbolic rape and physical violation of the queen. Although she has not been physically violated, she has been raped in the sense that all her dignity as a queen and as a woman has been stripped from her in this attack on herself, her family, and her home. Indeed, she is subjected to the indignity of escaping "almost naked," so stripped is she of her former robes of queenhood and feminine modesty that the system of aristocratic, feminine, and chivalric manners held in place.

In a later passage of the *Reflections*, Burke uses metaphors of dress and undress to meditate on the impact of the French Revolution on the nature of civilized man: "All the decent drapery of life is rudely torn off. All the superadded ideas, furnished from the wardrobe of a moral imagination, which the heart owns and the understanding ratifies as necessary to cover the defects of our naked, shivering nature, and to raise it to dignity in our own estimation, are to be exploded as ridiculous, absurd and antiquated fashion."[35] For Burke, the aristocratic, feminine, and chivalric systems of manners provided a "wardrobe" to cover and protect us from our base, brutish natures. Now that wardrobe has been tossed off and dismissed as "antiquated fashion."

Burke believes that Marie Antoinette preserved, in part, the "decent drapery of life" by bearing the threat of rape "with a serene patience, in a manner suited to her rank and race, and becoming the offspring of a sovereign distinguished for her piety and her courage; that, like her, she has lofty sentiments; that she feels with the dignity of a Roman matron; that in the last extremity she will save herself from the last disgrace; and that, if she must fall, she will fall by no ignoble hand."[36] The actual rape of the queen would have been the ultimate degradation, the "last disgrace." As a model of aristocratic nobility and feminine decorum, she must be willing to follow the example of Lucretia, the great Roman matron who took her own life to avoid the disgrace of rape. For Burke, the preservation of the queen's dignity symbolizes the survival of the last vestiges of the "lofty sentiments" upheld by the systems of aristocratic, feminine, and chivalric manners.

Burke concludes that once the "age of chivalry is gone . . . a king is but a man, a queen is but a woman; a woman is but an animal, and an animal not of the highest order."[37] Once people no longer pay homage to class hierarchies, a queen is nothing more than a woman and a king is nothing more than a man. Burke hints that the demise of the systems of aristocratic, feminine, and chivalric manners is more pernicious for women than it is for men. Once men no longer pay homage to the beauty and frailty of women, and once women no longer practice the virtue of modesty, men and women are stripped of the "wardrobe" that had raised them above the level of animals. Women become animals "not of the highest order" because men's greater natural strength makes them animals of a higher order. In short, women lose the power to civilize and tame men when the codes of chivalry and feminine decorum are discarded.

Burke's analysis of the origin and practice of civility extends beyond chivalric and feminine manners to aristocratic manners. In *Letter to a Noble Lord*, Burke defines the social role of the aristocracy as follows: "The nobility forms the chain that connects the ages of a nation, which otherwise (with Mr. Paine) would soon be taught that no one generation can bind another. . . . That is one fatal objection to all new fancied and new fabricated Republics (among a people, who, once possessing such an advantage, have wickedly and insolently rejected it), that the prejudice of an old nobility is a thing that cannot be made."[38] The aristocracy connects the generations of a nation by perpetuating the "prejudices"—or traditional behaviors and beliefs tested and sanctified by experience—that hold it together as a people. Aristocratic, feminine and chivalric manners are among these prejudices.

But what are aristocratic manners? In the *Reflections*, Burke refers to the "spirit of a gentleman" as one of the twin foundations of European civilization, along with religion.[39] Aristocratic gentlemen, through the ages, take as their social duty the preservation of learning, respect for rank, and the system of "noble" manners that set a nation's highest standard of civility. According to Burke, aristocratic manners are a highly intricate set of traditional social practices that pay homage to both class rank and scholarly learning. The aristocracy practices these manners, and the lower classes improve their own standard of civility by striving to emulate them. The noble family serves as a model for the social cultivation of all families. Burke thus concludes that aristocratic manners contribute to social and political stability.

Burke denounces the French revolutionaries for destroying the institutions of aristocracy and monarchy, and the correspondent system of noble manners, that characterized the traditional order of the ancien régime. He contends that the abstract doctrine of the "rights of man" cannot inspire the same love, devotion, and loyalty—and the same levels of civility and social stability—as a king or a lord:

> Nothing is left which engages the affections on the part of the commonwealth. On the principles of this mechanic philosophy, our institutions can never be embodied, if I may use the expression, in persons—so as to create in us love, veneration, or attachment. But

that sort of reason which banishes the affections is incapable of filling their place. These public affections, combined with manners, are required sometimes as supplements, sometimes as correctives, always as aids to law. . . . There ought to be a system of manners in every nation which a well-formed mind would be disposed to relish. To make us love our country, our country ought to be lovely.[40]

This passage uncovers the underlying "aesthetic-affective" reasons why Burke defends the patriarchal institutions of hereditary monarchy and aristocracy. The ideals of a nation—legal, moral, and civil—need to be "embodied" in actual persons, who represent the tradition of law and order that has been inherited from past generations. The "embodiment" of political and social institutions in particular members of the nobility, and the practice of aristocratic, feminine, and chivalric manners by these lords, queens, and kings, make a country, its laws, and its social order "lovely" in the eyes of the people. When a people loves and admires its aristocratic rulers, a high degree of civility and social stability ensues. Using his aesthetic theory as the ground for his political theory, Burke concludes that the abstract rights of man cannot possibly elicit these same affections—or the same civility or stability—because one cannot possibly love an idea as much as a person.

Burke admits that it is not only the Jacobins and the *philosophes* who are to blame for the demise of aristocratic manners, but also the aristocracy itself. He reproaches the French aristocracy for their failure to uphold the high standard of manners that was their safeguard against the revolt of the people: "Habitual dissoluteness of manners, continued beyond the pardonable period of life, was more common amongst them than it is with us; and it reigned with the less hope of remedy, though possibly with something of less mischief, by being covered with more exterior decorum. They countenanced too much that licentious philosophy which has helped to bring on their ruin."[41] The corruption of the aristocracy, and the "dissoluteness" of their manners, meant that they no longer endeared the people as the embodiment of lofty thoughts and noble deeds. As Burke writes in *Letter to a Noble Lord*, "when men in that rank lose decorum, they lose everything."[42] Likewise, in *Letter to William Eliot* (1791) he warns that "The great must submit to the dominion of prudence and of virtue, or none will long submit to the dominion of the great."[43] Burke predicts that crumbling hierarchies and civil unrest are inevitable once the aristocracy fails to uphold the standard of civility by which the rest of society models itself. Of course, it is questionable whether the aristocracy ever upheld these ideals. Marie Antoinette, for one, was widely rumored to have led a profligate and decadent lifestyle in the "noble" environs of Versailles.[44] Burke often glosses over the past, lax behavior of the French aristocracy to vilify the French Revolution for the disruption of the social and political hierarchies that, in his view, mirrored the natural order of things.

The Family as Cradle of Patriotism

According to Burke, the hierarchical family fosters the social bond of patriotism in addition to the social bonds of sympathy and civility. The hierarchical family is the foundation of the state insofar as it is the cradle in which man, the social and political animal, is nurtured. For Burke, the hierarchical family is the main little platoon that kindles sociability and patriotism, as revealed in a passage from the *Reflections*: "No man was ever attached by a sense of pride, partiality, or real affection to a description of square measurement. He will never glory in belonging to the Chequer No. 71, or any other badge-ticket. We begin our public affections in our families. No cold relation is a zealous citizen."[45] With the words "We begin our public affections in our families," Burke clearly identifies the function of the family with that of a "little platoon." Earlier in the *Reflections*, he defined a little platoon as a small social group that fosters the "public affections" that serve as "the first link in the series by which we proceed toward a love of our country and to mankind."[46] The family, alongside small communities such as churches, towns, and even the class to which a person belongs, form the little platoons that serve as the foundation of human social and political life.

Traditional boundaries of towns and counties demarcate the localities in which the little platoons of family and class flourish. Burke condemns the National Assembly for polluting the natural sources of public affection by erasing these boundaries and turning France into a utilitarian geometric grid. Burke contends that no one will ever have patriotic love for a "description of square measurement." Particular ties to relatives and neighbors inspire the public affection of patriotism. Burke offers a political version of Socrates' ladder-climb from physical love to love of truth in Plato's *Symposium*: from love of families, people pass to love of neighborhoods, love of habitual provincial connections, and, ultimately, love of country.

On the third day of the *Speech in General Reply*, Burke denounced Colonel Hannay, one of the minions of Warren Hastings, for oppressing Indians to the point that they unnaturally sought to flee both home and homeland. In a stunning passage, Burke celebrates love of family and love of country as the two strongest instincts found in humankind:

> Next to love of parents for their children, the strongest instinct, both natural and moral, that exists in man, is the love of country: an instinct, indeed, which extends even to the brute creation. All creatures love their offspring; next to that they love their homes: they have a fondness for the place where they have been bred; for the habitations they have dwelt in, for the stalls in which they have been fed, the pastures they have browsed in, and the wilds in which they have roamed. We all know that the natal soil has a sweetness in it beyond the harmony of verse. This instinct, I say, that binds all creatures to their country, never becomes inert in us, nor ever suffers us to want a memory of it. Those, therefore, that seek to fly their country can only wish to fly from oppression: and what other proof can you want of this oppression, when as a witness has told you, Colonel Hannay was obliged to put bars and guards to confine the inhabitants within the country?[47]

Like Aristotle, Burke draws parallels between the social behavior of animals and humans. Both animals and humans love their offspring first and foremost, and next of all love the place or country in which they dwell and raise their families. For this reason, Burke concludes that social, economic, or political oppression is at the root of any mass exodus from a country (a political and economic fact he knew personally as an Irishman living in exile from his homeland).

Burke believes that a person's place in the natural world, one's attachment to the land one lives on and the people one lives with, shapes one's nationalistic pride in one's country as a natural, social, and political entity, yet also tempers and balances one's capacity for patriotism. For this reason, Burke finds the patriotism of the French revolutionaries morally and politically circumspect. Not only did the revolutionaries redraw the borders of towns and counties, erasing the traditional markers of "local attachments," but they also sought to destroy the hierarchical family and replace its natural loves and loyalties with an unnatural, overzealous patriotic fidelity to the state.

In the *Fourth Letter on a Regicide Peace*, Burke argues that the destruction of the hierarchical family's role as the foundation of loyalty to the state entailed the total elimination of the distinction between public and private in France: "France has no public; it is the only nation I ever heard of, where the people are absolutely slaves, in the fullest sense, in all affairs, public and private, great and small, even down to the minutest and most recondite parts of their household concerns."[48] Burke suggests that the revolutionaries sought to destroy the hierarchical family for two reasons: (1) the hierarchical structure of the family subverted the legitimacy of the new egalitarian social and political order and (2) the newly founded and politically unstable French republic needed its citizens to be more devoted to the state than to their families. The revolutionaries thus transformed the state into one big egalitarian family, erased the distinction between public and private, and demanded citizens to revere the state with adoration formerly reserved for parents and the family itself.

The Family's Place in the Natural Order

Burke believed that the hierarchical family reflected and complemented the natural order of the universe as God ordained it. Upsetting the hierarchical order of the family meant it no longer mirrored the divinely sanctioned natural order. Burke concluded that the family—disconnected from its natural moorings—could no longer fulfill its natural purpose, the cultivation of the social bonds of sympathy, civility, and patriotism. Disconnected from the moral dictates of God's natural law, and from the hierarchical structure of the universe that He ordained, the family threatened to upset, rather than buttress, the stability of society and state. Yet Burke is not interested in defending or preserving unmitigated patriarchal power in any form. He defends hierarchical institutions to the extent that they contribute to the development of the essential social bonds that maintain the stability of society and state, and consistently denounces the abuse of patriarchal power for despotic ends.

Burke envisions the places of family, society, and state within the natural order in the following way. God, the Father of the Universe, stands at the top of the cosmic ladder, bestowing the natural law to his creation as the moral compass for the three levels of society in the temporal world. These three levels of society—state, civil society, and family (in descending order)—replicate the hierarchical and patriarchal order of the universe. Though it stands at the bottom of the cosmic ladder, the hierarchical family serves as the moral foundation for the upper levels of human society. The hierarchical family inspires the social bonds of sympathy, civility, and patriotism, which spur people to put their rational grasp of the natural law into action, and in turn encourages stability in the higher social spheres of civil society and the state.

Burke, like Aquinas and the Scholastic theologians who followed him, retains an Aristotelian view of the role of society and the state in perfecting raw, untutored human nature. For Burke, civil society and state are the arenas in which man realizes his telos, or purpose. In the *Reflections*, he defines the moral purpose of the state: "He who gave our nature to be perfected by our virtue, willed also the necessary means of its perfection—He willed therefore the state."[49] Burke establishes the state as one of the realms in which man's social nature is fully cultivated. In *An Appeal from the New to the Old Whigs*, he establishes the parallel purpose of civil society: "The state of civil society . . . is a state of nature; and much more truly so than a savage and incoherent mode of life. For man is by nature reasonable; and he is never perfectly in his natural state, but when he is placed where reason may be best cultivated, and most predominates. Art is man's nature. We are as much, at least, in a state of nature in formed manhood, as in immature and helpless infancy."[50] Burke outdoes even Rousseau with these paradoxes—and indeed, this passage can be read as a sharp retort to the *Second Discourse*'s stark divide between nature and society. Like Aristotle, Burke believes that man is by nature both a rational and a social animal. Thus, it is natural for human reason to be best nurtured within the realms of civil society and the state. To unravel the paradox: it is in man's nature to be nurtured within civil society. In this way, Burke collapses the distinction between the state of nature and civil society drawn to differing degrees by Hobbes, Locke, and Rousseau.

Such passages indicate Burke's debt to the Scholastic natural law tradition, rather than the modern social contract tradition of natural right. Parkin (1956) argues that Burke distinguishes between "natural rights" and "abstract natural rights" in *An Appeal from the New to the Old Whigs*. Abstract natural rights are hypothetical rights—such as those invoked by the French revolutionaries—that express our base needs and self-interest. Natural rights are moral rights dictated by the natural law and codified by the laws of the state that encompass both individual self-interest and duties to others.[51] According to Burke, a person's relationship to family, society, and state is not a matter of protecting abstract natural rights with contracts of convenience, but rather a matter of upholding the moral duties demanded by the natural law. For this reason, he denounces the French revolutionaries for turning both marriage and the state into shaky civil contracts easily dissolved by the "will" of the parties involved.

In *An Appeal from the New to the Old Whigs*, Burke offers a reinterpretation of the social contract from a natural law perspective:

> When we marry, the choice is voluntary, but the duties are not matter of choice. They are dictated by the nature of the situation. Dark and inscrutable are the ways by which we come into the world. The instincts which give rise to this mysterious process of nature are not of our own making. But out of physical causes, unknown to us, perhaps unknowable, arise moral duties, which, as we are able perfectly to comprehend, we are bound indispensably to perform. Parents may not be consenting to their moral relation; but consenting or not, they are bound to a long train of burthensome duties toward those with whom they have never made a convention of any sort. Children are not consenting to their relation, but their relation, without their actual consent, binds them to its duties; or rather it implies their consent because the presumed consent of every rational creature is in unison with the predisposed order of things. Men come in that manner into a community with the social state of their situation. If the social ties and ligaments, spun out of those physical relations which are the elements of the commonwealth, in most cases begin, and always continue, independently of our will, so without any stipulation, on our part, are we bound by that relation called our country, which comprehends (as it has well been said) "all the charities of all."[52]

In this passage, Burke draws a parallel between the bonds of the family and the bonds of the state to criticize the questionable notion of "consent" that underpins the social contract tradition of Hobbes, Locke, and Rousseau. He argues that obligations to one's country are like obligations to one's family: they are not a matter of choice or consent, but rather are dictated by the "predisposed order of things." Whether it be the marital bond, the bond between parent and child, or the bond between citizen and nation, the relationships between human beings rest on the inextricable "social ties and ligaments" that obligate people to serve one another's needs and interests. These "social ties" are not usually chosen, but rather arise from circumstances beyond the individual's control—such as an infant's dependency on her mother for nourishment, or a person's birth into a particular country and culture of origin. Burke rejects the modern social contract understanding of the origins of human society on the grounds that our "social ties" do not seem to arise from any kind of contractual agreement. For this reason, Burke reclaims the natural law understanding of how social ties and political communities develop: there are laws of nature established by God that quietly guide the origin and growth of human society.

In the *Reflections*, Burke explains how the British political system reflects this "order of the world": "Our political system is placed in a just correspondence and symmetry with the order of the world and with the mode of existence decreed to a permanent body composed of transitory parts, wherein, by the disposition of a stupendous wisdom, molding together the great mysterious incorporation of the human race, the whole, at one time, is never old or middle-aged or young, but, in a condition of unchangeable constancy, moves on through the varied tenor of perpetual decay, fall, renovation, and progression."[53] The British constitutional monarchy is "placed in a just correspondence and symmetry with the order of the world" insofar as generations of people pass through its stable and enduring political institutions. Like the universe itself, a long-standing and successful state is a "permanent body composed of transitory parts," not a contract whimsically made and unmade.

Burke continues by explaining the conservative political ramifications of his rejection of the social contract model of the state:

> Thus, by preserving the method of nature in the conduct of the state, in what we improve we are never wholly new; in what we retain we are never wholly obsolete. By adhering in this manner and one those principles to our forefathers, we are guided not by the superstition of antiquarians but by the spirit of a philosophic analogy. In this choice of inheritance we have given to our frame of polity the image of a relation in blood, binding up the constitution of our country with our dearest domestic ties, adopting our fundamental laws into the bosom of our family affections, keeping inseparable and cherishing with the warmth of all their combined and mutually reflected charities our state, our hearths, our sepulchres, and our altars.[54]

Again, Burke draws a parallel between the family and the state. He uses love of family as a "philosophic analogy" for the respect and affection due to the constitution of the state. He argues that the state stands in a "just correspondence" with the natural order when its laws and policies are treated with the same affection and respect one would give a "relation in blood." Political reform emulates the "method of nature" when it progresses conservatively, and demonstrates respect for the traditions that past generations have bequeathed to the present. Political reformers should always be aware of their transient place amid the enduring institutions of the state, and work not only to improve the state but also to perpetuate it.

In this spirit, Burke defends the principles of England's Glorious Revolution and distinguishes them from the principles of the French Revolution. The revolution of 1688, contrary to that of 1789, sought to preserve the tradition of hereditary monarchy. According to Burke, the terms of the peaceful settlement of the Glorious Revolution, "bind us and our heirs, and our posterity, to them, their heirs, and their posterity."[55] Through this bond between individual families and the royal family itself, the institution of hereditary monarchy secures and preserves the inherited rights and liberties of the people. Burke writes: "No experience has taught us that in any other course or method than that of a hereditary crown our liberties can be regularly perpetuated and preserved sacred as our hereditary right."[56] Hereditary succession in the monarchy secures the liberty of the English people not only because it promotes political stability, but also because English monarchy and English liberty are inextricably intertwined in the same constitutional tradition.

Just as the hereditary monarchy has a noble genealogy, the liberties of the people have a "pedigree": "Your subjects have inherited their freedom, claiming their franchises not as abstract principles as the 'rights of men' but as the rights of Englishmen and as patrimony derived from their forefathers."[57] Both the English monarchy and English liberty are founded on a tradition or family history. They are part of the patrimony that the English people derived from their forefathers as part of their rich constitutional inheritance. To reject hereditary monarchy, one of the major institutions of that constitutional tradition, is to risk losing the liberty that institution has helped to secure over the centuries.

Burke defends the institutions of hereditary property and aristocracy along the same lines. He argues that hereditary property and aristocracy are institutions that secure certain goods for citizens: namely, the perpetuation of a stable, secure society and the system of manners that underlies and fortifies it. These institutions and their corresponding goods are inextricably bound to the British constitutional tradition. For this reason, one cannot reject these institutions without rejecting the goods they entail and the constitutional tradition that produced them.

Burke begins by defending the virtues of hereditary property: "The power of perpetuating our property in our families is one of the most valuable and interesting circumstances belonging to it, and that which tends the most to the perpetuation of society itself. It makes our weakness subservient to our virtue, it grafts benevolence even upon avarice."[58] Interestingly, Burke claims that the most "valuable" quality of property is its ability to be passed from one generation to the next within a family. Not only does hereditary property maintain the stability of society by keeping property within a family line, but it also discourages avarice and encourages benevolence in property owners. The practice of transmitting property to one's children leads people to see themselves as brief caretakers of a gift passed from generation to generation.

Burke continues with a defense of aristocracy: "The possessors of family wealth, and of the distinction which attends hereditary possession . . . are the natural securities for this transmission."[59] There are two ways that aristocrats and aristocratic distinctions serve as the "natural securities" for the transmission of property and social stability. By maintaining a class of well-established families, aristocratic regimes make the transmission of property more secure and hence contribute to the stability of society as a whole. Aristocracy also helps to perpetuate society by maintaining the elite system of manners that gives society a noble character. According to Burke, it is never an evil to have a "large portion of landed property passing in succession through persons whose title it is, always in theory and often in fact, and eminent degree of piety, morals and learning."[60] Noble families often maintain the manners, piety, and learning that distinguish them as noble, and common families often elevate themselves by striving to emulate the manners, piety, and learning of the nobility.

The system of manners perpetuated by the institution of aristocracy is not the only means for elevating the common man to nobility. The main means is the principle of political inheritance that forms the basis of the British constitutional tradition. Burke delineates how the history of the British constitution can be seen as a kind of familial transmission of inherited rights, liberties, and franchises over the generations. Here, the populist dimensions of Burke's deployment of metaphors of aristocratic inheritance should not be overlooked. In his view, the liberties of the English people are an "entailed inheritance" and an "estate."[61] As a consequence, the common man—though effectively excluded from the ownership of property at the luxurious levels of the English nobility—possesses an "estate" more valuable than the wealth of any aristocrat. Political inheritance is what makes the common man and the House of Commons equal to the aristocracy and the House of Lords. No matter what one's rank in society, everyone shares in the same political inheritance of the constitution.

Burke also uses the metaphor of inheritance to establish the two ways that the hierarchical family serves as the foundation of the state. First, the most important "inheritance" families bestow on their children is the ability to share the natural affections that inspire the social virtues of sympathy, civility, and patriotism. Second, the hierarchical family is the foundation of the state insofar as the respect for the traditions inherited from one's ancestors is the best guide for political action.

Since the state is like a family writ large, we should treat it with the respect we would give to a family member. Burke suggests that citizens and statesmen alike ought to "approach the faults of the state as the wounds of a father, with pious awe and trembling solicitude."[62] He portrays revolutionaries as ungrateful children who would rather "hack that aged parent into pieces" than approach his wounds with care, awe, and respect.[63] For Burke, revolutionaries are not only parricides, but infanticides as well. He denounces those revolutionaries in whom "there is nothing of the tender, parental solicitude which fears to cut up the infant for the sake of the experiment."[64] The revolutionaries would cut the state to pieces and offer it on the altar of political experimentation, while Burke would rather preserve the state as one would care for a wounded father or a weak and innocent infant.

The Family Disordered

In Burke's political philosophy, the reader finds three main types of hierarchy—patriarchal, age, and class-based—within his conception of the natural order. Patriarchal hierarchies take several forms: men stand above women; fathers above children, husbands above wives, brothers above sisters, monarchs above subjects. The rule of men over women leads to the subordination of women within the family and their exclusion from a variety of roles in civil society and the state. The rule of fathers over children leads to the control of property, marital matches, and inheritances by the elder generation. The rule of husbands over wives leads to the husband's control over family property and finances. While age-based hierarchies generally intersect and blend with patriarchal and class-based hierarchies on every level of society, the moral significance of the age gap between parent and child remains one of the purest parallels to the natural order of things, particularly God's role as a guiding force within His creation, for Burke. As for class hierarchies, Burke, like his contemporaries, draws lines between the landed aristocracy of nobles and gentry, yeoman farmers, tenant farmers, laborers and cottagers, and paupers.[65] Ironically, Burke's own relationship to these class divisions is complicated by what Isaac Kramnick has perceptively called his "ambivalent" status as both a self-made man continually threatened by bankruptcy and a conservative political elite who eloquently defended the aristocracy.[66]

Burke contends that these three types of hierarchy should be found in each level of society—family, civil society, and state—for them to stand in "just correspondence" with the natural order. With regard to the family, he argues that it cannot foster the social bonds of sympathy, civility, and patriotism unless it incorporates patriarchal, age, and class hierarchies. If the family is not in synch with the natural order, it cannot serve as the moral and affective foundation for the upper levels of human society. Burke is indeed one of the last great political thinkers to craft a coherent vision of the political order within such a grand cosmological framework. Yet like all systems of thought, it is not without its flaws. While Burke's conception of sympathy encourages concern for the interconnectedness of humanity across cultures and regimes, it is partly compromised by the masculine bias of his aesthetic-affective moral philosophy. In a 1994 critique of Stephen K.White's interpretation of Burke's *Enquiry*, Linda Zerilli argues that Burke grounds his aesthetic-affective moral theory on contestable assumptions about the natural basis of cultural constructions of femininity and masculinity.[67] Mary Wollstonecraft, the earliest protofeminist critic of the moral implications of Burke's aesthetic theory, advanced a similar critique of Burke's assumption that physical differences in the sexes necessarily translate into separate sets of moral virtues for each sex. Wollstonecraft also questions Burke's assumption that only a family with patriarchal and class hierarchies can fulfill the vital role of the little platoon. As we will see in chapters four and five, while she challenges Burke's core assumptions about the necessity of certain social hierarchies and their synchronicity with the natural order, Wollstonecraft follows his ambitious approach to political thinking by theorizing the family and its relationship to society and government within her own theologically sophisticated conceptions of the cosmological order.

4

THE FAMILY AS CAVE, PLATOON, AND PRISON

The Three Stages of Wollstonecraft's Philosophy of the Family

Reinterpreting Wollstonecraft ✓

Mary Wollstonecraft, at the time she wrote *A Vindication of the Rights of Men* and *A Vindication of the Rights of Woman*, shared Burke's view of the family's role as the primary little platoon, or the affective space within which citizens are effectively formed. Although the *Rights of Men* vilifies Burke and his defense of the patriarchal hierarchies of the family of their time, Wollstonecraft shared Burke's understanding of what the moral, social, and political function of the family ought to be. In the *Rights of Woman*, Wollstonecraft echoes Burke's claim that "we begin our public affections in our families" by arguing that "if you wish to make good citizens, you must first exercise the affections of a son and a brother" and insisting that "few, I believe, have had much affection for mankind, who did not first love their parents, their brothers, their sisters, and even the domestic brutes, whom they first played with."[1]

Yet, contrary to Burke, she contended that a social revolution must overturn the oppressive patriarchal hierarchies of this little platoon for the goals of the American and French revolutions—greater equality and liberty for all—to be fully realized in all levels of society and politics. Wollstonecraft understood patriarchal hierarchies to include all the relationships and institutions—social, economic, and political—that privileged males over females. For this reason, her understanding of patriarchy encompassed all the sex-based and class-based hierarchies that perpetuated the male dominated social order. As Gunther-Canada (2001) has highlighted, Wollstonecraft's sweeping conception of patriarchy as a multilateral set of male-privileging hierarchies is best summed up in the clever phrase she coined to describe the beneficiaries of Rousseau's system of female education: the "male aristocracy."[2]

Contrary to Rousseau and Burke, Wollstonecraft thought that the patriarchal hierarchies of the family perverted, rather than inspired and supported, the natural affections that should foster the development of the moral, social, and political virtues that serve as the foundation of any stable and humane society. According to the author of the *Rights of Men* and the *Rights of Woman*, only once legal, educational, and political reform brought about the egalitarian transformation of the structure of the family, would it finally fulfill its natural role as the primary little platoon for shaping the virtuous citizens of the dawning republican age. Until then, the family would be a cesspool of vice, not a cradle of virtue.

Although Wollstonecraft was more radical than Rousseau and Burke, she never, at any point in her writing career, proposed a complete overhaul of family life. While she desired the egalitarian transformation of the relationships between husbands and wives and brothers and sisters, she sought to preserve the natural, yet temporary and cyclical, hierarchy between parents and their children. She called for reform in marriage, divorce, and property law that would encourage equality between spouses and siblings, but did not call into question the natural moral duty of parents to protect, educate, and discipline their dependent children, or the corresponding duty of children to respect and serve their parents even after they reach the age of majority.

Although she maintained the natural dependence of children on parents before they reached adulthood, and the natural duty of parents to care for their dependent children, she called for certain protective limits on the authority of parents over their offspring. She protested the physical abuse, emotional manipulation, and rote religious catechesis of children by tyrannical parents, and insisted that all children should be legally freed from parental control at the age of majority so that they could determine the course of their own lives and voluntarily perform the duty of respecting and caring for their elderly parents. With regard to her view of the proper extent, and ethical and political ends, of parental control over children, Wollstonecraft fits the mold cast most prominently by Locke and Rousseau. Locke, Rousseau, and Wollstonecraft all extensively discuss in their classic treatises on education how children need to be prepared for the rigorous demands of citizenship by the moral and intellectual instruction provided by their parents, but within certain authoritative limits. Yet among these three thinkers, Wollstonecraft emerges as the most trenchant critic of despotic power in all its forms, including the patriarchal hierarchies of family, civil society, and government.

While Wollstonecraft's debt to Rousseau, especially on the question of education, has been underscored by many scholars, current Wollstonecraft scholarship would benefit from studious attention to the unexpected parallels between Burke's philosophy of the family and her own. Scholars eager to situate Wollstonecraft and Burke at opposite poles of the political and philosophical spectrum—such as Claudia Johnson (1995) and Moira Gatens (1991)—call attention to the overt differences between them, while the equally important similarities between these ostensible rivals go unexplored.[3] The comparison to Burke reveals the morally conservative, Romantic, and Christian theological strands of Wollstonecraft's philosophy of the family that have been overlooked in many readings of her work.

Wollstonecraft and her philosophy of the family do not easily fit in any modern definition of feminism.[4] In particular, the theological principles that animate the moral theory of the bulk of her writings make her thought difficult to categorize under modern secular feminist labels. Nonetheless, scholarly understanding of her significance has unfortunately been constricted by labels that fail to capture the complexity of her thought. Wollstonecraft has been called a "revolutionary" republican feminist by Gary Kelly (1992), a radical feminist by Jennifer Lorch (1991), a care or difference feminist by Laurie Langbauer (1988), a liberal feminist by Zillah Eisenstein (1981), and a hybrid of liberal and care feminism by Daniel Engster (2001).[5] Wollstonecraft is none of the above alone, yet she is all of the above and more. As Virginia Sapiro (1992) has suggested, Wollstonecraft can be most accurately viewed as a protofeminist who anticipates certain aspects of our modern categories of liberal, republican, Christian, radical, and care feminism over the course of her philosophical development.[6]

Janet Todd and Moira Ferguson (1984) and Mary Poovey (1984), among others, have charged Wollstonecraft with exhibiting a lack of philosophical and personal rigor and consistency—especially with regard to the relationship between men and women, and the relationship between reason and feeling—over the course of her writing career.[7] In her landmark study, *A Vindication of Political Virtue: The Political Theory of Mary Wollstonecraft*, Sapiro strove to challenge the prevalent misperception of

Wollstonecraft's supposed inconsistencies by providing a systematic, thematic look at the continuity of her religious, moral, and political thinking across her corpus of writings. While her holistic view of Wollstonecraft's philosophy underscores the remarkable consistency of its principles and arguments over time, Sapiro's "bird's-eye" interpretive approach does not capture the complexity of its development through three distinct, yet interconnected, theological and political stages. To supplement and hopefully deepen Sapiro's vindication of Wollstonecraft as a political theorist of great originality and significance, this book calls attention to the important theological and political shifts in the philosophical development of her protofeminism over the course of her writing career.[8]

Twentieth-century feminist scholarship largely ignored the foundational role of theology in Wollstonecraft's moral and political philosophy. Patricia Michaelson (1993) and G. J. Barker-Benfield (1989) give her the inadequate title of "Christian Dissenter," and Melissa Butler (1988) frames her within the broad category of Enlightenment "natural religion," without delving into the theological nuances of her religious evolution.[9] The nineteenth-century scholars Emma Rauschenbusch-Clough (1898) and Elizabeth Pennell (1884) took greater care to illuminate the stages of Wollstonecraft's theological development, arguing that she shifted from Anglican Christianity to the rationalistic theology of Dissenting Christianity.[10] They sought to refute Godwin's boast that his once (embarrassingly) religious wife died an atheist and redeem Wollstonecraft as a good Christian in the eyes of the Victorians by revealing the Anglican and Dissenting Christian theological basis of her early and middle writings. Constrained by their Victorian milieu, they failed to address the undeniably Socinian (anti-trinitarian, unitarian) theology of her middle stage, and the deistic, and possibly atheistic, persuasion of her late theological position. Building on the theological orientation of these nineteenth-century readings of Wollstonecraft, yet treating her theological evolution as a subject of historical interest and philosophical significance, rather than as a means of biographical analysis, I regard Wollstonecraft as a traditional trinitarian Anglican in her early writings, a rationalistic Socinian Christian Dissenter in her middle writings, and a Romantic deist, skeptic, and possible atheist in her late writings.[11] Barbara Taylor (1997, 2003) has written two recent studies that similarly argue that Wollstonecraft passed through three distinct theological stages, but she refrains from drawing out the repercussions of Wollstonecraft's theological shifts for her philosophy of the family.[12]

Wollstonecraft's unconventional and adventurous life has rendered her a popular and recurring subject for biographies ever since her death in 1797. More biographical studies have been written of her life than full-length academic studies have been undertaken about her ideas—the best being Lyndall Gordon's recent intellectual biography, *Vindication* (2005).[13] A constant in the two-century tradition of Wollstonecraft scholarship has been the general consensus among her preeminent biographers that her writings fall into early, middle, and late stages.[14]

I demarcate the three stages of her writing career as falling between the years 1784 and 1788, 1788 and 1792, and 1793 and 1797. In the early stage (1784–1788), Wollstonecraft's Anglican theology shapes her pessimism regarding familial and political reform, yet inspires her hope for divine justice in the next life. In the middle stage (1788–1792), her radical, rationalistic, Socinian (unitarian) theology drives her optimism regarding the egalitarian reform of the family, society, and government. In the late stage (1793–1797), her deistic, skeptical, and perhaps atheistic worldview leads her to despair of reforming the family, society, and the state through direct political means, as well as realizing justice either in this life or the next.

Although Taylor (2003) also contends that Wollstonecraft had three distinct theological stages, she demarcates these stages and their ramifications for her philosophy differently. According to Taylor, Wollstonecraft's youthful orthodox Anglicanism left little impact on her early works, Wollstonecraft was more of a dissenting Christian Platonist in the years she wrote the two *Vindications*, and finally, Wollstonecraft abandoned theism in favor of pantheism in her later writings such as the *Letters Written during a Short Residence in Sweden, Norway and Denmark* (1796).[15] In contrast, I find much evidence of orthodox Anglican theology in Wollstonecraft's early writings from 1784 to 1788. Likewise, I argue that the influence of Christian variations of Platonism is more apparent in, and central to, her early writings than in her middle stage, in which the influence of Socinian Christology and Richard Price's moral theology is strong. Moreover, Wollstonecraft's late theology is better understood as deistic, rather than pantheistic, since she retains a view of God as the creator of the universe who is distinct, though distant, from his creation. Taylor's psychoanalytic reading of Wollstonecraft ultimately downplays the philosophical significance of her theological shifts, however, by emphasizing that Wollstonecraft's erotic love of God consistently animates her erotic desire for personal, social, and political transformation. In addition, Taylor's historical and biographical treatment of Wollstonecraft as a political thinker follows the long-established pattern of privileging the study of her life over her philosophy.

Unlike her many biographers, my methodological strategy is not to identify the personal events that triggered the shifts in Wollstonecraft's theological, philosophical, and political development; instead, I trace the changes in her theological views, and their influence on the development of her theory of the proper relationship between family, society, and government, through a close reading of her corpus of original writings. I contextualize the development of her thought, however, by pointing out the key biographical and historical landmarks that coincide with the main shifts in her theological and political ideas, and that Wollstonecraft and her biographers acknowledge as important influences on her thinking. The obvious autobiographical basis of many of her major works, including *Mary, a Fiction* (1788), *Original Stories from Real Life* (1788), *A Historical and Moral View of the Origin and Progress of the French Revolution* (1794), *Letters Written during a Short Residence in Sweden, Norway and Denmark* (1796), and *The Wrongs of Woman, or Maria* (1798) makes it impossible, to a certain degree, to dissociate the analysis of her philosophy from a discussion of the historical and personal events that shaped it. Her experience of the Terror during her stay in Paris, for example, drastically dampened her Jacobin fervor and ironically rendered her more sympathetic to Burke's prescient critique of the French Revolution, which she had remorselessly lambasted in the *Rights of Men*. Building on the traditional biographical schema that divides Wollstonecraft's life and works into three stages, this book uses the tripartite schema as a means for understanding the development of her philosophy of family-state relations and its theological underpinnings, not to dissect or analyze her romantic life.

The Family as Cave:
The Early Wollstonecraft, 1784–1788

Wollstonecraft's early stage of writing coincides with her work as a school owner and schoolteacher in the London neighborhood of Newington Green and her work as a governess for a noble family in Ireland. Although she had been raised Anglican, she attended a Dissenting Christian/ Presbyterian church in Newington Green that counted the famous Dissenters James Burgh and Richard Price among its preachers.

Her theological terms and arguments during her early stage of writing remained typically Anglican, however; she regularly invoked traditional Anglican Christian theological concepts such as the atonement, the trinity, and the divinity of Christ in her writings.[16] Yet exposure to the ideas of Burgh and Price probably influenced her shift toward a more radical, rationalistic, politically progressive unitarian theology in the middle stage of her writing career.

A deep-seated Christian political pessimism marks Wollstonecraft's early stage of writing. She views the patriarchal family, and the society it spawns, as a cave that traps humanity amid psychological delusion and moral corruption that can only be transcended by ascension to heaven, not attention to political reform. Her early works—*The Cave of Fancy* (1787), *Thoughts on the Education of Daughters* (1787), *Mary, a Fiction* (1788), and *Original Stories from Real Life* (1788)—feature a strict and didactic moral theory that blends this political pessimism with Christian natural law theory, a Romantic understanding of sensibility as both a moral and an aesthetic faculty of judgment, and an appreciation for the socializing power of the natural affections straight out of the classic texts of the Scottish Enlightenment. Her political pessimism seems to have its roots in the Augustinianism of Anglican Protestantism, which emphasized the bifurcation of the city of God, good angels and good people, from the city of the devil, evil angels and evil people, who largely hold sway over politics.[17] Like Augustine—who deeply shaped both the Roman Catholic tradition and the various strands of Protestantism, including the Church of England, that split from it—the early Wollstonecraft seeks a higher form of justice, and joy, than can be realized in any man-made government, one that is only possible in the forgiving embrace of the Almighty.

One of her earliest writings is a mysterious piece of children's fiction entitled *The Cave of Fancy* that she unfortunately never completed and was only published posthumously in 1798. Wollstonecraft draws from an eclectic collection of sources—Plato's *Republic*, the Anglo-Catholic tradition, and Rousseau's *Emile*—to compose her strikingly original story. *The Cave of Fancy* borrows and reworks the allegory of the cave from Plato's *Republic*, and introduces the crucial question that resounds throughout her writings: how are human beings to transcend the darkness, evil, ignorance, and oppression that dominate most of this mortal world? As Taylor (2003) has noted, Wollstonecraft's debt to Plato and Christian appropriations of Platonism (most famously through Augustine) is perhaps most obvious in this early fragment.[18] Yet Taylor admits that a direct tie between Wollstonecraft and the leading eighteenth-century Christian Platonists is hard to trace, while her references to Plato and especially various strands of the Christian tradition are quite common.[19] Taylor nonetheless persists in interpreting Wollstonecraft's writings through the lens of eighteenth-century Christian Platonism, an approach that obscures not only the theological import of her early, and orthodox, commitment to the Church of England, but the important changes she undergoes in her spiritual and political thinking over her writing career. While acknowledging the role that Platonic and Christian thought played in shaping not only her early writings but much of her corpus, I seek to uncover Wollstonecraft's originality in blending a range of philosophical and theological sources in *The Cave of Fancy* and other works, than to compartmentalize her mind in the terms of a single school of thought.

To understand Wollstonecraft's philosophy of the family and how it transformed over the course of her work, one must begin with a look at *The Cave of Fancy*. Since Wollstonecraft left the tale incomplete and unpublished, many scholars have overlooked the significance of this strange and intriguing story to her philosophical development. When read in the context of her other early writings, which are predominantly concerned with the role of faith in early female education, *The Cave of Fancy* seems to have been intended to serve as a didactic fairy tale for the discrete, imaginative, and enlightened moral instruction of children, free from crass, overt, boring, and conventional religious catechesis. The story sets the stage for a theme that reemerges, again and again, throughout her writings: namely, her view of humanity as struggling to emerge from the cave of oppression, suffering, and ignorance, either through belief in the effectiveness of moral, educational, political, or economic reform, or through faith that the insuperable injustices of this life will be ultimately redressed in the next, or tragically failing altogether.

Wollstonecraft's cave stands by an isolated beach inhabited only by a strange old man, Sagestus, who serves as a gaoler for the souls who need purification before passing from the mortal world to the afterlife. Sagestus is like Socrates, or Jesus, leading souls from darkness into the light; he frees them from the subterranean cave when the waves of water bubbling up from the center of the earth wash away the "dross contracted from the first stage of existence" that has blemished and burdened their spirits.[20] Wollstonecraft takes a traditional Catholic dogma—purgatory as the spiritual realm where souls are purified before entering heaven—and gives it her own imaginative twist for her Christian fairy tale.

Wollstonecraft, deeply influenced by her initial reading of *Emile* during her stay in Ireland as a governess in 1787, imagines in *The Cave of Fancy* the ideal moral education of a child outside of the traditional family. Sagestus finds a girl orphaned on the beach after a shipwreck, decides to adopt her, name her after himself (Sagesta), and educate her alone. Sagestus is like the tutor, and Sagesta like Emile. Cut off from society, and from conventional family life, he educates her through a series of highly orchestrated didactic episodes intended to cultivate her virtue and sensibility. His pedagogical method is counterintuitive and all-controlling: he aims to transform her natural goodness into a strong and stable moral character by keeping her in the isolation of the cave, introducing her only to the counterexemplary lives of a select few of the suffering souls who enter it. In short, Wollstonecraft transforms Plato's cave into a Dantean purgatory ruled by a Rousseauian tutor.

Wollstonecraft begins her philosophical exploration of the moral, social, and political significance of the family within this fantastical, fictional world. In the second chapter, Sagestus examines the bodies of Sagesta's parents for the indelible signs of character etched into their physiognomies. Noting the man's calm and benevolent countenance, Sagestus concludes that the girl's father was a warm-hearted saint, who was "all heart, full of forbearance, and desirous to please every fellow creature; but from a nobler motive than a love of admiration; the fumes of vanity never mounted to cloud his brain, or tarnish his beneficence."[21] The bitter lines on her mother's face, however, lead him to suspect that she was a superficial, belligerent, and unsympathetic woman. He dispassionately concludes that "the orphan was very fortunate in having lost such a mother. The parent that inspires fond affection without respect, is seldom a useful one."[22] Ironically, the orphan state of the girl is not tragic because the loss of the vicious mother is actually a gain, and the loss of the virtuous father can be rectified with his replacement by the old sage.

In *The Cave of Fancy*, as well as in all her later works, Wollstonecraft criticizes the same pattern of corrupt relationships in the patriarchal family: tyrannical, wastrel fathers; superficial, deluded, weak-willed mothers; adulterous spouses; dominating, greedy elder brothers; and vulnerable daughters deceived and destroyed by false ideals of love and marriage. The corrupt, patriarchal family is hardly the ideal place for raising a child with any soundness of character or acuteness of moral sensibility. Sagesta thus gains by being orphaned on the beach with the wise old tutor Sagestus.

Wollstonecraft intended Sagestus to educate Sagesta through exposure to the counterexemplary lives of a series of souls who enter the cave. She only wrote one chapter along these lines, however, before abandoning the project. In chapter three, a female spirit enters the cave for purification and tells Sagesta her story. She married a man she did not love, while loving another man who died young, and then wasted her life pining for the dead man instead of loving the living—whether it was her husband or strangers in need of her charity. Right before her own death, she helps a girl whose mother is sick and whose father is out to sea, and realizes, too late, that "life may thus be enlivened by active benevolence, and the sleep of death, like that I am now disposed to fall into, may be sweet!"[23] She laments, in the cave, that she wasted her life and love pining after the dead lover, instead of devoting herself to charity and the love of her family:

> Worthy as the mortal was I adored, I should not long have loved him with the ardour I did, had fate united us, and broken the delusion the imagination so artfully wove. His virtues, as they now do, would have extorted my esteem; but he who formed the human soul, can only fill it, and the chief happiness of an immortal being must arise from the same source as its existence. Earthly love leads to heavenly, and prepares us for a more exalted state; if it does not change its nature, and destroy itself, by trampling on the virtue, that constitutes its essence, and allies us to the Deity.[24]

Passionate romantic love is often delusional, myopic, and selfish; for the early Wollstonecraft, the only true love is love of God and the selfless love of virtue and charitable love of humanity that springs from it. The story of the soul found in chapter three of *The Cave of Fancy* illustrates the unfortunate fact that human beings rarely aspire to ground their romantic feelings on love of God. For this reason, romantic love is usually dishonest and deceitful and spreads ripples of moral corruption throughout society as deluded lovers become warring spouses, and warring spouses become tyrannical parents.

The Cave of Fancy is one of Wollstonecraft's first theoretical attempts to deal with the problem of corruption in the patriarchal family. The story presents this form of the family as a cave that enslaves its tenants without hope of escape. The mystical cave of Sagestus, in contrast, purifies the souls that enter its gates, and prepares them for transcendence of the sad mortal life that began with birth into a corrupt family. Sagesta, educated apart from society, represents the hope of escaping the corruption of the patriarchal family. Yet Wollstonecraft's answer to Rousseau's *Emile* suffers from the same practical flaw she attributed to its predecessor; she knows full well that there is no possibility of turning Sagesta's fantastical education into general practice, let alone public policy. The early Wollstonecraft, bound steadfast to an Anglican creed drenched in a fatalistic, political Augustinianism, wants to drive home the point that transcendence from the cave of human corruption is only possible when we shed this mortal coil and pass into the next life. Wollstonecraft continues in a similar theoretical and theological vein in three of her other early works, *Mary, a Fiction*, *Thoughts on the Education of Daughters*, and *Original Stories from Real Life*.

Mary, a Fiction, Wollstonecraft's first novel, builds on the pessimistic theme that arises in *The Cave of Fancy* and culminates in her last work and novel *The Wrongs of Woman*: namely, that the patriarchal hierarchies of the family have corrupted human interaction in all spheres of society, and unfortunately social, educational, and political reform can offer little or no promise of change. *Mary, a Fiction* is a theological novel, not a political novel. The author upholds Christian charity as the only positive force for ameliorating the ineradicable evil in the world, and clearly demarcates the limits of positive social change in this mortal world of sin and death.[25] We are born into the cave of the patriarchal family and the corrupt society it spawns, and must await the next life for complete release from its shadows and chains.

There are no positive visions of family life in *Mary, a Fiction*. The heroine, Mary, is born into what Wollstonecraft believed to be a typical patriarchal upper-class family of her time. Mary's mother, Eliza, is an indolent, superficial, weak, and dependent woman, who married for rank rather than love, and who bestows "the warmest caresses" on her "beautiful dogs," while showing no affection for her husband or her children.[26] Mary's father, Edward, is an adulterous, gluttonous tyrant who lords over his wife and children. A luxurious and leisurely lifestyle corrupts the character of both parents and leaves them without any of the ennobling virtues of the hard-working middle class.

Like the selfish aristocratic mothers Rousseau criticizes in the first book of *Emile*, Eliza hands her children over to the care of nurses so that she can play with her dogs. When she grows bored with her pets, she directs her attention toward her children, neglecting her daughter and lavishing love on her son—partly out of jealousy of her daughter's youth and beauty, and partly out of slavish regard for her son's unmerited role as heir of the family estate. Only when Mary's brother dies, making her the heiress of the family fortune by default, does her mother start taking an interest in her education. Unfortunately, she cares nothing for the education of her daughter's mind, but only for the cultivation of superficial feminine "accomplishments" that will attract a suitor.

Because of the practice of primogeniture, a relative who claims to be the next male heir disputes whether Mary is entitled to inherit the estate. He colludes with Mary's father to arrange her marriage to a cousin in order to unite the two branches of the family and their estates. As with all the arranged marriages portrayed in Wollstonecraft's works, it is a loveless match. The two are in no hurry to settle down together, so he leaves her for his education on the continent. The only sentiment shared between the couple is mutual dislike: "In one thing there seemed to be a sympathy between them, for she wrote formal answers to his formal letters."[27] Mary faces the tragic prospect of following the path of her parents into a marriage lacking love, respect, or friendship, and perpetuating the corrupt pattern of family relationships found in her childhood home. Fearful of this fate, Mary equates marriage with slavery, and pledges to escape its chains: "I will work, she cried, do anything rather than be a slave!"[28] She arranges to postpone their cohabitation for a year, and supports herself through her own labors and savings.

Mary travels to Lisbon to help an ailing friend. She meets a family "of rank" traveling in Lisbon, who are superficial, silly, and concerned with appearing more noble than their coat of arms entails them to be: "They were people of rank; but unfortunately, though of an ancient family the title had descended to a very remote branch—a branch they took care to be intimate with; and servilely copied the Countess's airs. Their minds were shackled with a set of notions concerning propriety, the fitness of things for the world's eye, trammels which always hamper weak people."[29] Here enters a theme that recurs throughout Wollstonecraft's early and middle writings: namely, the foolishness of those who venerate the traditional class hierarchy and its system of manners. In the *Rights of Men*, she likewise suggests that the lower and middle classes, "by apeing the manners of the great," are as morally decadent as the actual aristocrats.[30] Until the ferocity and incivility of the Terror chasten her radical egalitarianism, Wollstonecraft shares none of Burke's respect for the social role that traditional class-based manners play in encouraging and reinforcing moral actions.

In *The Cave of Fancy* and *Mary, a Fiction*, Wollstonecraft plots the fate of her heroines so that they must face the dangerous delusions of romantic love. Just as the female soul recounts to Sagesta how her passion for a dead lover prevented her from loving her husband, family, and fellow humanity, Mary realizes that her idealized love for Henry, a man she met in Lisbon, will keep her from making the best of a bad, but inescapable, marriage with her husband: "Could she set a seal to a hasty vow, and tell a deliberate lie; promise to love one man, when the image of another was ever present to her—her soul revolted."[31] After Henry dies in her chaste embrace—in a scene reminiscent of Julie's dying embrace with her cousin Claire in Rousseau's *Julie*—she vows to channel her unspent affections into charity toward the poor, but she never completely frees her heart from the hold of her dead lover. She never learns to love her husband, and their childless marriage never creates a family that serves as a forum for moral and civic formation.

Wollstonecraft uses Mary's unhappy childhood and adult homes to illustrate why the patriarchal family fails to foster the affections that form the basis of the moral, social, and political virtues. If Mary had been free to marry the man she loved instead of submitting to an arranged marriage for the sake of maintaining the family estate in the male line, the love shared in her family would have inspired all of its members to act benevolently and charitably, not only toward their kin, but toward ever-widening circles of society. The patriarchal family, with its warped power struggles between husband and wife and brother and sister, perverts the growth of the natural affections and prevents them from developing into the virtues that maintain a stable and humane society.

Wollstonecraft's theological beliefs are the driving force behind the plot and message of *Mary, a Fiction*. The novel would be more aptly labeled a spiritual journey than a romance. Mary, her fictional counterpart, consistently upholds her faith in the benevolence of God and his providence, and places her hopes for happiness and justice in the life hereafter, rather than in this world. Mary learns to see herself, from a young age, as part of God's family, rather than the corrupt families into which she has been born and married. Parental neglect leads Mary to develop a religious faith and sensibility: "She began to consider the Great First Cause, formed just notions of his attributes, and, in particular, dwelt on his wisdom and goodness. Could she have loved her father or mother, had they returned her affection, she would not so soon, perhaps, sought out a new world."[32] Bereft of an affectionate family life, the child precociously concludes, "only an infinite being could fill the human soul, and that when other objects were followed as a means of happiness, the delusion led to misery."[33] She concludes that love of family, and all things mortal, is an uncertain foundation for human happiness, and that love of God is the only solid ground to stand on.

The neglected young Mary is practically orphaned, like Sagesta, yet meditates alone on the meaning of the universe, without the help of a tutor like Sagestus. Her solo contemplations lead her to accept the beliefs of the Church of England, the faith to which Wollstonecraft adhered throughout her youth and young adulthood. Mary prepares herself, without parental injunction, for the reception of the Anglican "gospel" sacraments of baptism and communion at age fifteen. She cannot sleep the night before receiving the sacraments because she so "eagerly desired to commemorate the dying love of her great benefactor," Jesus Christ.[34]

Mary views God through a traditional Protestant lens: He is her Father, the Creator, and Jesus Christ, her personal savior, and her only truly reliable friend. On her trip to Lisbon, she reflects, "When she had not any one she loved near her, she was particularly sensible of the presence of her Almighty friend."[35] When she meets Henry in Lisbon, they discuss the theological differences among Catholicism, Protestantism, and Deism. She weighs the value of both "Romish tenets" and "deistical doubts," and open-mindedly concludes that "apparently good and solid argument might take their rise from different points of view" and that "those she should not concur with had some reason on their side."[36] Yet exposure to different religious perspectives does not weaken her faith, but rather strengthens her conviction that Anglican Protestantism is the truth, in contrast to the "gross ritual of Romish ceremonies" or the empty skepticism of deism.[37]

Wollstonecraft's orchestration of Mary and Henry's poignant joint reception of the sacrament of communion on his deathbed, as a symbol of their love for each other and of God, suggests the author's pious reverence toward the sacraments of the Church of England. Her married state prevents Mary from sharing the sacrament of marriage with her dying lover, but the joint reception of communion suggests the Christian understanding of marriage as the union of two souls in Christ. Recalling Julie's transcendent love for St. Preux in Rousseau's *Julie*, Mary views Henry as her true soul-mate, even after his death and her marriage to another man.

During a storm while sailing from Lisbon to England, Mary associates the fearful might of the tempest with the impenetrable wisdom and unstoppable will of God.[38] Threatened by the ferocity of the sea, she places her hopes in divine providence and the promise of justice and happiness in the afterlife, and stoically concludes, "Everything material must change; happiness and this fluctuating principle is not compatible."[39] On returning to England, she devotes herself to helping a poor family wrecked by the storm. Rather than reproducing the same destructive patterns of family life found in her own homes, she channels her affections into charitable acts toward the sick, elderly, and poor who have been abandoned by their own families and oppressed by the unjust sex-based and class-based hierarchies of English society.

Thus, Mary creates an alternative "family" life outside of the bounds of the patriarchal family. She abandons the hope of building an ideal marriage or family in this world and instead strives to assuage the pain of the broken families that already exist. Above all, she looks forward to the pure love, uncorrupted by bodily passions, shared between souls in the afterlife. The final line of the novel encapsulates the heroine's Christian otherworldliness and longing for release from the cave of conventional family life and marriage: "In moments of solitary sadness, a gleam of joy would dart across her mind—She thought she was hastening to that world where there is neither marrying, nor giving in marriage."[40] Here Wollstonecraft alludes to Matthew 22:30, "For in the resurrection they neither marry, nor are given in marriage, but are as angels of God in heaven." For the early Wollstonecraft, marriage is a fetter of the material world from which the soul is liberated in its passage to heaven. The early Wollstonecraft had no hope for the whole-scale reform of the family in this world, only hope for patchwork attention, inspired by Christian charity, to its ineradicable problems. Instead, she looked to heaven, where the burdens of family, marriage, and romantic love would no longer hinder the spiritual development of the human soul.

Given her pessimism regarding the possibility of the wide-scale reform of the family, society, and politics, it is not surprising that the early Wollstonecraft, animated by a deep Christian faith, devotes her attention instead to the reform of the individual soul. Her early works—*The Cave of Fancy*, *Mary, a Fiction*, *Thoughts on the Education of Daughters*, and *Original Stories from Real Life*—focus largely on the role of childhood moral and religious education as a preparation for both the moral challenges of adulthood and divine scrutiny of the soul in the afterlife. For the early Wollstonecraft, religious and moral education are inextricably intertwined. She directs the heroine of *Mary, a Fiction* to claim that moral education, without Christian faith, will fail: "Christianity can only afford just principles to govern the wayward feelings and impulses of the heart: every good disposition runs wild, if not transplanted into this soil; but how hard it is to keep the heart diligently, though convinced that the issues of life depend on it. . . . Good dispositions, and virtuous propensities, without the light of the Gospel, produce eccentric characters."[41] The early Wollstonecraft rejects the Aristotelian assumption that habitual practice of the virtues, combined with a rational capacity for prudential moral judgment, is enough to produce and sustain a solid moral character. Following Augustine, she contends that reason, habit, and prudence founder without the "light of the Gospel"—or faith in Jesus Christ as the ultimate moral and spiritual guide—to direct the actions of the sinful, weak-willed human being.

She echoes this sentiment in *Thoughts on the Education of Daughters*, when she defends Christian moral theology against the excessive rationalism of Deism: "It is the fashion now for young men to be Deists. And many a one has improper books sent adrift in a sea of doubts—of which there is no end. . . . Reason is indeed the heaven-lighted lamp in man, and may be safely trusted when not entirely depended upon; but when it pretends to discover what is beyond its ken, it certainly stretches the line too far, and runs into absurdity."[42] Putting an Enlightenment spin on a classic gospel metaphor, she calls reason "the heaven-lighted lamp in man," but admonishes parents to teach their daughters the limits of reason, and the need for revealed religion, in moral decision-making.[43]

In the preface to *Original Stories from Real Life*, she emphasizes that reason and religion are not incompatible means of moral education. Rather, the rational capacity of children to grasp and understand the nature of God and the obligation to obey His moral laws should not be underestimated: "Systems of Theology may be complicated; but when the character of the Supreme Being is displayed, and He is recognized as the Universal Father, the author and center of Good, a child may be led to comprehend that dignity and happiness must arise from imitating Him; and this conviction should be twisted into, and be the foundation of every inculcated duty."[44] If a governess leads a child to rationally grasp the nature of God as the "author and center of Good," she shows the child the path to Christian charity. With her faith fortified by a philosophical understanding of God as the creator of the laws that govern man and nature, the child seeks to follow God's moral law by "imitating Him" and His infinite capacity for mercy toward humanity.

As Mrs. Mason—the formidable fictional governess of *Original Stories*—explains to her young charges: "We serve a long-suffering God; we must pity the weakness of our fellow creatures, we must not beg for mercy and not show it; we must not acknowledge that we have offended, without trying to avoid doing so in the future. We are to deal with our fellow creatures as we expect to be dealt with. This is practical prayer!"[45] The early Wollstonecraft envisions God not as the distant, detached watchmaker of Deism, but rather as the "long-suffering" God of the Judeo-Christian tradition—the God of the Old Testament who patiently and mercifully embraced his prodigal people again and again, and the God of the New Testament who suffered human pain and death in order to redeem the sins of humanity. Hence, her early works stress that the only worthwhile moral education for children is one that teaches the "practical prayer" of imitating the "long-suffering" patience, mercy, and charity of the biblical God.

The cultivation of sympathy is central to the theory of moral and religious education found in Wollstonecraft's early works. She defines sympathy as a "natural affection" that inspires emotional identification with the needs and feelings of others. The natural affection of sympathy may be cultivated through moral habituation and religious education to serve as the emotional basis of social virtues such as patience, mercy, and charity. Ideally, the family should serve as an affective space in which parents train their children to extend their experience of sympathy from the narrow kinship circle to ever-widening circles of society. The sympathy first shared between parent and child should serve as an emotional springboard for the habitual practice of compassion toward neighbors and strangers, fellow citizens, and foreigners. Unfortunately, the patriarchal family fails to serve this vital social role because its unjust hierarchies corrupt and pervert the emotional bonds shared between its members and render it unfit for schooling children to be merciful, charitable, and compassionate.

Since she lacks hope in the possibility of egalitarian social or political reform of the family, the early Wollstonecraft contends that love of God, not love of family, is the only authentic source for the sympathy that inspires the practice of the moral and social virtues. Whether in her own voice, or the voice of Mary or Mrs. Mason, the early Wollstonecraft grounds her moral theory on this simple psychological premise: love of God inspires love of His creation. Love of God's creation, in turn, inspires a radically egalitarian sympathy with His other creatures—not just one's own kin, class, country, or species, but all of God's family. The primary goal of her early prescriptions for childhood moral and religious education is to cultivate this faith-based sense of egalitarian sympathy with all the members of God's great family.

In *Thoughts on the Education of Daughters,* Wollstonecraft outlines a generally conservative vision of early childhood education for
girls. This work is often dismissed as an undistinguished representative
of the genre of staid religious treatises on female education that were
popular at the time, such as John Gregory's *A Father's Legacy to his
Daughters* (1774) or James Fordyce's *Sermon to Young Women* (1787).
Many feminist scholars have been perplexed by the general conservatism of this educational treatise written only five years before the
more radical proposals of *A Vindication of the Rights of Woman.* What
has been overlooked in this work is the Anglican theology driving its educational philosophy. Hence, scholars have tended to underestimate and
misunderstand the significance of *Thoughts on the Education of Daughters* to Wollstonecraft's theological and philosophical development.[46]

Thoughts on the Education of Daughters fits snugly into the theological, philosophical, and political framework set by her other early
works. She reveals an admiration for many of the child-rearing principles
of Rousseau's *Emile,* such as the importance of maternal breast-feeding
for strengthening the health of infants and the natural emotional bond between mother and child. Yet she also roundly criticizes Rousseau, and his
predecessor Locke, for what she perceives as the utopian idealism of
their proposals for improved parenting and childhood education. The
early Wollstonecraft proposes a more piecemeal approach to the repair of
the troubles inherent in the families of her time, much like Burke suggests a gradualist approach to political reform in the *Reflections.* She
suggests that children be educated at home by their parents, rather than
by servants, because strict parental discipline is essential for their proper
moral development. She suggests that women should not marry young
because they cannot be expected to "improve a child's understanding
when they are scarcely out of the state of childhood themselves."[47]

Yet the early Wollstonecraft never proposes a complete overhaul of
the structure of the family to redeem its corruption. Rather, she consistently defends a number of hierarchies of the family of her time: children ought to respectfully submit to the authority of their parents, and
wives ought to cheerfully submit to their separate duties in the domestic
realm. One of the first things that children should be taught is "a proper
submission to superiors," particularly their parents.[48] Likewise, women
should accept their place in the home and seek to discharge their
domestic duties as best they can. For example, Wollstonecraft argues
that women should learn a bit of "physic" in order to care for the health

of their families more effectively, on the grounds that "every kind of domestic concern and family business is properly a woman's province."[49] The point of female education should be "to prepare a woman to fulfill the duties of a wife and a mother."[50]

The primary focus of *Thoughts on the Education of Daughters* is the use of religious and moral education to give women the strength of character to cope with the inescapable problems of family life and the sinful human condition in general. Wollstonecraft expresses her fear for the girls "who are entering the world without fixed principles" of reason and religion to guide their actions, especially in the profound matters of love, marriage, and motherhood.[51] She suggests that the most important lesson parents can teach their daughters is a humble sense of their "infirmities" combined with a deep gratitude for Christ's atonement for their sins: "A true sense of our infirmities is the way to make us Christians in the most extensive sense of the word. A mind depressed with a weight of weaknesses can only find comfort in the promises of the Gospel. The assistance there offered must raise the humble soul; and the account of the atonement that has been made, gives a rational ground for resting in hope until the toil of virtue is over, and faith has nothing to be exercised on."[52] Girls who place their faith in Christ's atonement and resurrection possess a "rational ground for resting in hope until the toil of virtue is over." Their Christian faith will give them the strength to imitate their Lord as best they can, graciously accept the burdens of womanhood and the injustices of this mortal life, and look with hope toward the eternal happiness of heaven.

Wollstonecraft insists that parents should not fear if they cannot protect their daughters from the pain and suffering that befalls them, for God will be a "kind parent" to them:

> Though I warn parents to guard against leaving their daughters to encounter such misery; yet if a young woman falls into it, she ought not be discontented. Good must ultimately arise from every thing, to those who look beyond this infancy of their being; and here the comfort of a good conscience is our only stable support. . . . It is true, tribulation produces anguish, and we would fain avoid the bitter cup, though convinced its effects would be the most salutary. The Almighty is then the kind parent, who chastens and educates, and indulges us not when it would tend to our hurt. He is compassion itself, and never wounds but to heal, when the ends of correction are answered.[53]

Wollstonecraft firmly believes that God is a "kind parent" who "never wounds but to heal." He "chastens and educates" his children through trials and tribulations that strengthen their character and faith. Likewise, parents must model themselves after their Father in heaven, in order to set a good moral example for their children.

For example, Wollstonecraft asks parents to behave in a manner appropriate to the sabbath, so that their children (and servants) do not lose respect for them or the dignity of the church:

> It is unfortunate, that such a day is either kept with puritanical ex-actness, which renders it very irksome, or lost in dissipation and thoughtlessness. Either way is very prejudicial to the minds of children and servants, who ought not to be let run wild, nor con-fined too strictly; and, above all, should not see their parents or masters indulge themselves in things which are generally thought wrong. . . . Such a close attention to a family may appear to many very disagreeable; but the path of duty will be found pleasant after some time; and the passions being employed this way, will, by degrees, come under the subjection of reason . . . I never knew much social virtue to reside in a house where the sabbath was grossly violated.[54]

Wollstonecraft identifies the violation of the sabbath with the demise of "social virtue" in the home. If parents disrespect God and his day of rest, then their children will follow suit and disregard the moral authority of both their heavenly and human superiors. The natural sympathy between child and parent, creature and Creator, will no longer inspire the practice of the social virtues of mercy, compassion, patience, and charity.

In order to encourage their children to practice the moral and so-cial virtues, parents must instill in them a "habitual reverence" for God, His creation, and His law: "If the presence of the Deity be inculcated and dwelt on till an habitual reverence is established in the mind, it will check the sallies of anger and sneers of peevishness, which corrode our peace, and render us wretched, without any claim to pity. . . . Our phil-anthropy is a proof, we are told, that we are capable of loving our Cre-ator. Indeed, this divine love, or charity, appears to me the principal trait that remains of the illustrious image of the Deity, which was originally stamped on the soul, and which is to be renewed."[55] Love of God checks the sinful tendencies of the human character, and instead inspires acts of "philanthropy" and "charity" toward others that imitate the "divine love" of the Creator for his creation. Wollstonecraft notes that benevolence is "the first, and most amiable virtue . . . often found in young persons that afterwards grow selfish."[56] Although the instinct for benevolence develops naturally in young children who enjoy affectionate, loving, and sympathetic relations with their parents, it is usually extinguished in the treacherous atmosphere of the patriarchal family.

Wollstonecraft complains that women, corrupted by the current system of moral education, devote too much of their love and charity to their own families: "They fix not in their minds the precedence of moral obligations, or make their feelings give way to duty. Goodwill to the whole human race should dwell in our bosoms, nor should love to individuals induce us to violate this first of duties, or make us sacrifice the interest of any fellow-creature, to promote that of another, whom we happen to be more partial to."[57] As a partial remedy to this problem, Wollstonecraft suggests that parents encourage their daughters to perform acts of charity toward neighbors and strangers. The practice of charity will teach the girls to feel sympathy for the whole of God's family, not just for their own family. As in the opening chapters of her *Original Stories*, she also encourages parents to use stories of the kind treatment of insects and animals to inspire them to "exercise humanity" toward all of God's creation.[58]

Although the early Wollstonecraft desires the wide-scale practice of egalitarian sympathy toward all members of God's creation, she does not yet translate this spiritual and ethical mission into a platform for the egalitarian transformation of family, society, and state, as in her middle stage. Her Anglican-Augustinian political pessimism prevents her from idealistically embracing egalitarian sympathy as a potentially revolutionary force for transforming family, society, and state. It is clear that the author of *Thoughts on the Education of Daughters* looks beyond the family, society, and politics to God for the locus of human happiness and virtue. The family, in its lamentably, yet inescapably, corrupt form, serves as the first moral training-ground and obstacle course for the soul to endure and ultimately transcend on its journey toward union with its Creator. Wollstonecraft continues with this blend of Christian political pessimism and moral idealism in her collection of children's stories, *Original Stories from Real Life*.

Original Stories is the culmination of Wollstonecraft's early stage of writing, and the literary and philosophical completion of the unfinished work *The Cave of Fancy*. Mrs. Mason, the formidable governess assigned to educate the misbehaving, ill-mannered girls Mary and

Caroline, resembles her predecessor Sagestus. Like Sagestus, she is a Socratic figure who leads her pupils out of the cave of ignorance and immorality and into the light of truth and virtue. Like Sagestus, Mrs. Mason also resembles the tutor from Rousseau's *Emile* with her all-controlling pedagogical method. Mary and Caroline, likewise, call to mind the character of Sagesta. All three girls stand opposite the blank slate that is Emile. Parental neglect of their proper moral, religious, and intellectual education has rendered them corrupt and "shamefully ignorant" at a pitifully young age.[59] Only through subjection to the rigorous method of moral education supplied by their tutors, Sagestus and Mrs. Mason, can their souls be saved. Mrs. Mason tells Mary and Caroline nightmarish stories of human vice and suffering, and then leads them, through a series of detached, didactic questions, to understand why they must define their lives against these dire moral counterexamples. She shows the children how to live a virtuous life amid the darkness of our corrupt, mortal existence while preparing for transcendence from the cave into the eternal joy and light of heaven.

While Mrs. Mason shares the ascetic otherworldliness of Sagestus, she seems to be of a darker stripe than the wise hermit of *The Cave of Fancy*. William Blake portrayed Mrs. Mason as a Christ-like, maternal, yet grim figure in his stark, subversive illustrations for the second edition of Wollstonecraft's book.[60] *Original Stories* anticipates the macabre moralism of the Brothers Grimm, and the brutal realism of Victorian children's fiction, with Mrs. Mason's showcase of human horror stories. Most of the tales she tells Mary and Caroline for their moral edification are unbearably, even implausibly, tragic. In one sense, Mrs. Mason's stories play the same didactic role as the fantastical "hard cases" found in contemporary moral philosophy. Yet while contemporary ethicists use hard cases as part of an abstract philosophical argument, rather than a description of reality, Wollstonecraft intends the extreme pathos of her stories to serve as a realistic reminder of the bitter nature of mortal existence. Mrs. Mason's stories are both "original"—fantastic, extreme, hard cases—and "from real life"—dark reflections of the cave in which human beings are bound.

The antiheroes of Mrs. Mason's stories experience the brunt of their suffering within the confines of families corrupted by arbitrary social hierarchies based on sex and class. The "History of Jane (Fretful)" provides the example of a girl whose character is ruined by the inept parenting of ignorant nurses and a weak-willed mother. Without adequate moral discipline, the girl becomes an angry and imperious tyrant.

Mrs. Mason mournfully recounts how Jane kicks and kills a pregnant dog, and even drives her mother to an early grave with her fits of rage. The unsung villain in the story is the patriarchal system of education that produces generation after generation of weak women incapable of passing anything onto their daughters but their vices. Yet "The History of Jane" serves not as a clarion call for educational reform, but rather as a warning for young girls to preserve their souls from sinking into the moral pitfall of an unruly temper.

In "Mrs. Trueman vs. Lady Sly," Mrs. Mason turns to the topic of marriage and the moral pitfalls it presents. She recounts the story of two young cousins who benefit from the charity of the same wealthy patroness. One of the cousins, Miss Trueman, has lost her estate to her eldest brother due to the practice of primogeniture. The other cousin—Lady Sly—resents that the fortune she would have solely inherited from her patroness will be split with the impoverished Miss Trueman. Through all sorts of wily tricks, Lady Sly makes the patroness distrust, hate, and disinherit Miss Trueman.

Miss Trueman unfortunately marries an "old rake whom she detested" out of desperation for financial security, and suffers a sad fate as a miserable wife: "She tried in vain to please him, and banish the sorrow that bent her down, and made wealth and all the pleasures it could procure tasteless."[61] Miss Trueman is betrayed more by her own poor moral judgment than the machinations of her evil cousin. Her decision to marry a man for his wealth, rather than respect for his virtue, is the real cause of her demise. Miss Trueman falls prey to madness, and her husband locks her in a madhouse, like Maria in *The Wrongs of Woman*. In both "Miss Trueman vs. Lady Sly" and *The Wrongs of Woman*, Wollstonecraft portrays the patriarchal family, with its practices of primogeniture and arranged marriage, as a madhouse in which women are unfairly trapped.

Unlike *The Wrongs of Woman*, however, the story of "Miss Trueman vs. Lady Sly" does not even propose the reform of the laws surrounding marriage, divorce, and the inheritance of property. Instead, the story aims to teach children the importance of valuing virtue, in oneself and others, above all else. Mrs. Mason's story places its hopes not in the transformation of the family and society at large, but in the salvation of the souls who learn from Miss Trueman's woes.

In "The Story of Crazy Robin," Mrs. Mason tells the bizarre and tragic tale of a family reduced to harrowing poverty by an extortionate landlord. Starvation strikes and kills the members of the family, one by one. Eventually, only the bereaved father—Robin—is left to weep over the dead bodies of his children. His pet dog provides his only source of sympathy and comfort, until, pathetically, it too dies. Ultimately, Robin loses his mind. "The Story of Crazy Robin," read from a political perspective, is a grim account of how the aristocratic class system and its unjust property laws destroy poor families without land of their own. Yet the point of the story, as told by Mrs. Mason, is not to rally support for property reform. Mrs. Mason's intention is to teach Mary and Caroline that charity toward all of God's creatures is the only stable and lasting human investment. Mrs. Mason wants Mary and Caroline to realize that they, too, could suffer the cruel fate of Crazy Robin; thus, they should care for all of God's creatures, whether a dog or the smallest spider, for they never know when, in a time of dire need, an insect or an animal might be their only friend.

What is strange and disturbing about "The Story of Crazy Robin" is its extreme pessimism and defeatism in the face of the horrors of human poverty. The author expresses no hope for economic or legal reform that could alleviate the suffering of the poor. Wollstonecraft, as in all her early writings, mournfully accepts poverty as an inescapable part of human existence, and posits compassion and charity as the only means for ameliorating the pain of the poor and sharing in the spiritual solidarity of human suffering. The stories of Jane, Miss Trueman, and Crazy Robin all share the same moral: the sins of individuals, not social forces that lie beyond individual control, are the only cause of human misfortune that we can effectively check. Thus, moral reform of the individual, not social and political reform, is the proper means for tempering the brunt of the injustices we inevitably face in life.

Indeed, as Eleanor Flexner (1972) points out, the author of *Original Stories* believes very much in original sin as the cause of human misfortune.[62] For Wollstonecraft, God is not a vicious punisher—he is the loving, forgiving God of the New Testament. Human beings have themselves to blame for their misfortunes, not their Creator. Although God's omniscience meant that He foresaw the Fall of humanity, He did not directly cause it. The social forces that bring about human misery are the product of individual human sins. Yet the early Wollstonecraft, moved by an Anglican-Augustinian political pessimism based on a strong sense of the pervasiveness and invidiousness of original sin in all human activity, sees redemption of the individual soul as more feasible than reform of the family or the entire society.

The early Wollstonecraft thus faces the problem of the cave with more of an Augustinian resignation to fate than a boundless Enlightenment optimism. In *The Cave of Fancy* and *Mary, a Fiction*, Wollstonecraft portrays the patriarchal family as a cave that traps people in a life of vice, conflict, and despair in this mortal world. The cave of the family might be partly transcended in this life by redirecting the love and affection that, in an ideal world, might have animated a healthy family life, to acts of selfless Christian charity. A life of Christian charity prepares the soul for full transcendence of the cave of the family, and the greater cave of this mortal world, through death and passage to God's family in heaven. The early Wollstonecraft reserves some faint hope that educational reform, modeled after her proposals in *Thoughts on the Education of Daughters* and *Original Stories from Real Life*, might affect some positive, yet modest, changes in family life and society at large, but she harbors no dream of building a utopia on earth. Children, if raised in the manner outlined in her early educational treatises, can learn to suffer and shoulder the pains of the human condition with humility, dignity, and charity, but can only hope to fully transcend the ignorance, depravity, and oppression of this world when their immortal souls enter the light of heaven.

The Family as Little Platoon: The Middle Wollstonecraft, 1788–1792

A fearless political optimism regarding the potential for reform of the family, society, and government marks the middle stage of Wollstonecraft's writings. Fueled by republican political sympathies, the middle Wollstonecraft seeks to turn the family into a training-ground for virtuous, patriotic, civic-minded citizens for the new republican order erupting in the wake of the French Revolution. A linear theory of human progress, standard in Enlightenment philosophies of history, and radical Dissenting Christian theological principles provide the unified philosophical basis of her middle works. From her belief in God's creation of humanity in His own image, she derives her belief in the fundamental equality of all human beings in the eyes of God, and in turn her political commitment to the realization of equal rights and liberties for all humanity, regardless of sex, class, or country. Following the lead of Enlightenment heroes such as Voltaire, Kant, and Paine, the middle Wollstonecraft believes in unlimited human progress—moral, intellectual, social, political, and economic—through the spread of modern science, rationalism in philosophy and religion, print culture and free public debate, and egalitarian rights-based republican politics. The middle stage of her writing career produced her two most famous works of political theory— the *Rights of Men* and the *Rights of Woman*. It is in these treatises that Wollstonecraft elevates herself to the level of the philosophical giants of her time; she assaults Burke in the *Rights of Men*, subverts Rousseau in the *Rights of Woman*, and upholds herself as the exemplar of a new egalitarian politics that seeks to liberate both men and women from the cave of social and political oppression in *this* world, rather than waiting for divine justice in the *next*.

The middle stage of Wollstonecraft's writing career coincides with her work for Joseph Johnson's publishing house in London and her presence in his social circle of fellow theological and political radicals. A gradual shift from traditional Anglican trinitarian theology to a progressive and rationalistic Socinian (unitarian) Dissenting Christian theology accompanied her shift from an Anglican-Augustinian political pessimism to the Christian republican political optimism of her mentor Richard Price. Abandoning the pessimistic view of earthly life that emerges from the traditional Anglican view of the doctrines of original sin and the atonement, Wollstonecraft embraced the more abstract, rationalistic, and politically progressive theology of the London Dissenters who were also the core British supporters of the republican cause in France. The combination of progressive theology and radical politics in turn changed her view of the family and its role in society and politics.

Wollstonecraft's evolving theological and political views helped her to develop a conception of the family's potential function parallel to Burke's notion of the little platoon. Yet her transition to the more optimistic and radical political perspective of the rational Dissenters also led her to believe that the hierarchical structure of the family could be successfully discarded in favor of a more egalitarian one. What she and Burke are left in common is their understanding of the family as a kind of training-ground in which people experience the affections of domestic life, learn the moral virtues, and are formed and shaped as citizens within the limited hierarchy of the parent-child relationship.

Although Wollstonecraft does not use Burke's term "little platoon," she follows Burke in her subversive, feminized deployment of military terms and images to convey her moral outrage at war and violent abuses of power, while subtly shoring up her own domestic idyll.

In the opening pages of the *Rights of Woman*, Wollstonecraft sympa-
thetically compares the plight of women to that of male soldiers; despite
their difference in sex, both are victims of the hierarchies of the patriarchal order. She writes, "Every corps is a chain of despots, who, submitting and tyrannizing without exercising their reason, become dead
weights of vice and folly on the community."[63] She likewise compares
women to both "despots" and "coquettish slaves," because they participate in a dialectical process of domination and submission with their
male counterparts under the current patriarchal system.[64] In Wollstonecraft's new republican world, women are not to remain at the oppressed level of soldiers, but both men and women are to transcend the
vicious cycle of tyranny and slavery that characterizes all relationships
in the patriarchal order.

Like many republican political thinkers of the late eighteenth century, including Rousseau, Wollstonecraft stood as a powerful critic of the
deleterious moral effects of standing armies on both soldiers and the nation itself. Yet unlike Rousseau, she only mildly and nostalgically supports citizen-soldiers as a moral alternative for republican self-defense,
and instead leans more passionately toward pacifism as the only truly
moral stand toward war and violence. She argues against the view that if
women were citizens, they should have to serve in the military, on the
grounds that military service is not a prerequisite, but a barrier to, true
civic virtue for either sex: "Though I have compared the character of a
modern soldier with that of a civilized woman, I am not going to advise
them to turn their distaff into a musket, though I sincerely wish to see the
bayonet converted into a pruning-hook."[65] Wollstonecraft's statement of
her pacifist sympathies adds a protofeminist twist to the Old Testament
metaphor of turning "swords into plowshares"—a woman will not exchange her distaff for a musket, yet a man's bayonet will be replaced with
a pruning hook. Wollstonecraft's juxtaposition of images of spinning and
gardening alongside images of weaponry transport us from the realm of
war to the realm of domesticity, just as Burke's addition of a diminutive
adjective to the word platoon turns this sublime bastion of militaristic
male bonding into a feminized sphere of socialization in which local and
domestic affections develop into the "beautiful" virtues of sympathy, civility, and a moderate patriotism. While Burke may beautify the platoon
by making it small and social, rather than sublime and war-like, the middle Wollstonecraft revolutionizes it, ridding it of patriarchal hierarchies,
but retaining its affectionate tutelary environment, its benevolent parental
hierarchy, and its socializing and civic-minded function.

The middle Wollstonecraft builds her hopes for the transformation of the family into an affective, and effective, platform for political reform on the foundation of a rationalist Dissenting Christian theology akin to the thinking of Richard Price and Joseph Priestley. Price and Priestley debated extensively about the nature of God, the soul, human agency, and biblical revelation in their extensive correspondence, as published in *A Free Discussion of the Doctrines of Materialism and Philosophical Necessity* (1778). While both adopted a broadly rationalistic approach to theology, Price considered himself an Arian Christian, while Priestley identified himself as a Socinian Christian. Wollstonecraft drew from both Price and Priestley's schools of thought while constructing her own unique rationalist Dissenting Christian theological system during her middle stage of writing. As Rauschenbusch-Clough (1898) argues, the middle Wollstonecraft resists an easy fit into the standard theological categories of her time (or ours) because her theological system is in many ways genuinely original.[66]

The Dissenting Christians were all the non-Anglican Protestants in England from the late seventeenth century to the mid-nineteenth century. In return for their support of the Glorious Revolution and the ascent of William of Orange to the throne, the Dissenters gained the right to practice their alternate forms of Christianity under the Toleration Act of 1689. Richard Price and Joseph Priestley counted themselves among the Dissenters. Both were raised Presbyterian; Price preached at the Presbyterian church on Newington Green that Wollstonecraft attended during her early stage of writing, and later in the 1790s Priestley replaced Price as the morning preacher at the Gravel Pit Chapel in London. Both men left the traditional Calvinism of their Presbyterian youth for the rationalistic Arianism and Socinianism that permeated their preaching and their writings on moral philosophy, science, theology, and politics during their adult lives as ministers and public intellectuals.[67]

Arianism is an anti-trinitarian theological position in the Christian tradition that originated with the theologian Arian in the fourth century. Arian was excommunicated by the Church for claiming that Jesus is a creature made by God, rather than cosubstantial with God. His views were defeated by the theologian Origen's trinitarian view of the cosubstantial nature of the Father, Son, and Holy Spirit that was institutionalized by the Council of Nicea in 325. Arian argued that Jesus preexisted with God the Father before the incarnation, but as a creature he was not eternal like the Father. Arian still held that Jesus was the Messiah, sent by God into the world to redeem sin and destroy death, but insisted that he was subordinate to God Himself. Early Arianism still called for the worship of Jesus and permitted prayer to him, but the Arianism of the Enlightenment called for nonadorantism—no worship of Jesus, only worship of God the Father.

Socinianism is also an anti-trinitarian theological position in the Christian tradition that originated in the sixteenth century. The Italian theologian Fausto Sozzini (1539–1604) authored the doctrine, namely, that Jesus was neither cosubstantial with God the Father and the Holy Spirit (as Origen insisted) nor a preexistent creature (as Arian contended). Rather, Jesus was a man of exemplary character, a prophet, and the messiah sent by God to save humanity not through the mystery of the atonement, but rather through the moral example of his life and teachings. Hence, Socinians likewise upheld the doctrine of nonadorantism. Socinianism is the theological precursor to nineteenth- and twentieth-century Unitarianism. Unitarian theology argues that God is one, not three, and only the one God may be worshiped.

Price blended his Arianism with a rationalistic moral theology. Price contended that both voluntarism—the claim that God's will is the source of the moral law—and empiricism—the claim that moral standards are a product of human sensory and social experience—render morality arbitrary. In contrast, Price argued that the moral law, though a part of God's nature, existed independently of His will. Because God possesses perfect moral excellence, He subjects His omnipotent will to the rule of the moral law. According to Price, the moral law is rational and fully graspable by reason alone, though the revelation of scripture is complementary to it.[68]

Priestley's theology diverged significantly from Price's, not only in its Socinian Christology, but also in its necessitarianism and materialism. Priestley disagreed with Price that the soul was a spiritual substance and that human beings possessed free agency. Priestley believed that the soul and body were not distinct, that everything in the universe, including what we call the "mind" or "soul," was formed from matter, and that death marked the end of human life until God chose to resurrect the body. As a Newtonian materialist, Priestley also denied the existence of human free will. Like atoms bombarding one another in space, human actions followed an unchangeable course, propelling each other forward like a chain of tumbling dominoes. Priestley's blend of necessitarianism, rationalism, and radical theology led him to believe that history was incontrovertibly progressing on a divinely predetermined course toward ever-expanding religious and political freedom.[69]

The middle Wollstonecraft adopted a Socinian Christology, like Priestley, while following Price in matters of moral theology. Like Price, she believed in human free agency and that the soul was an immortal, spiritual substance distinct from the mortal body. Like Price, she rejected voluntarist and empiricist accounts of morality, and contended that the moral law is objective, universal, graspable by reason, and exists independently of God's will while constituting part of His nature. As with both Price and Priestley, she believed that humankind was moving inexorably toward the realization of greater religious and political freedom; but, like Price, she believed that human free will, and the good and evil that result from human choices, is one of the divinely ordained motors for human history, alongside the laws of nature and providence itself.

Like Price and Priestley, the middle Wollstonecraft conceived of God as sharing a personal relationship with his creatures, especially humankind, whom He created in His image. In the *Rights of Men*, she pays tribute to the primary bond between Creator and creature and upholds it as the ultimate source of solace for all humanity:

> What else can fill the aching void in the heart, that human pleasures, human friendships can never fill? What else can render us resigned to live, though condemned to ignorance? What but a profound reverence for the model of all perfection, and the mysterious tie which arises from a love of goodness? What can make us reverence ourselves, but a reverence for that Being, of whom we are a faint image? . . . when friends are unkind, and the heart has not the prop on which it fondly leaned, where can a tender suffering being fly but to the Searcher of hearts?[70]

The middle Wollstonecraft's God is not the distant watchmaker of Voltaire's deism, but rather the personal God of the Christian tradition, ✓ the "Seacher of hearts" who knows each and every human being as intimately as a father knows his children.

Like Price and Priestley, the middle Wollstonecraft is first and foremost a rationalist. She insists that the natural religious feeling that fills the human heart is not simply a product of emotion, but rather is guided and directed by reason. It is God's gift of reason that distinguishes human beings from animals and elevates them closer to their Creator: "In what respect are we superior to the brute creation, if intellect is not allowed to be the guide of passion? Brutes hope and fear, love and hate; but, without a capacity to improve, a power of turning these passions to good or evil, they neither acquire virtue nor wisdom. Why?

Because the Creator has not given them reason."[71] According to Wollstonecraft, it is reason that defines humankind's religious instinct to worship the rational Being that made them in His image. She accuses Burke of having an irrationalist view of the human impulse to worship God, and contends that it is not just feelings, but the "refinement of the affections" and the "cultivation of the understanding" through the exercise of reason, that engender genuine religiosity.[72]

Like Price, the middle Wollstonecraft defines religion as a subspecies of morality.[73] Both thinkers view the trappings of religious ritual and tradition as secondary and superficial compared to the sacred importance of using one's reason to understand and abide by God's moral law. She defines her rationalistic account of morality against Burke and his traditonalist view of the cohesion between manners and morals: "What indeed would become of morals, if they had no other test than prescription? The manners of men may change without end . . . the more man discovers of the nature of his mind and body, the more clearly he is convinced, that to act according to the dictates of reason is to conform to the law of God."[74] For Wollstonecraft, the only solid and unchanging foundation for morality is reason itself, both the means of grasping and the substance of God's law. Manners, tradition, custom, and culture are subject to change and therefore do not provide a sufficiently stable basis for a rational, objective, universal code of morality.

In *Rights of Men*, Wollstonecraft derides Burke's worshipful praise for Queen Marie Antoinette, and his portrayal of her as the embodiment of a lost age of civility and chivalry. She also condemns Burke for his vilification of Price as a dangerous political radical in the opening pages of the *Reflections*. In contrast, she presents the sage Dr. Price as the symbolic antidote to Burke's luminous queen, in a moving paean to his piety:

> I could almost fancy that I now see this respectable old man, in his pulpit, with hands clasped, and eyes devoutly fixed, praying with all the simple energy of unaffected piety; or, when more erect, inculcating the dignity of virtue, and enforcing the doctrines his life adorns; benevolence animated every feature, and persuasion attuned his accents; the preacher grew eloquent, who only labored to be clear; and the respect that he extorted, seemed only the respect due to personified virtue and matured wisdom. Is this the man you brand with so many opprobrious epithets?[75]

Price is to Wollstonecraft what Marie Antoinette is to Burke. Yet Wollstonecraft uses Price as a symbol of what the queen is not: the virtues of the soul rather than the beauties of the body, the inner harmony that attends a life of moral action, rather than the pomp and splendor of external shows of grace and manners. It is Price's internal virtue that animates him with "benevolence" and "the simple energy of an unaffected piety" and renders him admirable in Wollstonecraft's eyes, whereas it is the queen's external beauty and dignified manners that make her an idol for Burke. For Wollstonecraft, Price and the queen represent opposite poles of the ethical spectrum: the life of true moral virtue and the life of duplicitous and superficial manners.

Like Price and Priestley, the middle Wollstonecraft identifies herself as a Dissenting Christian, and defends the right to religious freedom won by Dissenters during the Glorious Revolution. She insists that Price and other Dissenting Christian ministers stand for freedom of religious association, not for radical political dissent. Both Price and Wollstonecraft advise those who feel constrained by the liturgy of the Church of England and "cannot find any mode of worship outside the church, in which they can conscientiously join, to establish one for themselves."[76] After her early years spent as a devout member of the Church of England, the middle Wollstonecraft defines herself against the orthodoxy of the established church and identifies her freedom of thought as a springboard for a richer and more authentic form of faith. In the *Rights of Men*, she gently rebukes "the timid fears of some well-meaning Christians, who shrink from any freedom of thought" that prevent them from thinking independently about theological matters. It is clear that she still conceives of herself as a Christian, but as a Dissenter, not an Anglican.

Much of the *Rights of Men* is devoted to an attack of Burke's defense of the Roman Catholic Church in France and the Church of England. She criticizes the institutional hierarchy of both the Roman Catholic and Anglican Churches, arguing that it fosters a culture of servility and obsequiousness on the one hand, and worldly ambition and abuse of power on the other. She rails against "popery," priestly offices, and the sacraments as the institutionalization of the separation between religion and morality: "What, but the rapacity of the only men who exercised their reason, the priests, secured such vast property to the church, when a man gave his perishable substance to save himself from the dark torments of purgatory; and found it more convenient to indulge his depraved appetites, and pay an exorbitant price for absolution, than listen to the suggestions of reason, and work out his own salvation: in a word, was not the separation of religion from morality the work of the priests?"[77] Instead of relying on their own reason to grasp God's moral law and "work out (their) own salvation," Catholics enslave themselves to a priesthood that grants them forgiveness in exchange for charitable donations. As one would expect of an Enlightenment Protestant, Wollstonecraft's anti-Catholicism is the one constant throughout her theological development; what changes from her early to her middle stage is the application of the same critique of Roman Catholicism to the practices of the Church of England.

Finally, like Priestley, the middle Wollstonecraft adopts a Socinian view of Jesus Christ and his relationship to God and humanity. In her early writings and letters, Wollstonecraft often referred to the divinity of Christ. In her middle period, she moves away from the traditional trinitarianism of her Anglican upbringing and embraces a Socinian understanding of Christ's nature. She still deeply reveres Christ as the Messiah, but she does not conceive of him as anything but a man chosen by God to redeem humanity through his exemplary moral example and teachings. Wollstonecraft, Priestley, and other Socinians believed that Christ saved individual human beings not through the mystery of the atonement, but rather through the emulation of his moral example.

The *Rights of Men* offers several clues to this shift in Wollstonecraft's theological development. In a strikingly emotional and revealing passage, she suggests that Burke's traditionalism is incompatible with the radical teachings of Jesus Christ: "Or, to go further back; had you been a Jew— you would have joined in the cry, crucify him!—crucify him? The promulgator of a new doctrine, and the violator of old laws and customs, that not melting, like ours, into darkness and ignorance, rested on Divine authority, must have been a dangerous innovator, in your eyes, particularly if you had not been informed that the Carpenter's Son was of the stock and lineage of David."[78] Wollstonecraft paints a portrait of Jesus from the perspective of Socinian Dissenting Christianity: He is an innovator, a radical, a "violator of old laws and customs." His "new doctrine" rests on "Divine authority" but he himself is not divine. He is a man not a god, a "Carpenter's Son" who is of the "stock and lineage of David." Her choice of words here is very telling: the middle Wollstonecraft sees Jesus not as the Son of God and an equal part of the Trinity but as a carpenter's son chosen to be a prophet and messiah by the one and only God. She sees Jesus as the teacher of a radical new ethic that has radical personal, social, and political consequences. She accuses Burke of professing an anti-Christian moral and political philosophy; the defense of tradition and private property seem to matter more to him than the defense of the poor, oppressed, enslaved, and downtrodden whom Jesus called humankind to serve.

Throughout the *Rights of Men*, it is clear that Wollstonecraft suspects Burke to be a crypto-Catholic, or perhaps even an atheist. She casts aspersions about the authenticity of his faith, and suggests that, even if he is religious, he worships the institutions of the Christian church (whether in England or France) and admires their social and political power, rather than living a truly "revolutionary" life as a Christian devoted to the amelioration of poverty and the care of the weak. In a powerful passage, she suggests that he is a religious hypocrite whose profession of Christian faith has been politically, not spiritually, motivated. She quotes a speech he made about the regency crisis in 1789, in which he disrespectfully and perhaps impiously compared the abused and beaten Christ to the mad King George:

> Observe, Sir, that I called your piety affectation.—A rant to enable you to point your venomous dart, and round your period. I speak with warmth, because, of all hypocrites, my soul most indignantly spurns a religious one; and I very cautiously bring forward such a heavy charge, to strip you of your cloak of sanctity. Your speech at the time the bill for a regency was agitated now lies before me. Then you could in direct terms, to promote ambitious or interested views, exclaim without any pious qualms—"Ought they to make a mockery of him, putting a crown of thorns on his head, a reed in his hand, and dressing him in a raiment of purple, cry, Hail! King of the British" Where was your sensibility when you could utter this cruel mockery, equally insulting to God and man? Go hence, thou slave of impulse, look into the private recesses of thy heart and take not a mote from they brothers eye, till thou hast removed the beam from thine own.[79]

Although she does not worship Jesus as God, the middle Wollstonecraft still deeply reveres him as the greatest moral exemplar in human history and, as such, deplores Burke's disrespectful use of Good Friday as a mocking metaphor for the regency crisis. She even reprimands Burke with a reference to Luke 6:41–43, calling him to take the "beam" from his own eye before taking the "mote" out of his brother's. She presses Burke to critically examine the apparent hypocrisy in his own public statements about religion before accusing Price and other pious Dissenting Christians of professing dangerous theological and political ideas.

The most important shift in Wollstonecraft's theological development from her early to her middle works is her reinterpretation of the problem of evil. As a devout Anglican, she believed in the pervasiveness of original sin and the redemptive necessity of Christ's atonement for the sins of humanity. God threw Adam and Eve out of Eden because they freely chose to disobey His will. Adam and Eve brought the curse of sin and death not only on themselves, but also on every generation of humankind to follow them. In the corrupt, postlapsarian world, in which moral and natural evil ran amuck, human beings were plagued by sin, disease, and death. Only through the sacrifice of the Son of God on the cross was humanity offered the possibility of redemption: belief in His resurrection guaranteed humanity freedom from sin and death. Yet there remained a disparity between the postlapsarian world and the paradise that awaited humanity in heaven. For the early Wollstonecraft and other orthodox Anglicans, this world remained a cave in which sin and corruption ruled, and from which the soul longed to be liberated.

As a Socinian Dissenting Christian, she discards the orthodox doctrines of original sin and the atonement in favor of a theodicy with more progressive implications for society and politics. In the *Rights of Men*, she argues that God, if omnipotent, must have not only foreseen, but must have originally planned, the presence of physical and moral evil in the world.[80] In the *Rights of Woman*, she debunks account of the origin of evil found in both the Genesis story and, in secularized form, in Rousseau's *Second Discourse*. She contends "the paradoxical exclamation, that God made all things right, and that error has been introduced by the creature, whom he formed, knowing what he formed, is as unphilosophical as impious."[81] In the *Rights of Men* she argues that God brought evil into the world for the sake of the "education of his children."[82] Yet she resists a utilitarian understanding of the presence of evil in the world; God does not inflict pain and hardship on some of his creatures so that a greater number might flourish: "To suppose that, during the whole or part of its existence, the happiness of any individual is sacrificed to promote the welfare of ten, or ten thousand, other beings is impious. But to suppose that the happiness or animal enjoyment of one portion of existence is sacrificed to improve and ennoble the being itself, and render it capable of more perfect happiness is not to reflect on the either the goodness or wisdom of God."[83] God intended the human struggle with evil to cultivate in each and every individual soul the capacity for, and the practice of, moral virtue. God allowed evil in the world, so it may lead to the moral betterment of individual souls, and, ultimately, the whole of humanity. This shift in her theodicy allowed the middle Wollstonecraft to become a Christian political optimist. No longer did she think that the presence of evil rendered the world a cave that could only be escaped by the liberation of death. Instead, she now viewed the world, and the microcosm of the family, as a little platoon in which we are strengthened, rendered capable of using our strengths to change the world for the better, and made worthy of God's reward in heaven.

Daniel Robinson has argued that it is not Wollstonecraft's *Rights of Men*, but the *Rights of Woman*, that marks a turning point in her theology. He argues: "*A Vindication of the Rights of Woman* marks the point at which the theodicy of *Mary* develops into the feminist strategy of the *Wrongs of Woman*. In this work, evil is a fact of female existence and Wollstonecraft uses the language of suffering to expose the futility of theodicy and the reckless asceticism of providential resignation. She understands that theodicy may soothe a theologically troubled individual but does little to assuage the evils of society."[84] I agree with Robinson that the author of the *Rights of Woman* rejects the otherworldliness, religious fatalism, and Anglican-Augustinian political pessimism of her early works. I contend, however, that theology continues to play a foundational role in her moral and political theory throughout her middle stage, beginning with the *Rights of Man* and continuing through the *Rights of Woman*. She did not intend the systematic and philosophical answer to the problem of evil offered consistently throughout the *Rights of Men* and the *Rights of Woman* to serve solely as a psychological salve for the "theologically troubled individual." Rather, the theodicy offered in the *Rights of Men* and the *Rights of Woman* forms the underlying foundation for her newfound Christian republican political optimism. Robinson correctly notes the drastic difference in the treatment of theodicy in Wollstonecraft's two novels *Mary, a Fiction* and *The Wrongs of Woman*, but misidentifies the *Rights of Woman* as the linchpin in the philosophical transition.

This change of mind provoked the middle Wollstonecraft to embrace a more optimistic view of the possibility of social and political progress. She argued that even though moral and physical evil were an inescapable part of human life, the "business of the life of a good man should be, to separate light from darkness; to diffuse happiness, whilst he submits to unavoidable misery. And a conviction that there is much unavoidable wretchedness, appointed by the grand Disposer of all events, should not slacken his exertions: the extent of what is possible can only be discerned by God."[85] The burden of evil was not an excuse for humanity to sullenly accept their present misery and place their hopes in the justice of the next life. Neither was it an excuse, as the early

Wollstonecraft would have it, for rejecting the possibility of large-scale social justice in favor of practicing good works on a small scale. Rather, the presence of evil in the world should serve as a challenge to good men and women; it should inspire them to conquer suffering, promote virtue, and spread happiness as much as is possible. She builds her new Christian republican political optimism on the ground that only God knows the "extent of what is possible." For this reason, humankind should not "slacken their exertions" when fighting against the seemingly insuperable obstacles that moral and natural evil place before the realization of social and political progress.

While the early Wollstonecraft extolled the virtue of charity, she did not propose, or even consider feasible, any political program to help the plight of the poor. The middle Wollstonecraft, fueled by her progressive theology, seeks to transform the private virtue of charity into a political virtue:

> And is the humane heart satisfied with turning the poor over to *another* world, to receive the blessings this could afford? If society was regulated on a more enlarged plan; if man was contented to be the friend of man, and did not seek to bury the sympathies of humanity in the servile appellation of master; if, turning his eyes from ideal regions of taste and elegance, he labored to give the earth he inhabited all the beauty it is capable of receiving, and was ever on the watch to shed abroad all the happiness which human nature can enjoy; he who, respecting the rights of men, wishes to convince or persuade society that this is true happiness and dignity, is not the cruel oppressor of the poor, nor a short-sighted philosopher—He fears God and loves his fellow-creatures. Behold the whole duty of man! The citizen who acts differently is a sophisticated being.[86]

In this optimistic and charitable spirit, the *Rights of Men* and the *Rights of Woman* advocate many legal and political reforms that would encourage more economic and social equality between the classes and the sexes. The middle Wollstonecraft wants the state to act as a "good parent" by equitably treating all of its "children" regardless of class, wealth, or sex.[87] She writes that only a state that cares for its citizens with such equity will inspire, in turn, the "natural affection" that a beloved child returns to a loving parent.[88] This natural affection serves as the basis for the practice of the civic virtues that keep a state stable, prosperous, and at peace.

In the *Rights of Men*, she writes movingly about the relationship between her faith and her desire for moral and political reform: "The blessings of Heaven lie on each side; we must choose, if we wish to attain any degree of superiority, and not lose our lives in laborious idleness. If we mean to build our knowledge or happiness on a rational basis, we must learn to distinguish the possible, and not fight against the stream. And if we are careful to guard ourselves from imaginary sorrows and vain fears, we must also resign many enchanting illusions: for shallow must be the discernment which fails to discover that raptures and ecstasies arise from error."[89] It is clear from this passage that Wollstonecraft has moved beyond the Christian political pessimism of her early works to a more optimistic, though still Christian, view of the possibility of human happiness in this world. It is telling that she writes, "the blessings of Heaven lie on each side": meaning, blessings lie both in this life and in the next. We are obligated to appreciate, use, share, and spread the blessings of this life, while recognizing the limits placed on human happiness in this world by our mortality and the darker side of our nature. The middle Wollstonecraft offers a realistically hopeful, not a hopelessly utopian, view of moral and political progress. She neither wants humanity to be paralyzed by the "laborious idleness" and "vain fears" that pessimism instills, nor to succumb to the empty, "enchanting illusions" professed by utopian reformers.

Like Richard Price, the middle Wollstonecraft adopted a metaphysical understanding of human rights as the foundation for her political theory. She espoused the belief that the equality of all souls, and God's gift of reason to each and every human being, entails a commitment to equal rights to men and women alike:

> in my eye all feelings are false and spurious, that do not rest on justice as their foundation and are not concentred by universal love. I reverence the rights of men. Sacred rights! For which I acquire a more profound respect, the more I look into my own mind; and, professing these heterodox opinions, I still preserve my bowels; my heart is human, beats quick with human sympathies—and I FEAR God! I bend with awful reverence when I enquire on what my fear is built. I fear that sublime power, whose motive for creating me must have been wise and good; and I submit to the moral law which my reason deduces from this view of my dependence on him. It is not his power that I fear—it is not to an arbitrary will, but to unerring REASON that I submit. . . . This fear of God makes me reverence myself. Yes, Sir, the regard I have for honest fame, and

the friendship of the virtuous, falls far short of the respect which I have for myself.[90]

In this passage from the *Rights of Men*, Wollstonecraft upholds God as the father of the universal moral law based on reason. Like Price, the middle Wollstonecraft believes that God is reason itself; hence, He does not have an "arbitrary will" and subjects Himself to the demands of His own moral law. Wollstonecraft writes that she "fears" and "reveres" God and His rational moral law, because as His creation she is dependent on Him and thus subject to His will. Her "fear" of God makes her "reverence" herself because she as his human creature is endowed with reason and the power to govern herself with it. The power of reason is the little spark of the divine within her and all human creatures. Consequently, she contends that the gift of reason is what separates man from beast. Animals, guided simply by emotion and instinct, carry on an amoral existence, whereas humans may use their God-given (and God-emulating) reason to regulate their feelings and passions to live a virtuous life.

In this passage from the *Rights of Men,* Wollstonecraft criticizes Burke for the emotive basis of his moral theory. She contends that feelings alone are "spurious" guides to moral judgment because they are not based on (1) justice (God's rules of reason) and (2) universal love (benevolence toward all humanity based on respect for the rationality in each and every human creature). Because humans possess the God-given gift of reason, they respect themselves as mirrors of the divine and respect each other as equals in the eyes of God. The middle Wollstonecraft thus argues that respect for human rationality—within oneself, in others, and as a reflection of God's rational moral law—is the basis for human rights. Because she reveres God, His moral law, and herself, she reveres the rights of man.

The middle Wollstonecraft defines the natural rights of man in a Lockean fashion: "The birthright of man, to give you, Sir, a short definition of this disputed right, is such a degree of liberty, civil and religious, as is compatible with the liberty of every other individual with whom he is united in a social compact, and the continued existence of that compact."[91] Following Locke, Wollstonecraft upholds civil and religious liberty as basic rights of humanity. By civil and religious liberty she means the freedom to speak and act as one wishes in matters of religion and politics so long as this does not interfere with the liberty of other citizens to do the same, or threaten the security and stability of the social contract that protects and makes possible the practice of these

God-given rights. Like Locke, she conceives of government in terms of a contract between the people to establish a government, respect certain civil rights and accept certain public duties in the name of preserving peace and prosperity among themselves. Just as Price professed in his sermon *The Love of our Country* (1789), Wollstonecraft viewed the Glorious Revolution, the American Revolution, and the early stages of the French Revolution as the three prime examples of enlightened modern peoples who determined their own political destiny by agreeing to forge a new social contract that would better protect their freedom, peace, and prosperity.

In the *Rights of Men*, Wollstonecraft opposes her conception of natural, God-given rights to Burke's conception of legally guaranteed rights as a historical inheritance from our forefathers: "It is necessary emphatically to repeat, that there are rights which men inherit at their birth, as rational creatures, who were raised above the brute creation by their improvable faculties; and that, in receiving these, not from their forefathers but from God, prescription can never undermine natural rights."[92] She views Burke's ideal of liberty as materialistic, not only because she believes that he portrays rights as purely historical and political constructions, but also because he places so much emphasis on the right to property: "Security of property! Behold, in a few words, the definition of English liberty. And to this selfish principle every nobler one is sacrificed. The Briton takes the place of the man, and the image of God is lost in the citizen!"[93] Wollstonecraft goes so far as to claim that Burke has a historicist and materialist understanding of rights that would justify slavery in the name of protecting the property rights of the slaveholder, whereas her metaphysical understanding of natural rights construes slavery as an "atrocious insult to humanity" and God Himself.[94]

Wollstonecraft concludes the *Rights of Men* with two powerful lines that charge Burke with an insidious theological and political pessimism while upholding herself as the champion of an optimistic and progressive Christian political vision: "nature and reason, according to your system, are all to give place to authority; and the gods, as Shakespeare makes a frantic wretch exclaim, seem to kill us for their sport, as men do flies. But neither open enmity nor hollow homage destroys the intrinsic value of those principles which rest on an eternal foundation, and revert for a standard to the immutable attributes of God."[95] In these lines, Wollstonecraft suggests that what she perceives as the foundation of Burke's political theory—authority and tradition—is shoddy and weak because ultimately it is lost in the darkness of unwritten history. The immutable attributes of God, on the other hand, provide the strongest possible foundation for Wollstonecraft's political theory. She also suggests that Burke's account of the origin of rights is historicist and empirical, and hence morally arbitrary. Without an immutable, universal, objective standard for justice, she asks, how can human beings be judged definitively right or wrong in their actions? The line quoted from Shakespeare's *King Lear* reveals the depths of her cynicism toward what she perceives as Burke's empiricism and historicism. What are we but flies, killed arbitrarily for sport by capricious gods, if there is no ultimate standard of justice by which to judge either divine or human conduct? Rather than accept this nihilistic portrait of the human condition, Wollstonecraft insists that there is an immutable, objective, universal moral law, to which all rational beings, even God Himself, are bound, and that provides the metaphysical basis for the natural rights any good government should strive to protect.

Of course, the irony is that Burke and Wollstonecraft share a very similar moral philosophy that combines elements of Christian natural law theory with elements of the Scottish Enlightenment school of moral thought. Both Burke and Wollstonecraft view the natural affections as the motivational force behind the practice of the rationally grasped, universal, God-given moral law. Wollstonecraft (perhaps purposefully) misreads Burke in two crucial ways, leading her to misrepresent him as a nihilistic traditionalist. She ignores the repeated affirmations of his belief in an immutable, God-given moral law, which can be found throughout the *Reflections*. She also ignores his consistent argument that customs, laws, manners, and other traditional social codes of conduct serve only as the external, physical supports of this unchanging, metaphysical law. For Burke, customs, laws, and manners are the material means by which people are encouraged to practice the moral law they rationally know is right to do.

Wollstonecraft perhaps understood that she was overstating her criticism of Burke's traditionalism by unfairly ignoring its theological foundation. What Wollstonecraft rightfully feared about Burke's traditionalism is the ever-present reality of the passive acceptance and purposeful perpetuation of oppressive and unjust laws and customs. She would agree with Burke that good laws and customs encourage people to put their rational grasp of the moral law into action. But as she argues in the *Rights of Men* and the *Rights of Woman*, unjust laws and customs (such as primogeniture or the unsatisfactory education of girls) have the opposite effect: they promote bad behavior, crime, and economic and political oppression.

Burke understood that bad laws and customs were a source of sin and evil, not a spring of social benevolence. His relentless criticisms of the use of the Irish penal code to oppress Catholics are a fine example of his own intolerance for preserving such dangerous traditions. Wollstonecraft simply felt that in his *Reflections* he failed to confront and disparage the bad laws and customs that held the French nation in their suffocating grasp. Her criticism of Burke's failure to fully extend his sympathy toward the poor and oppressed of France is perhaps her most poignant and timeless insight into the moral deficit of the *Reflections*.

The middle Wollstonecraft's belief in natural, equal, God-given rights led her to make a political commitment to the destruction of dangerous, unnatural hierarchies in the family, society, and state that foster inequality between the sexes, classes, and fellow citizens. As in her early stage of writing, the middle Wollstonecraft perceives the family as the basic building block of society and hence establishes it as the fundamental unit of study in her political theory. In the *Rights of Men* and the *Rights of Woman*, Wollstonecraft identifies the family as the linchpin for her hopes for the egalitarian transformation of society and politics. She no longer views the patriarchal family as a cave of moral corruption and hierarchical oppression that is inescapable in this earthly life. The patriarchal family, though corrupt, can be transcended through legal and educational reform. The first step—outlined in the *Rights of Men*—is the reform of the unjust, patriarchal laws regulating marriage, property, and inheritance that have institutionalized the patriarchal family and its legacy of sex and class-based oppression. The second step—found in embryonic form in *Thoughts on the Education of Daughters*, but brought to a radical political conclusion in the *Rights of Woman*—is the reform of childhood education, particularly the education of girls. Only once these reforms have precipitated its egalitarian transformation can the family serve as a little platoon that inspires genuine and lasting affectionate bonds between relatives, neighbors, and fellow citizens and inculcates the moral, social, and political virtues necessary for sustaining a stalwart and dutiful republican citizenry.

It is the explicit task of the *Rights of Woman* to design an educational system that will produce women, strong in body, mind, and character, who are capable of performing the roles of spouse, parent, and citizen as the equals of men. As we will see in chapter five, it is Wollstonecraft's hope that the implementation of this educational system, perhaps at first in republican France, will break down Burke's divide between the sublime and the beautiful, the masculine and the feminine, and the public and domestic spheres, while accepting his identification of the family as the source of all that is sociable. The *Rights of Woman* is also Wollstonecraft's main response to Rousseau's *Emile*. In it she argues that Emile's progressive education, denied to Sophie by Rousseau, should be extended to girls. She sees physical education as the foundation for moral, intellectual, and civic education. For both Rousseau and Wollstonecraft, the education of the female body has radical consequences for the body politic. While Rousseau proposes, like Plato's Socrates in Book V of the *Republic*, that the equal treatment of boys and girls in matters of physical education will lead to the destruction of the family, Wollstonecraft thinks that equal physical education will lead to the positive transformation of the family without destroying it altogether.

In the *Rights of Woman*, Wollstonecraft calls for the establishment of a national system of coeducational public day schools in which girls and boys, rich and poor, would all be provided the same education until the beginning of puberty. There would be a big playground at the school where all the young children would mix together in their outdoor games. She believes that coeducation will not only promote greater strength of body, mind, and character in girls, but will also foster friendship, cooperation, and a feeling of equality between the sexes in the long term. Physical exercise would take primacy over all other forms of education, for no school subjects would "encroach on gymnastic play in the open air" and the children would never be "confined to any sedentary employment for more than an hour at a time."[96] Although Wollstonecraft agrees with Rousseau that men are by nature physically stronger than women, she does not draw the conclusion that girls and boys should be given completely different physical, moral, intellectual, and civic educations. On the contrary, she concludes that even though the sexes differ in physical strength, they are both rational creatures, whose souls are equal in the eyes of God, and who share the same "eternal standard" of virtue and thus deserve the same education in body, mind, and character.[97]

The *Rights of Woman*'s system of equal education would help precipitate the egalitarian transformation of the family alongside the reforms of marriage, property, and inheritance law proposed in the *Rights of Men*. Equal physical, moral, intellectual, and civic education would help to eradicate the unnatural, socially constructed hierarchies between men and women that previously inhibited the flourishing of the natural affections of family life, and the development of the moral and civic virtues that grow from these affections. The family could finally fulfill its natural function by encouraging children to extend their natural affection for their parents outward toward others, through ever-widening circles of society. When the family assumes this role, children learn to practice the virtues—such as loyalty, charity, honesty, trust, and sociability—that foster a sense of community and stability among neighbors and fellow citizens.

The women produced by this new system of education would realize that "their first duty is to themselves as rational creatures, and the next, in point of importance, as citizens, in that which includes so many of a mother."[98] Motherhood and political citizenship are not incompatible in the *Rights of Woman* as they are in *Emile*. Although motherhood may be one of the civic duties of women, it is not the only way that women can experience citizenship in their ideal republic, since they will possess equal civil and political rights alongside men. For the author of the *Rights of Woman*, women would be better citizens if they earned their own subsistence through occupations outside the home that encourage strength and independence of body, mind, and character. Wollstonecraft suggests that women could be doctors, nurses, farmers, shopkeepers, and even politicians. She hints that women should be represented in Parliament, implying both that women should be awarded suffrage and that there should be women politicians.

If progressive men in positions of power, such as Talleyrand in republican France, allow the implementation of this new system of education, the middle Wollstonecraft believes that the little platoon of the family would be positively transformed, consequently triggering egalitarian reform in all levels of society and the state. She envisions the rise of an egalitarian family filled with "more observant daughters, more affectionate sisters, more faithful wives, more reasonable mothers" who would all be, in turn, "better citizens."[99] The family, finally freed from the corrupt, socially constructed hierarchies that plagued it in the past, could finally serve as the cradle of the natural affections that inspire and enable the practice of the moral and civic virtues. She insists, however, that women will only become "good wives and mothers" if men "do not neglect the duties of husbands and fathers."[100] For the middle Wollstonecraft, the egalitarian transformation of the family hinges on the moral transformation of *both* men and women. Indeed, her educational system has the ambitious ethical aim of producing men and women capable of understanding and practicing marriage as a "friendship" between equals who are bound together by affection and rational respect for one another as fellow creations and servants of God.[101]

Although the middle Wollstonecraft hopes for the egalitarian transformation of the relationships between spouses and siblings through the reform of education and the laws concerning marriage and the inheritance of property, she does not call for the complete eradication of the hierarchy between parents and children. While she rails against the tyrannical abuse of power that some parents wield against their children, she accepts that the dependence of children on their parents is the basis for the temporary hierarchy between them. She counsels parents to view themselves as caretakers and educators who train children to gradually accept the responsibilities of adulthood: "Few parents think of addressing their children in the following manner, though it is in this reasonable way that Heaven seems to command the whole human race. It is your interest to obey me until you can judge for yourself; and the Almighty father of all has implanted an affection in me to serve as a guard to you whilst your reason is unfolding; but when your mind arrives at maturity, you must only obey me, or rather respect my opinions, so far as they coincide with the light that is breaking in on your own mind."[102] In return, parents should expect their children to care for them in their old age, when the natural hierarchy is reversed between them: "The simple definition of the reciprocal duty, which naturally subsists between parent and child, may be given in a few words: The parent who pays proper attention to helpless infancy has a right to require the same attention when the feebleness of age comes upon him."[103] The hierarchy between parent and child is morally justified in Wollstonecraft's eyes because it involves the practice of the "reciprocal duty" to care for one another in different stages of life; thus, respect for the natural hierarchy between parent and child reinforces the understanding of their fundamental equality as human beings radically dependent on one another for their survival, happiness, and prosperity.

The Family as Prison:
The Late Wollstonecraft, 1793–1797

This optimistic, linear, classic Enlightenment narrative of human progress pervades Wollstonecraft's middle stage of writing only to gradually dissolve between the composition of *Letter on the Present Character of the French Nation* in 1793 and *The Wrongs of Woman, or Maria* in 1797. Her firsthand experience of the Terror during her sojourn in Paris seems to have precipitated her disillusionment with unitarian theology and its attendant rationalistic moral philosophy and radical republican political progressivism. The jaded republican radical could not make sense of the problem of moral and political evil as posed by the Terror within this rationalistic theological, moral, and political framework. In her late stage of writing, her theological views slowly devolved from the unitarianism of her middle works to the Romantic deism and skepticism of *Letters Written during a Short Residence in Sweden, Norway, and Denmark* (1796) and ultimately to the pessimistic protofeminism, and possible atheism, of *The Wrongs of Woman.*

In *Letter on the Present Character of the French Nation*, she writes poignantly about the shift in her theological and political views that residence in revolutionary France has occasioned:

> Before I came to France, I cherished, you know, an opinion, that strong virtues might exist with the polished manners produced by the progress of civilization; and I even anticipated the epoch, when, in the course of improvement, men would labor to become virtuous, without being goaded on by misery. But now, the perspective of the golden age, fading before the attentive eye of observation, almost eludes my sight; and, losing thus in part my theory of a more perfect state, start not, my friend, if I bring forward an opinion, which at the first glance seems to be leveled against the existence of God! I am not become an Atheist, I assure you, by residing at Paris: yet I begin to fear that vice, or, if you will, evil, is the grand mobile of action, and that, when the passions are justly poised, we become harmless, and in the same proportion useless.[104]

Wollstonecraft assures her readers that she has not become an atheist as a result of witnessing the Terror, but she reveals the striking change in her worldview that the traumatic experience has triggered. She has lost faith in the God of unitarian Dissenting Christianity and His benevolent, rational, and progressive plan for the development of humanity to its highest moral, intellectual, and political form. She no longer views evil as something to be overcome or overthrown; she accepts it as the "grand mobile" of human action, the irresistible driving force behind all human activity.

In her *Historical and Moral View of the Origin and Progress of the French Revolution* (1794), she doubts the possibility of training human beings to dampen their passions and vices in order to practice the ratio-nalistic moral theory of Burgh, Price, and her own two *Vindications*. She derides the rationalistic political optimism of the French and British radicals, from Robespierre and the Gironde to Paine and Godwin, who believed that extreme political reform could easily restructure the insti-tutions of education and government so as to promote a more egalitarian social order: "But, from the commencement of the revolution, the mis-ery of France has originated from the folly or art of men, who have spurred the people on too fast; tearing up prejudices by the root, which they should have permitted to die gradually away."[105] Ironically, like Burke, she calls for prudence and caution in all attempts at social and political reform, and condemns the rash actions of the revolutionaries in France, despite her support of the ultimate end of their cause. She echoes this point in her *Letters Written during a Short Residence in Sweden, Norway and Denmark*, wherein she concludes her "compara-tive reflections" on the culture and politics of Scandinavia, France, and England by signaling the limited, and even dangerous, effect of "benev-olent" but naïve, radical reformers: "Innumerable evils still remain, it is true, to afflict the humane investigator, and hurry the benevolent re-former into a labyrinth of error, who aims at destroying prejudices quickly which only time can root out, as the public opinion becomes subject to reason."[106] Continuing in a strikingly Burkean fashion, she ar-gues that humane political reform is a gradual, time-sensitive process that is attentive to the particularity of a nation's culture and history, and its current "understanding" of what is moral and rational: "An ardent af-fection for the human race makes enthusiastic characters eager to pro-duce alteration in laws and governments prematurely. To render them useful and permanent, they must be the growth of each particular soil, and the gradual fruit of the ripening understanding of a nation, matured by time, not forced by an unnatural fermentation."[107] In these passages, Wollstonecraft's unspoken debt to Burke's organic conception of politi-cal development indicates the extent to which the first and foremost critic of the *Reflections* eventually became a latent follower of its central philosophical teaching.

In the *Letters,* Wollstonecraft's emerging pessimism moves beyond the pragmatic and ethical issue of the effectiveness of radical political reform into deeper existential questions concerning human nature and the meaning and progress of human civilization. Observing the bleak, uninhabited shores of Scandinavia, Wollstonecraft composes a morose meditation on the inevitability of poverty and overpopulation that eerily parallels the dark forecast of her contemporary Malthus:

> The view of this wild coast, as we sailed along it, afforded me a continual subject for meditation. I anticipated the future improvement of the world, and observed how much man had still to do, to obtain of the earth all it could yield. I even carried my speculations so far as to advance a million or two of years to moment when the earth would perhaps be so perfectly cultivated, and so completely peopled, as to render it necessary to inhabit every spot; yes, these bleak shores. Imagination went still farther, and pictured the state of man when the earth could no longer support him. Where was he to fly to from universal famine? Do not smile: I really became distressed for these fellow creatures, yet unborn. The images fastened on me, and the world appeared a vast prison.[108]

As in her early and middle writings, she exhibits a universal sympathy for the plight of the human race, but now doubts whether Christian charity or social and political reform will have any lasting impact on its condition. The world appears to her "a vast prison"—a stark and pessimistic image that also recurs throughout her final novel, *The Wrongs of Woman.*

The late Wollstonecraft anticipates not only Malthus but also Darwin. During her Scandinavian journey, witnessing the impressment of soldiers in northern Germany spurs a melancholy meditation on how individual lives are ultimately dwarfed by the survival of the species of as a whole. Self-consciously emulating her literary hero Hamlet, when he observes Fortinbras assembling his army in Denmark, she ponders the sad fate of the soldiers heading to their slaughter:

> Arriving at Schleswig, the residence of Prince Charles of Hesse-Cassel, the sight of the soldiers recalled all the unpleasing ideas of German despotism, which imperceptibly vanished as I advanced into the country. I viewed, with a mixture of pity and horror, these beginnings training to be sold to slaughter, or be slaughtered, and fell into reflections, on an old opinion of mine, that it is the preservation of the species, not of individuals, which appears to be the design of the Deity throughout the whole of nature. Blossoms only come forth to be blighted; fish lay their spawn where it will be devoured: and what a large portion of the human race are born merely to be swept prematurely away. Does not this waste of budding life emphatically assert, that it is not men, but man, whose preservation

is so necessary to the completion of the grand plan of the universe? Children peep into existence, suffer and die; men play like moths about a candle, and sink into the flame: war, and "the thousand ills which flesh is heir to," mow them down in shoals, whilst the more cruel prejudices of society palsies existence, introducing not less sure, though slower decay.[109]

No longer does she affirm the personal God of Christianity who cares for the salvation and moral health of individual souls, but rather believes in the distant, abstract Deity of deism who designed the natural world with the sole and limited intent of preserving the human species. Taylor (2003) suggests that the *Letters* reveal Wollstonecraft's shift to pantheism, or a worldview in which the distinction between nature and God, creation and Creator, is erased, and the divine is conceptualized as immanent in all aspects of material life, including the human self.[110] A careful reading of the *Letters,* however, shows that Wollstonecraft still appeals to the distinction between Creator and creation. For example, hidden within a barbed remark on the hypocritical inability of the "dissenters" to truly lay aside "all the pomps and vanities of life" that they condemn (perhaps especially in the Church of England and its Roman Catholic roots) is Wollstonecraft's plaintive notation of the nobility of grand church architecture, and how these and other worldly "beauties" force even the "sorrowing heart" to pay the most "sublime homage" to "the Deity" in the "acknowledgment that existence is a blessing."[111] Her spiritual affirmation of the need to recognize and honor the Deity's responsibility for our existence suggests that she remained a deist, and did not veer into pantheism, during this time. While Wollstonecraft's lyrical meditations on nature in the *Letters* certainly shaped the pantheistic spirituality of Romantic writers of the nineteenth century, her own "God-talk," and her portrayals of her own, or her fictional characters', conversations with or meditations on God as a metaphysical entity independent of the individual human consciousness, suggest the centrality of the distinction between God and His creation, and her resultant commitment to some form of theism, at least through the time of the composition of the *Letters.* Taylor is apt in celebrating the creativity of the late Wollstonecraft's theological worldview, however. It is during her Scandinavian journey that we see Wollstonecraft develop a new faith— a Romantic deism that blends a mystical appreciation of the wonder of Creation and a stubborn belief in the immortality of the soul with an abstract, philosophical, and often cynical and melancholic view of God as the impersonal Creator of paradoxical world laced with both great beauty and terrible evil.

While in Scandinavia, Wollstonecraft acts as an anthropologist, observing the family life of the denizens of the towns and cities she visits. She bitterly criticizes the harmful child-rearing practices: children are bound in smelly, sweaty clothes, fed with unhealthy food and the milk polluted by the unsavory diets of their nurses, and infected by the diseases carried by these nurses. Anticipating the anger and cynicism of *The Wrongs of Woman*, she laments the injustice of an economic system that forces poor women to nurse other women's babies, while paying other poor women to nurse their own, and drives fathers away from their wives and children to avoid the expense: "There was something in this most painful state of widowhood which excited my compassion, and led me to reflections on the instability of the most flattering plans of happiness, that were painful in the extreme, till I was ready to ask whether this world was not created to exhibit every possible combination of wretchedness."[112] The corrupt state of the Scandinavian family leads her to speculate that the Deity created the world to display all the possible forms of evil. The unexpectedly corrupt state of these families, cut off from civilization, amid the natural world that Rousseau so romanticized, confirms what the Terror taught her—namely, that evil is the irresistible driving force behind the motions of both the natural world and human history.

Wollstonecraft, by the time she writes *The Wrongs of Woman,* views the patriarchal family, and the corrupt society it spawns, as a prison that is terribly difficult to escape. Educational, social, legal, and political reform was once the key to unlocking the prison door, but the late Wollstonecraft expresses little hope in the possibility of such reforms succeeding. For the author of *The Wrongs of Woman*, the brute fact of human misery, particularly the oppression of women, is the fundamental reality; there is little hope for the transcendence of oppression in this life, and no evident hope for justice in the next. As Rauschenbusch-Clough (1898) notes, a slow movement toward "silence" on the question of God's existence characterizes the late Wollstonecraft's writings.[113] While the late Wollstonecraft never publicly renounced her faith in the existence of a Deity who created the world and remains distinct (and distant) from it, she grows quiet on the subject of her faith. Unfortunately, Godwin's public, and indeed inappropriate, statements on the subject have been taken as her own views, a leap of judgment that Rauschenbusch-Clough judiciously advised against. While Wollstonecraft's silence in *The Wrongs of Woman* on God and His relationship to human experiences of justice in this life or the next opens the door to speculation about her loss of faith and its possible impact on her political thought, it cannot be used as conclusive evidence for the materialist Godwin's (perhaps self-serving) suggestion of her late-life atheism.

The Wrongs of Woman begins on a gothic note: the heroine, Maria, finds herself locked against her will in an asylum by her abusive, unfaithful, exploitative husband after she attempts to flee from him with their infant daughter. He has stolen away her child, her property, and her liberty. The asylum is a metaphor for the prison of Maria's marriage, and the prison that the late Wollstonecraft cynically believes the patriarchal family, and the society it spawns, is for all women, in all classes, in all stages of life. Contemplating her enslavement to her husband within the bonds of coverture, and the near impossibility of divorce, Maria laments, "Marriage had bastilled me for life."[114] The late Wollstonecraft equates the plight of wives trapped in unhappy marriages with the plight of the political prisoners held in the Bastille in prerevolutionary France. Yet her hopes for the continued advances of democratic freedom in republican France far exceed her hopes for the liberation of women from traditional patriarchal institutions. Thus, a sense of futility and powerlessness plagues the heroine of her final novel. Maria, faced with the fact of her imprisonment, asks herself, "And to what purpose did she rally all her energy? Was not the world a vast prison, and women born slaves?"[115] The late Wollstonecraft dwells morbidly on the fact of women's oppression without focusing on law and politics as a positive means for its transcendence.

In the pivotal point in the novel, Maria realizes the depth of her husband's depravity after he attempts to sell her sexual favors to one of his friends, treating his wife like a prostitute. Rejecting her husband transports her into an almost mystical realization of the oppressed state of women as a whole and her solidarity with them:

> How I had panted for liberty—liberty, that I would have purchased at any price, but that of my own esteem! I rose, and shook myself; opened the window, and methought the air never smelled so sweet. The face of heaven grew fairer as I viewed it, and the clouds seemed to flit away obedient to my wishes, to give my soul room to expand. I was all soul, and (wild as it may appear) felt as if I could have dissolved in the soft balmy gale that kissed my cheek,

or have glided below the horizon on the glowing, descending beams . . . My present situation gave a new turn to my reflection; and I wondered (now the film seemed to be withdrawn, that obscured the piercing sight of reason) how I could, previously to the deciding outrage, have considered myself as everlastingly united to the decided outrage, have considered myself as everlastingly united to vice and folly! "Had an evil genius cast a spell at my birth; or a demon stalked out of chaos, to perplex my understanding, and unchain my will, with delusive prejudices?"[116]

Maria's own oppression leads her to identify with the oppression of all women, the phenomenological starting point of modern radical feminist political philosophy: "I pursued this train of thinking; it led me out of myself, to expatiate on the misery peculiar to my sex. 'Are not,' I thought, 'the despots for ever stigmatized, who, in the wantonness of power, commanded even the most atrocious criminals to be chained to dead bodies? Though surely those laws are much more inhuman, which adamantine fetters to bind minds together that never can mingle in social communion'"![117] Is this the dawn of the modern feminist consciousness? If so, it is transient. The "film" falls from Maria's eyes, allowing her to see for the first time the chains that have bound her in the prison of the patriarchal family, but escape, she finds, is dangerous and woefully incomplete. The law prevents her from obtaining a divorce from her husband, and thus she remains "chained" to him, in a bond more gruesome than even a convicted murderer chained to the corpse of his victim. In her first novel, *Mary*, at least, there was the hope of transcending the evils of this world in the next life. In *The Wrongs of Woman*, there is only the recognition of the chains, without the promise of a liberator to lead one out of the prison-cave into the light. Symbolically, Maria's husband limits the impact of her mystical moment of feminist consciousness by locking her against her will in her room.

In her final novel, Wollstonecraft moves from the optimistic, Christian republican feminism of her middle stage to a kind of protofeminist pessimism. At one point, she has Maria ask darkly, "Why was I not born a man, or why was I born at all?"[118] Like a feminist Job, the late Wollstonecraft can see nothing but inordinate suffering and injustice plaguing her and all women, and lacks faith in the possibility of moving beyond it:

But I lose all patience—and execrate the injustice of the world— folly! Ignorance! I should rather call it; but, shut up from a free circulation of thought, and always pondering on the same griefs, I writhe under the torturing apprehensions, which ought to excite only honest indignation, or active compassion; and would, could I view them as the natural consequence of things. But, born a woman—and born to suffer, in endeavoring to repress my own emotions, I feel more acutely the various ills my sex are fated to bear—I feel that the evils they are subject to endure, degrade them so far below their oppressors, as almost to justify their tyranny; leading at the same time superficial reasoners to term that weakness the cause, which is only the consequence of short-sighted despotism.[119]

Maria recognizes that the oppression of women is based on and sustained by unjust social practices that render women so weak that it is difficult to rise above their degradation. Yet she is not inspired to feel "honest indignation" or "active compassion," but rather "grief" and "torturing apprehensions," regarding the plight of womankind. She is numbed and muted by grief, rather than moved by compassion and indignation to try to change things for the better.

The late Wollstonecraft discards Christian metaphysics, the prior ground of her conception of inalienable universal human rights. The early and middle Wollstonecraft believed all human beings to be equal in the eyes of God, and therefore desired both sexes, and all classes and races, to be treated with equal respect in society and politics. The late Wollstonecraft, without this universalistic view of the fundamental equality of all human beings serving as the metaphysical foundation of her political theory, instead uses her own particular painful experiences of oppression and discrimination to generalize about the plight of womankind and to build a phenomenological foundation for a pessimistic protofeminism. The pessimistic protofeminism of *The Wrongs of Woman* lacks faith in the possibility of using political, legal, or providential means for the transcendence of human suffering, particularly the pain of women, the most oppressed half of humanity. The late Wollstonecraft focuses myopically on the oppression of women and the material inequalities (biological, economic, social, and political) that build an insuperable barrier between them and the experience of freedom and equality. At the end of *The Wrongs of Woman*, the judge's hostility toward Maria's case for divorce from her cruel husband and her defense of her lover Darnford against the charge of seduction powerfully signifies Wollstonecraft's loss of faith in legal reform of coverture and divorce law in the British society of her time.

The striking contrast between the title of her middle-stage masterpiece, *A Vindication of the Rights of Woman*, and the title of her final novel, *The Wrongs of Woman*, says it all. In *The Wrongs of Woman*, there is no longer hope in either political or spiritual redemption, but rather only the sad recognition of the brute fact of the corrupt state of the family, women's oppression, and the fundamental unfairness of human life. No longer is educational reform and the legal reform of the family the simple key to the transformation of society and politics at large; instead, the corruption of the patriarchal family threatens to relentlessly spread and infect ever-widening circles of human society.

The only hope expressed in Wollstonecraft's final, incomplete works—*The Wrongs of Woman, Letters on the Management of Infants*, and *Lessons*—is the possibility that future generations of women might escape the prison of the patriarchal family. Wollstonecraft drafted several endings to *The Wrongs of Woman* before she died. All but one of these endings is dreadfully pessimistic about the possibility of escaping the prison of the patriarchal family, especially through reform of the patriarchal laws that regulate marriage, divorce, and inheritance. The single unambiguously optimistic ending, in which the heroine, Maria, revives from an attempted suicide and declares that she will live for the child she thought was dead, suggests that hope might lie in motherhood itself.

Wollstonecraft's other two incomplete works from this era, *Lessons* and *Letters on the Management of Infants*, propose strategies to new parents for the progressive moral, intellectual, and physical education of infants and young children. The late Wollstonecraft seems to lose faith in religious redemption and direct, radical legal and political reform, but retains a residual faith in the socially transformative power that mothers and fathers wield as educators of the moral and political actors of the next generation. For the late Wollstonecraft, the prison of the patriarchal family might not be unlocked from the *outside*, by radical politics, but might be unlocked from the *inside*, by successive generations of morally sound parenting.

Several contemporary feminist readings of *The Wrongs of Woman* have suggested that the dark novel reveals the extent to which Wollstonecraft lost faith altogether in recovering a place for marriage and family in her protofeminist politics. For Claudia Johnson (1995) and Andrew McCann (1999), the novel is an early challenger of "the ideology of heterosexual love" and points toward a "homosocial" community as its ethical and sentimental successor.[120] Likewise, Janet Todd (1992) suggests the novel stands in tension with the "claustrophobic nuclear family unit" and Lori Langbauer (1988) argues that it upholds single motherhood within an all-female support network as its viable alterna-tive.[121] The terrible consequences of Maria's sexual and romantic rela-tionships with men both inside and outside of marriage, and her reliance on a female friend (Jemima, who attends to her in the asylum) to help her with rescuing her daughter, are used as evidence of Wollstonecraft's (at least implied) interest in moving beyond heterosexual marriage to-ward an all-female model of marriage, family, and child rearing. Yet a close reading of the novel in the context of her other late writings re-veals that while *The Wrongs of Woman* suggests a deep-seated disillu-sionment with the prison of the patriarchal family and the effectiveness of radical politics as a means for exiting it, Wollstonecraft persists in imagining the possibility of the gradual, grassroots transformation of marriage into an affectionate, respectful, equal friendship between a man and a woman and the intensification of both parents' loving in-volvement, perhaps especially the father, in the marital project of child rearing. *The Wrongs of Woman* is rarely read in conjunction with its con-temporary unfinished works *Lessons* and *Letters on the Management of Infants*. The comparison of these works is the key to understanding the transfigured, yet enduring, presence of marriage and the family in her late stage of writing.

Godwin speculated that Wollstonecraft probably composed *Lessons* in 1795 for her infant daughter Fanny Imlay, although Lyndall Gordon has recently argued that this work was likely written during her pregnancy with her second child, the future Mary Shelley.[122] The work traces a child's development from infancy to early childhood. The goal of these lessons is to teach children how to respect the feelings and needs of others through experience and error, rather than rigid rules and discipline. The entire family—mother, father, and siblings—play essen-tial roles in this educational process.

In *Lessons,* Wollstonecraft portrays the mother as the primary caregiver and educator of infants, but emphasizes the important role of the father in fostering proper early child development. Wollstonecraft joyfully celebrates the vital role of the father in child rearing in *Lesson VII:* "Away you ran to papa, and putting forth your arms around his leg, for your hands were not big enough, you looked up to him and laughed. What did this laugh say, when you could not speak? Cannot you guess by what you now say to papa? Ah! It was, play with me, papa!—play with me! Papa began to smile, and you know that the smile was always—Yes."[123] Wollstonecraft's ideal father, as found in her *Lessons,* cares for and plays with the children, plants the family garden, and tends to his wife when she is sick. The father is as integral to the children's lives as the mother. The fictional family who stars in Wollstonecraft's *Lessons* is intact and happy, with mother, father, and siblings living together in a single home filled with love and affection. Her dream of transforming the corrupt, patriarchal family into an egalitarian little platoon lives on in these *Lessons*, but sadly Wollstonecraft did not finish the book before her death just as she left behind her hopes of using radical political reform to bring the egalitarian family into existence.

Wollstonecraft's untimely death also prevented her from moving beyond the composition of a few pages of *Letters on the Management of Infants*. The extant table of contents reveals that Wollstonecraft hoped to write an extensive treatise on the progressive prenatal and postnatal care of infants from pregnancy to the second year of life. In the first and only complete letter, she expresses her hope that her progressive ideas on pregnancy, childbirth, and infant care would "be found most useful to the mothers in the middle class; and it is from them that the lower imperceptibly gains improvement."[124] She suggests that middle-class women might read her work and change the way babies are raised in all classes, so that "a third part of the human species" might no longer "die during their infancy."[125] While Wollstonecraft never finished her revolutionary treatise on the management of infants, fragments of the *Letters* reveal that she at least retained the hope of gradually improving the lives and health of mothers and infants through the spread of progressive education and medicine across classes and generations. The first *Letter* also suggests that Wollstonecraft remains a consistent critic of the aristocratic class system and its corrosive effects on the upper, middle, and lower classes, and a consistent celebrant of the rise of an expansive, socially dominant, morally sound, and economically independent "middle" class to check both the corruption of the upper classes and the oppression of the poor, throughout her three stages of writing.

Although she despairs of realizing effective, direct, and radical legal and political reform that would bring about the egalitarian transformation of the family, the late Wollstonecraft never suggests the abandonment of family life, marriage, or joint parenting between fathers and mothers. While the early Wollstonecraft identifies the family as the earthly locale for the moral redemption and education of the individual prior to the full realization of justice and happiness in God's family in the afterlife, and the middle Wollstonecraft exudes faith in the power of radical politics to spur the egalitarian transformation of the family, society, and state, the late Wollstonecraft simply places what meager hopes she has for the positive transformation of humanity in good parenting rather than politics or religion. The middle Wollstonecraft's hopeful political outlook on the possibility of the transformation of the family renders her a model for compromise between the fearful conservatism of Rousseau and Burke's defenses of the patriarchal, sex-roled family and the political pessimism of *Mary, a Fiction* and *The Wrongs of Woman*. Nonetheless, chapter five's comparative look at Burke and Rousseau through the critical lens of Wollstonecraft's *Rights of Men* and *Rights of Woman* paves the way for understanding the enduring commonalities between the trio's familial-political ideals.

5

WOLLSTONECRAFT, BURKE, AND ROUSSEAU ON THE FAMILY

Friends *and* Foes

A Sibling Rivalry

Wollstonecraft remarks in the *Rights of Woman* that "in every age there has been a stream of popular opinion that has carried all before it, and given a family character, as it were, to the century."[1] She uses this observation to buttress her argument for a combination of private and public education as the only effective means for changing the dominant culture of an age, and to highlight how exclusively private, family-based education simply reinforces the "stream of popular opinion" that characterizes the times, rather than systematically transforms it. Her use of the term "family character" to describe the spirit of a century also implicitly illuminates the centrality of the family to European political thought of the "long" eighteenth century. By challenging the supposedly enlightened notion—promoted most famously by Locke and Rousseau—that "a private education can work the wonders which some sanguine writers have attributed to it," Wollstonecraft underscores the dubious faith that her late seventeenth- and eighteenth-century philosophical predecessors had in the family as the perhaps only necessary forum for physical, moral, intellectual, and civic education.[2]

Yet, as we have seen, Wollstonecraft retains the family as her most compelling subject of analysis in her political philosophy, throughout all three stages of her writing career. Pragmatically, Wollstonecraft makes her own contribution to the "family character" of the century by supporting the reform, and not the rejection, of the family, and proposing a

Burhan

creative hybrid of family-based education and public coeducation in day schools. Philosophically, Wollstonecraft reveals her enduring concern with the "family character" of the times by critically engaging the thought of Burke and Rousseau on the question of the family and its relationship to politics in her two major treatises, *A Vindication of the Rights of Men* and *A Vindication of the Rights of Woman.*

Wollstonecraft's comparative critique of Rousseau and Burke in her two *Vindications* is largely implicit: her joint assessment of the two thinkers runs quietly under the surfaces of the texts. While the *Rights of Men* attacks Burke's *Reflections* and his *Enquiry,* and much of the *Rights of Woman* critiques Rousseau's novels *Julie* and *Emile,* she only directly compares or contrasts Burke and Rousseau twice in the two works. Early in the *Rights of Men,* Wollstonecraft directly contrasts Burke and Rousseau. She allies herself with Rousseau, and chastises Burke for the theatrical tears that he shed for Queen Marie Antoinette in the *Reflections*:

> Misery, to reach your heart, I perceive, must have its cap and bells; your tears are reserved, very naturally considering your character, for the declamation of the theatre, or for the downfall of queens, whose rank alters the nature of folly, and throws a graceful veil over vices that degrade humanity; whilst the distress of many industrious mothers, whose helpmates have been torn from them, and the hungry cry of helpless babes, were vulgar sorrows that could not move your commiseration, though they might extort an alms. "The tears that are shed for fictitious sorrow are admirably adapted," says Rousseau, "to make us proud of all the virtues which we do not possess."[3]

While she and Rousseau feel genuine sympathy and shed natural tears for the degradation of humanity, Burke reveres the "graceful veils" of civilization that cover its corruption and pull humanity farther away from nature.

Later in the *Rights of Men,* however, she compares the two thinkers and sets herself in opposition to both of them: "There appears to be such a mixture of real sensibility and fondly cherished romance in your composition, that the present crisis carries you out of yourself; and since you could not be one of the grand movers, the next best thing that dazzled your imagination was to be a conspicuous opposer. Full of yourself, you make as much noise to convince the world that you despise the revolution, as Rousseau did to persuade his contemporaries to let him live in obscurity."[4] In this passage, she portrays herself as the voice of reason and truth, while her rivals appear as hypocritical men led astray by passion and sensibility to contradict their own philosophies through their public actions.

What, then, is the philosophical relationship between Wollstonecraft, Burke, and Rousseau? Are they friends or are they foes? Conventional wisdom and traditional scholarship—spurred by Burke's own condemnation of Rousseau as the "insane *Socrates* of the National Assembly"—uphold Burke and Rousseau as philosophical and political archenemies.[5] Following Burke's *Reflections* and *Letter to a Member of the National Assembly*, many late eighteenth- and early nineteenth-century counterrevolutionary works pilloried Rousseau as the philosopher responsible for inspiring the French Revolution.[6] Even to the present day, many scholars—such as Ritchie (1992), Stanlis (1991), Courtney (1963), Canavan (1960), and Parkin (1956)—have persisted in situating Rousseau and Burke at opposite ends of the philosophical and political spectrum.[7] Moving beyond this common polarization, this chapter highlights how the familial-political ideals of Rousseau and Burke, together with Wollstonecraft's, represent a kind of sibling rivalry for the interpreter to analyze and disentangle: recognition of their vital differences should be a step toward the appreciation of their equally significant, though often obscured, similarities.

More than two centuries ago, during the middle stage of her writing career, Wollstonecraft uncovered some important similarities between Rousseau and Burke's views of the family and femininity that have escaped the notice of the handful of scholars—such as Cameron (1973), Osborn (1940), and Cobban (1929, 1964)—who have undertaken systematic comparative studies of Rousseau and Burke's moral and political theories.[8] Although the passages from the *Rights of Men* that open this chapter are the only two instances in which Wollstonecraft directly compares or contrasts Burke and Rousseau, the arguments she uses to critique *Emile, Julie,* the *Reflections* and the *Enquiry* are very similar. Reading Wollstonecraft's *Rights of Men* and *Rights of Woman* side by side reveals to the reader that Burke and Rousseau are friends when it comes to the questions of what the role and structure of the family should be and what the role of women should be in civil society and the state.[9] The two treatises implicitly compare Burke and Rousseau's ideas on the family, morality, manners, and the role of women in society. Wollstonecraft accuses the two thinkers of denying women the same rational capacities as men and, hence, the same capacity for morality, and, ultimately, salvation in the eyes of God. With reasoning similar to Burke's critique of *Julie* in *Letter to a Member of the National Assembly*, Wollstonecraft censures the same novel for its dangerous ideals of romantic love. Yet she underscores the hypocrisy of Burke's condemnation of Rousseau by demonstrating that his own conceptions of feminine beauty and feminine manners pose equally dangerous threats to the moral fiber of the family. Through a close reading of the *Rights of Men* and the *Rights of Woman*, one learns that Burke and Rousseau share much more in common than either of them probably would have ever admitted.

Yet neither is Wollstonecraft a clear-cut enemy of Rousseau and Burke. As a young governess, the early Wollstonecraft read and admired Rousseau's *Emile*, yet she concluded that his philosophy of education would be fair and effective only if it were extended to girls. Like Paine and other London radicals of the time, the middle Wollstonecraft admired the Burke who defended the American Revolution, yet abhorred the Burke who then turned to denounce the French Revolution. Complicating her relationship with his thought further, the late Wollstonecraft found herself employing a Burkean critique of radical political reform after witnessing the Terror and its aftermath.

Wollstonecraft's evolving account of the family's place in the political order thus shares important parallels with the ideas of Rousseau and Burke that extend through all three stages of her writing career. All three thinkers agree that the family should direct the natural affections of domestic life toward the inculcation and practice of the moral and civic virtues that hold society and the state together in a stable and humane fashion. They also each call attention to how the family stands in a symbiotic relationship with the state, and emphasize the significance of the psychological experience of small spaces and local places to human moral and civic development within the family. Yet they differ on the question of what the best structure of the family is, and, in turn, diverge on the issue of what political regimes their ideal family forms ought to undergird. Burke and Rousseau defend patriarchy and sex-role differentiation in the family, while Wollstonecraft, in the middle stage of her career, calls for the egalitarian transformation of the family through educational and legal reform. While Burke understands the hierarchical structure of the family to be a cross-cultural moral foundation for a variety of regime types, including the British constitutional monarchy he famously defends in the *Reflections*, Rousseau argues that his ideal republican state would find its moral backbone in patriarchal, sex-roled, agriculturally self-sufficient families of the rural countryside. On the other hand, Wollstonecraft believes that only the egalitarian family, free from the conflicts caused by patriarchal hierarchies, will allow for the full flourishing of the moral and civic virtues within a fully egalitarian, and hence legitimate, republic. While her disgust for the patriarchal family and its detrimental impact on humanity extends through all three stages of her writing career, her hopes for the egalitarian transformation of the family radiate most strongly during the middle stage of her writing career—the time when she composed her provocative parallel critiques of Rousseau and Burke in her twin *Vindications*.

Wollstonecraft's Parallel Critiques
of Burke and Rousseau's
Views of the Family

Wollstonecraft's *Rights of Men* is not simply a critique of Burke's *Reflections*. The first published response to the *Reflections* is much more than just a negative analysis of Burke's polemic against the French Revolution. Wollstonecraft's critique of Burke in her first *Vindication* sets the stage for the exposition of her own substantive moral and political theory, particularly her own philosophy of the family.[10] Perhaps her most potent critical insight into Burke's work is the recognition that his fear of the destruction of the sex and class-based hierarchies of the family amid the social and political tumult of the French Revolution is central to his argument in the *Reflections*. It is on this fear that she grounds her greatest hopes, and constructs her positive proposal for the transformation of the family from its corrupt, patriarchal state into its ideal, egalitarian form. In the *Rights of Woman*, she expands on this radical proposal, and outlines how the present system of female education must be overturned in order to spur the egalitarian transformation of the family, and, in turn, civil society and the state. Her main target in the *Rights of Woman* is Rousseau's philosophy of the family and female education as set forth in *Emile*.

The *Rights of Man*'s critique of Burke's defense of the sex- and class-based hierarchies of the family in the *Reflections* parallels the *Rights of Woman*'s critique of Rousseau's reimagining of the family in the *Emile*. Likewise, the *Rights of Man*'s critique of Burke's aesthetic theory in the *Enquiry* parallels the *Rights of Woman*'s critique of

Rousseau's theory of female education in *Emile*. By studying these parallels, the reader realizes that these two supposed foes are really friends when it comes to the questions of how the family should be structured and what role women should play within it.

Burke and Rousseau's Defense
of Familial Hierarchies

In the *Rights of Men*, Wollstonecraft rejects Burke's defense of aristocracy and hereditary property (guided by the principle of primogeniture) on the grounds that these institutions establish unnatural hierarchies among human beings and contribute to the moral decay of families rich and poor. Her arguments are strikingly similar to Rousseau's critical analysis of the morally corrosive effects of the economic, social, and political inequalities of modern civilization in the *Second Discourse*. She argues that the system of "hereditary property" and "hereditary honors" supported by Burke in the *Reflections* has only served to refine "manners at the expense of morals" during the course of European civilization.[11] Both the working poor and the idle aristocracy become "vulgar" under this system of hereditary property. While the poor must work to "support the body" at the expense of cultivating the mind, the rich who are coddled in the "lap of affluence" never have to develop either their minds, bodies, or characters and so simply degenerate into hedonistic creatures of "habit and impulse."[12] The gravest problem with the aristocratic class system is that it prods the lower classes to try to imitate the nobility and pretend to be wealthier than they are. Wollstonecraft writes: "How much domestic comfort and private satisfaction is sacrificed to this irrational ambition! It is a destructive mildew that blights the fairest virtues; benevolence, friendship, generosity, and all those endearing charities which bind human hearts together, and the pursuits which raise the mind to higher contemplations . . . are crushed by the iron hand of property!"[13] Under the current class hierarchy, she laments, "irrational ambition" subverts the growth of the natural affections and, in turn, the formation of the "fairest virtues" and "endearing charities" which "bind human hearts together." The "domestic comfort" of family life, and the moral tenor of public life, suffer terribly as a consequence.

In rebuttal of Burke's defense of hereditary property in the *Reflections*, Wollstonecraft extensively details how the institution of primogeniture causes the moral corruption of the family.[14] By sacrificing the interests of the youngest children for the sake of the eldest son, primogeniture perverts the "natural parental affection" that should be expressed unconditionally and equally to each child.[15] Primogeniture forces elder daughters into the legal prostitution of arranged marriage and drives younger daughters into convents and younger sons into exile. The fear of losing their family inheritance incites children to lie in order to avoid a father's angry curse. Primogeniture encourages late, loveless, and adulterous marriages, turns husbands into gallants and wives into coquettes who neglect their marriages for the sake of adulterous affairs, and permits parents to wield *lettres de cachet* to imprison children who refuse to marry the persons chosen for them. Tragically, primogeniture splits the family apart for the sake of preserving the family estate.

So that the extremes of luxury and poverty will no longer pervert the moral development of both rich and poor, and the privileging of the eldest son will no longer corrupt the natural affections of the family, Wollstonecraft insists that "property ought to be fluctuating."[16] With this goal in mind, she demands the abolition of aristocracy, aristocratic estates, and primogeniture. In counterpoint to Burke's defense of these familial hierarchies, Wollstonecraft envisions the egalitarian transformation of the family and society at large after the abolition of these inegalitarian institutions.

First, a child "would be freed from implicit obedience to parents and private punishments, when he is of an age to be subject to the jurisdiction of the laws of his country."[17] Once they reached the age of reason, children would no longer be subject to the rule of their parents and no longer would they be subject to forced marriages. There would be more equality between people, and they would realize that "true happiness arose from the friendship and intimacy which can only be enjoyed by equals."[18] Men would give up gaming for virtuous ambitions; women would give up coquetry to be rational women and good mothers who suckle their own children and fulfill their part in the social contract; and love would take the place of gallantry. Natural parental affection, which Wollstonecraft calls the "first source of civilization," would be restored once all children are loved equally and favored only insofar as their merit deserves.[19] Luxury, effeminacy, and idiotism would no longer plague noble families, because personal merit and manly industry would be the gauge for the distribution of property. The vulgarity of the rich and the poor would fade away, for the virtue of individual merit and industry would supercede the effeminizing and animalizing vices of luxury and poverty. Aristocratic estates filled with superficial, superfluous objects of architectural luxury would be replaced with pastoral farms that are more pleasing and useful to the people.

In this future enlightened age, where a "garden more inviting than Eden" would grow, there would be bliss and harmony in the family, the school, the playing fields, the church, and the state, that Wollstonecraft, in her early years, thought only would be experienced in heaven.[20] No longer would poor laborers be alienated from the land they worked and dwelled on; instead, they would possess their own little farms, carved out of former aristocratic estates: "Why cannot large estates be divided into large farms? . . . This sight I have seen, the cow that supported the children grazed near the hut, and the cheerful poultry were fed by the chubby babes, who breathed a bracing air, far from the diseases and vices of cities."[21] Here we see Wollstonecraft's pastoral vision of the ideal family, obviously inspired by her devoted reading of Rousseau's *Emile* and *Julie*. It is an idyllic family farm, set far from the vices of cities, where children can grow strong in body, mind, and character, in touch with their natural selves. "Domestic comfort" and "civilizing relations" with one's family would soften labor and make life contented.[22] No longer torn apart and corrupted by conflicts over hereditary property, families would be a haven of comfort, civility, and contentment. Natural affection between parent and child, brother and sister, husband and wife would no longer be perverted and stunted by unnatural hierarchies.

Yet in the *Rights of Woman*, Wollstonecraft criticizes Rousseau's vision of the ideal family along much the same lines as she criticizes Burke's defense of primogeniture and aristocracy in the *Rights of Men*. Although she embraces the rural, pastoral quality of Rousseau's ideal family, she contends that both Burke and Rousseau's ideals of the family foster unnatural hierarchies and moral corruption among human equals. Burke's hierarchical family reinforces socially constructed hierarchies based on sex and class so that the aristocrat and the eldest male reign supreme. Although he ostensibly abhors the social inequality and moral corruption of eighteenth-century European civilization, Rousseau's vision of the ideal family also remains laden with patriarchal hierarchies.

First, Wollstonecraft objects to Rousseau's relegation of women to the domestic realm in which they are isolated from the public life of civil society and the state. Wollstonecraft criticizes Rousseau's segregation of women within the family on the grounds that it does not account for the equal rational capacities of the sexes and the equal potential for the sexes to exercise the same moral and civic virtues in both the domestic and public spheres. To Rousseau's claim that he has empowered Sophie and Julie, his fictional ideals of womanhood, as "empresses" of the domestic realm, Wollstonecraft retorts "I do not wish them to have power over men; but over themselves."[23] Self-mastery, not mastery of others, is the moral goal of Wollstonecraft's political theory. Whether it is the unnatural rule of men over women, or the unnatural rule of women over men, such hierarchical power struggles should be discarded in favor of egalitarian power-sharing.

Furthermore, she contends that women cannot possibly perform the duties and responsibilities of motherhood and wifehood properly if they are not educated to exercise their rational capacities, achieve mastery of their passions, and practice the same moral and civic virtues expected of men. For Wollstonecraft, there is no sex to virtue because there is no sex to the human soul; in the eyes of God, all souls are equal and thus equally subject to His unchanging moral laws. She thus views Rousseau's exclusion of women from full participation in the civic and commercial activities of the public realm as metaphysically ungrounded. She concludes that women should not be excluded from the public sphere because they are perfectly capable of exercising the public virtues.

She also criticizes Rousseau's "help meet" ideal of marriage; she asserts that women are not by nature needy of a patriarch's guidance. Wollstonecraft acknowledges that men are physically stronger than women, but does not accept that this physical dominance legitimates any kind of moral, social, or political authority over their female counterparts. For this reason, she finds both Rousseau and Milton's "help meet" ideals of marriage flawed. To Rousseau's claim that women need the rational guidance of their fathers and husbands, she retorts, "Husbands—as well as their helpmates—are often only overgrown children."[24] Following the argument of Rousseau's *Second Discourse* to its logical conclusion, she concludes that wives *and* husbands are equally incapable of genuine moral autonomy under the present trappings of European civilization. Even Rousseau's radical reformulation of education in *Emile* is not enough to remedy the situation, since it preserves the patriarchal, sex-roled structure of the family. Extending the reach of Enlightenment egalitarianism from the state to the family, Wollstonecraft contends that the "the divine right of husbands" must be demystified and deconstructed just as the "divine right of kings" has been debunked.[25] Only then will men and women enjoy an equal chance to practice the moral and civic virtues in the realms of family, civil society, and state, and prepare their souls for God's scrutiny in the next life.

Burke and Rousseau's Defense
of Traditional Femininity

The uncanny resemblance of Wollstonecraft's critiques of Burke's *Enquiry* and Rousseau's *Emile* squarely strikes the reader of the two *Vindications*. Her parallel critiques of Rousseau and Burke lead one to suspect that she thought they shared virtually the same aesthetic theory, which in turn justified their joint designation of women's proper place as within the domestic sphere and their dual advocacy of traditional feminine manners and different forms of education for the sexes. As discussed in chapter three, Burke's *Enquiry* associates the "sublime" with largeness, hardness, strength, men, nature, and the public realm of war and politics, and the "beautiful" with smallness, softness, weakness, women, culture, and the domestic oasis of the family. Burke pivotally identifies beauty as a "social quality" because it draws people into relationships with those people and things that they find attractive and desire to love.[26] Making clear the ethical and social relevance of his aesthetic theory, Burke also categorizes the virtues according to his schema of the sublime and the beautiful. For Burke, those virtues that inspire love, such as tenderness, are "beautiful." In contrast, those virtues that inspire awe, such as courage, are "sublime." Burke accordingly associates the beautiful virtues with the domestic realm occupied by women and the family, and the sublime virtues with the public realm occupied by men.

It is precisely this bifurcation of the moral virtues according to the socially constructed categories of masculinity and femininity that angers Wollstonecraft. She takes issue with Burke's general identification of the "beautiful virtues" with women and the "sublime virtues" with men. She blames Burke for perpetuating the stereotype of women as helpless, irrational creatures incapable of genuine morality whose only purpose is to please men with their beauty: "You may have convinced them that littleness and weakness are the very essence of beauty; and that the Supreme Being, in giving women beauty in the most supereminent degree, seemed to command them, by the powerful voice of Nature, not to cultivate the moral virtues that might chance to excite respect, and interfere with the pleasing sensations they were created to inspire."[27] Women who take Burke's *Enquiry* to heart will not "cultivate the moral virtues that might chance to excite respect" for fear that such sublime virtues might compromise their feminine attractiveness.

Wollstonecraft's main concern is that Burke's view of femininity and feminine virtue stands in opposition to the Christian doctrine of salvation.

She challenges Burke: "If beautiful weakness be interwoven in a woman's frame, if the chief business of her life be (as you insinuate) to inspire love, and Nature has made an eternal distinction between the qualities that dignify a rational being and this animal perfection, her duty and happiness in this life must clash with any preparation for an exalted state."[28] Christian theology—from Thomas Aquinas to Wollstonecraft's own mentors, the Dissenters James Burgh and Richard Price—demands that human beings use their reason to grasp God's unchanging moral laws and practice the universal set of moral virtues applicable to men and women alike. Wollstonecraft worries that if women are discouraged from using their reason to practice the entire spectrum of the moral virtues, they cannot be expected to rise above an animalistic existence and achieve the level of rational self-mastery necessary for the salvation of the soul.

   Not only are women's souls placed in jeopardy by Burke's aesthetic theory, but so too are the well-being of their marriages and children. Wollstonecraft laments that the Burkean aesthetic holds such sway in society that many a woman forgets to care for her children to tend to her adulterous affairs, but "never forgets to adorn herself to make an impression on the senses of the other sex."[29] Women who define themselves in terms of their beauty alone are nothing but "vain inconsiderate dolls," incapable of the moral autonomy necessary to direct their own lives and the moral leadership necessary to direct the lives of their children.[30] Wollstonecraft believes that women will be "prudent mothers and useful members of society"[31] only once they are no longer slaves to the ideal of beauty codified in Burke's *Enquiry* and perpetuated by the present system of female education. Wollstonecraft additionally argues on the basis of social utility that women should be educated to fulfill their intellectual and physical potential if only to improve the condition under which future generations are raised.

   It is to the topic of female education that Wollstonecraft turns more fully in the *Rights of Woman*. Through the lens of Wollstonecraft's two *Vindications*, Book V of Rousseau's *Emile* looks like an application of Burke's aesthetic theory to the problem of female education. Although there is no evidence that Rousseau took Burke's *Enquiry* as a model for his own theory of female education and feminine manners, Wollstonecraft's criticisms of the two thinkers' underlying aesthetic assumptions reveal that they share many presuppositions about the nature of women and their beauty.

   Wollstonecraft rejects Rousseau's reification of traditional femininity in the figure of Sophie for the same reasons she rejects Burke's definition of feminine beauty in the *Enquiry*. Like Burke, Rousseau identifies and glorifies weakness—physical, sexual, and intellectual—as the hallmark of feminine beauty. In order to cultivate and refine their "natural" feminine tendency toward weakness, Burke and Rousseau suggest that girls and women be confined, physically, socially, and intellectually, so that their bodies, minds, and wills remain weak and vulnerable. For this reason, Wollstonecraft accuses both Burke and Rousseau of confusing what is natural and what is artificial in the female condition. Both Burke and Rousseau treat feminine beauty as a static facet of the existing social order, and suggest that weakness and smallness are two of its unchanging qualities.

Wollstonecraft blames the corrupt institutions of European civilization for perpetuating this warped ideal of feminine beauty. True feminine beauty—which displays both a "physical and a moral beauty"—won't be realized until the egalitarian transformation of the family and female education spurs a "revolution in female manners."[32] The epitome of feminine beauty would no longer be weakness, but rather strength of body, mind, and character. By strength of body Wollstonecraft means "natural soundness of constitution" not the "robust tone of nerves and vigor of muscles which arises from bodily labor."[33] The goal of egalitarian physical education will not be to turn women into muscular men, but rather to give them the physical fitness and health necessary for the development of strong minds and characters. Wollstonecraft predicts that a healthy, natural "dignified beauty" will radiate from the girls and women who experience this revolution in female education.[34]

Although Wollstonecraft freely admits "bodily strength seems to give man a natural superiority over women," she argues that the traditional restriction of female physical activity exaggerates the effective difference in strength between the sexes.[35] She furthermore suggests that advances in the egalitarian education of the sexes would largely overcome the present difference in strength between men and women. She acknowledges that Rousseau allows Sophie more freedom of movement in her childhood than previous theorists of female education permitted young girls. Yet she still blames Rousseau's theory of female education for reinforcing the unnatural and unhealthy ideal of feminine weakness by centering the activity of Sophie around the dolls, chores, and constricting clothes of the domestic realm, while Emile romps outdoors. She laments, "To preserve personal beauty, woman's glory! The limbs and faculties are cramped with worse than Chinese bands, and the sedentary life which they are condemned to live, whilst boys frolic in the open air, weakens the muscles and relaxes the nerves."[36]

Sophie's physical weakness renders her dependent on her father and, later, her husband, for protection and financial support. Her intellectual weakness renders her incapable of understanding the "rational religion" professed by the Savoyard Vicar, and thus leaves her no choice but to be blindly obedient to the dictates of the Catechism. Her physical vulnerability, and her tendency toward sexual weakness, demand that she be educated to practice the virtue of modesty. According to Rousseau, she must be modest not only to preserve her honor but most of all to preserve her allure from the taint of sexual experience and overexposure. Rousseau focuses every aspect of Sophie's education—even what little intellectual training, physical exercise, and moral teaching she receives—on the goal of rendering her more beautiful and attractive in the eyes of Emile.

Wollstonecraft decries the moral failures that beset women who are raised to be blindly obedient to patriarchal and church authority, narrowly concerned with the domestic domain, and desperately striving to appear both chaste and alluring to the men that surround them. She upholds Sophie as the symbol of the moral failure of her fellow women:

> Yet in what respect can she be termed good? She abstains, it is true, without any great struggle, from committing gross crimes; but how does she fulfill her duties? Duties! In truth she has enough to think of to adorn her body and nurse a weak constitution. With respect to religion, she never presumed to judge for herself; but conformed, as a dependent creature should, to the ceremonies of the church which she was brought up in. . . . These are the blessed effects of a good education! These are the virtues of man's help-mate![37]

Wollstonecraft questions whether Sophie can be termed "good" if her physical, sexual, and intellectual weakness prevents her from performing the duties demanded of her as a daughter, wife, mother, and servant of God. She may not commit "gross crimes," but she hardly qualifies as a paragon of moral and civic virtue. Indeed, in *Emile and Sophie*, Rousseau depicts Sophie as precisely the kind of adulterous wife that Wollstonecraft predicted Burkean aesthetics and Rousseauian education would inevitably produce. While Rousseau partly blames the corruption of Parisian city life for Sophie's downfall, Wollstonecraft would have retorted (if she had read the unpublished sequel to *Emile*) that the defects in Sophie's moral education rendered her vulnerable to the temptations she faced in Paris.

Wollstonecraft's parallel critiques of the *Enquiry* and *Emile* suggest that, in her eyes, Burke's aesthetic theory and Rousseau's educational theory fail for the same reasons. First, both theories veer toward moral relativism by defining virtue differently for men and women, rather than applying a single moral standard to all humanity. Grounding her philosophical position on the theology of Socinian Dissenting Christianity, the middle Wollstonecraft contends that there is no "sex to mind," no "sex in souls," and "no sex to virtue."[38] She believes that the human soul and the human mind possess the same moral and intellectual capacities, whether they occupy a male or female body. She believes that God legislates his moral laws for all of humanity, and prescribes a set of moral virtues for men and women to grasp by reason and put into practice alike. Consequently, Wollstonecraft argues that even "if women are by nature inferior to men, their virtues must be the same in quality, not in degree, or virtue is a relative idea; consequently, their conduct should be founded on the same principles, and have the same aim."[39] In this provocative thought-experiment, Wollstonecraft grants to her critics, for the sake of argument, the possibility that women might be "by nature inferior to men," but uses this premise of her opponents to show that any differences in mental or physical capacities between the sexes do not necessitate any differences in moral standards between them.

Second, both theories overestimate the power of beauty to serve as a stable and lasting magnetizing force in social and romantic relationships. Wollstonecraft notes that both men and women fade in attractiveness as they age; hence, she claims physical attraction should never be the sole foundation of any social relationship, especially the lifelong covenant of marriage. Friendship—the love and respect shared between equals hailed by Wollstonecraft as "the most holy band of society"—instead should be the foundation of marriage.[40] She revels in the irony that Rousseau admits "beauty . . . will not be valued or even seen after a couple have lived six months together" and "artificial graces and coquetry will likewise pall on the sense." "Why then," she pointedly asks, "does he say that a girl should be educated for her husband with the same care as for an eastern harem?"[41]

With these criticisms of her rivals in mind, Wollstonecraft calls for the egalitarian transformation of the family and female education: "It is time to effect a revolution in female manners—time to restore to them their lost dignity—and make them, as a part of the human species, labour by reforming themselves to reform the world."[42] Contrary to Burke and Rousseau, she longs for a "revolution in female manners" rather than a return to a traditional understanding of the proper women in the family and the world at large. Wollstonecraft sees l as the true Rousseauian by extending her rival's theory of education to women. She claims that "civilized women are, therefore, so weakened by false refinement, that, respecting morals, their condition is much below what it would be were they left in a state nearer to nature."[43] Women have been the worst victims of the corruption spread by the hierarchical institutions of European civilization; only when they are reeducated along the same lines as Emile to balance the demands of nature and society will they be liberated from the chains of "false refinement." Only then will they return to a state "nearer to nature" that enables them to perform the moral and civic duties of domestic and public life as prudent mothers and civic-minded citizens.

The Common Ground between Wollstonecraft, Burke, and Rousseau

Although she delivers a powerful critique of their defenses of familial hierarchies and traditional femininity, Wollstonecraft's own philosophy of the family shares important parallels with the ideas of Rousseau and Burke. They each hold differing conceptions of the best structure of the family, and deploy their respective ideals of the family toward supporting divergent political ends. Yet their view of the moral, social, and political function of the family remains fundamentally the same: each highlights the crucial role of the family in cultivating the affectivity necessary for human moral development and the formation of human social and civic identities.)

    Although he praises Plato's *Republic* as the best work on education ever written, Rousseau reserves some of his most vitriolic criticism for the ancient philosopher's argument for the destruction of the family. In Book V of the *Republic,* Plato's Socrates toys with the idea that the destruction of the private family is necessary for the construction of a perfectly just regime free from conflict between familial and political loyalties. For this reason, he suggests that the children of the warrior class should be raised in common while their fathers and mothers equally share the burden of defending the state. Rousseau bristles at the suggestion that the private family ought to be sacrificed for the sake of fortifying patriotism. He argues, to the contrary, that the private family is the cradle of all the public virtues:

> I speak of that subversion of the sweetest sentiments of nature, sacrificed to an artificial sentiment which can only be maintained by

them—as though there were no need for a natural base on which to form conventional ties, as though the love of one's nearest were not the principle of the love one owes the state; as though it were not by means of the small fatherland which is the family that the heart attaches itself to the large one; as though it were not the good son, the good husband, and the good father that make the good citizen![44]

Rousseau likens the family to a "small fatherland" in which the "good son, the good husband, and the good father" learn how to be a "good citizen." It is through the love that one feels for one's family that one learns how to love the state to which one's family belongs. The affective ties of the family serve as the "natural base" for the "conventional ties" of patriotism and the other civic virtues.

Like Rousseau, Burke defends the hierarchical family as the source of the social bonds that hold society together in a civilized fashion. Illustrating his theory of the distinction between the sublime and the beautiful, Burke takes a military term—the platoon—and by rendering it "little," transforms it into a term of endearment and domestication. A platoon is a tight, close-knit group of soldiers irrevocably bound by the shared experience of war and fear of death; likewise, a "little platoon" is a group of people, inextricably tied together by natural and public affections, who share a vital common bond through family, land, work, or politics.[45] The little platoon experiences the same intense sense of community as the military platoon, but the former belongs to the realm of the beautiful, whereas the latter belongs to the realm of the sublime. For Burke, the hierarchical family is the most important little platoon insofar as it fosters the development of the natural and public affections that serve as the motivational force behind the practice of the moral, social, and civic virtues.

Wollstonecraft, likewise, celebrates the family as the nursery of the moral and civic virtues. Like Adam Smith, Wollstonecraft was one of the first supporters of a national system of public education for children. She believed, like Talleyrand-Périgord—the former bishop and French revolutionary to whom she dedicated the *Rights of Woman*—that public education should aim to form civic-minded citizens. Yet she recognized the limits of public education in realizing this goal:

Public education, of every denomination, should be directed to form citizens; but if you wish to make good citizens, you must first exercise the affections of a son and a brother. This is the only way to expand the heart; for public affections, as well as public virtues, must ever grow out of the private character, or they are merely meteors that shoot athwart a dark sky, and disappear as they are gazed at and admired. Few, I believe, have had much affection for mankind, who did not first love their parents, their brothers, sisters, and even the domestic brutes, whom they first played with. The exercise of youthful sympathies forms the moral temperature; and it is the recollection of these first affections and pursuits that gives life to those that are afterwards more under the direction of reason.[46]

Public education cannot substitute for the moral education gained within the family. It is the "first affections" of family life—love of parents, brothers, sisters, and even pets—that transform into the "public affections" and "public virtues." It is the "recollection of these first affections" that inspires one to practice the moral virtues in the public realm among neighbors, strangers, and fellow citizens. For this reason, Wollstonecraft identifies "marriage as the foundation of almost every social virtue."[47] It is through the institution of marriage that families are born, and it is through family life that children learn to love and respect others as they do themselves.

Wollstonecraft defines "natural parental affection" as that which "makes no difference between child and child, but what reason justifies as pointing out superior merit."[48] She recognizes this form of parental affection as the "first source of civilization" because it teaches children to respect each other as equals while honoring the distinctive achievements of one another.[49] Families guided by such natural parental affection serve as schoolhouses for the kind of egalitarian politics that Wollstonecraft hopes the American and French Revolutions will help to usher into European civilization.

Yet Wollstonecraft recognizes that human selfishness and corrupt laws and social institutions warp the natural impulses of parental affection. Hence, she opens the chapter on parenting in the *Rights of Woman* with the cutting line, "Parental affection is, perhaps, the blindest modification of perverse self-love."[50] Parents regularly abuse the power they hold over their children for the sake of selfishly pursuing the social-climbing goals set by the system of aristocracy and primogeniture. Wollstonecraft also notes that "it is the irregular exercise of parental authority that first injures the mind, and to these irregularities girls are more subject than boys."[51] The abuse of parental authority leads to the corruption of children's minds and morals. Children unloved by their parents, lacking proper rewards and punishments for their actions, and ignorant of the difference between right and wrong, cannot help but fail to practice the moral and civic virtues in later life. The character of girls suffers the most because they endure the most severe tyranny and relish the least affection; how can girls feel equally loved when their eldest brothers are favored above all?

Wollstonecraft argues that the restoration of natural parental affection represents the first step toward a "revolution in female manners." Both the tyrannical patriarch and the weak, inattentive mother pose threats to the development of girls strong in mind, body, and character. Wollstonecraft upholds the care of infants as a "grand duty annexed to the female character by nature."[52] Like Rousseau, she condemns aristocratic women who abandon their infants to wet nurses so that they can pursue adulterous affairs rather than care for the needs of their children. Wollstonecraft questions whether mothers who hire wet nurses and governesses to care for their children will ever develop a strong affectionate bond with them: "Natural affection, as it is termed, I believe to be a very faint tie, affections must grow out of the habitual exercise of a mutual sympathy; and what sympathy does a mother exercise who sends her babe to a nurse, and only takes it from a nurse to send it to school?"[53] Wollstonecraft observes that the "natural affection" shared between mother and child will fade quickly if it is not reinforced by the "habitual exercise of a mutual sympathy." Children raised by nurses love them more than their own mothers, and adulterous mothers care more for their lovers than their children. Like Rousseau, she considers the care of infants to be the "indispensable duty" of mothers because it "gives birth to affections that are the surest preservatives against vice."[54] Children raised by loving, attentive mothers experience the "first affections" of family life that spur the development of the moral and civic virtues and discourage the practice of vice.

With such "enlightened maternal affection" guiding family life, Wollstonecraft's ideal egalitarian family can finally be realized.[55] The egalitarian transformation of the family, according to Wollstonecraft, does not demand the destruction of the private family, the abandonment of motherhood, or the subversion of parental authority. Unlike Burke and Rousseau, she believes that women can travel between the domestic and public spheres while remaining committed to motherhood. She contends that women should be granted citizenship if they must serve as the primary educators and caretakers of future citizens. Women should also enjoy the freedom to pursue careers, but nature obliges them to put t. "grand duty" of motherhood first when they are rearing young children. Wollstonecraft takes what's best about Rousseau and Burke— namely, their common view of the family as the primary tutelary space in which citizens are formed through the forging of emotional bonds with particular people and places—and remedies their patriarchalism with her insistence that the egalitarian family can better serve this crucial educative role. Wollstonecraft retains Burke and Rousseau's commitment to preserving a nondespotic parent-child hierarchy in the family, and similarly believes that such a hierarchy is essential for the family to perform its tutelary function. Integral to all three views of child rearing and education is the notion that knowledge must be imparted, and habits must be inculcated and reinforced, from the top down. Without the guidance of parents and other elders, children would be lost, Lockean blank slates, written on randomly by empirical experience, rather than purposefully shaped into adults capable of genuine moral autonomy.

Their common understanding of the political function of the family renders Rousseau, Burke, and Wollstonecraft friends on a related set of issues. First, each understands the family to exist in a symbiotic relationship with the state. For each, the moral and emotional contours of the dominant form of family life are projected into a nation's form of government, for better or for worse. The family, as an organic entity living interdependently with the broader social and political structures that surround it, can either be a corrective to, or an instigator of, moral and political decay. As Wollstonecraft argues in the *Rights of Woman*, "A man has been termed a microcosm; and every family might also be called a state. States, it is true, have mostly been governed by arts that disgrace the character of man. . . . Thus morality, polluted in the national reservoir, sends off streams of vice to corrupt the constituent parts of the body politic; but should more noble, or rather, more just principles regulate the laws, which ought to be the government of society, and not those who execute them, duty might become the rule of private conduct."[56] In this passage, Wollstonecraft sets up the family and the state like reflections in a set of mirrors facing one another, projecting infinite, embedded images of the other. Just as the state reflects the moral qualities of the family, the family reflects the moral qualities of the state; thus, it is difficult, if not impossible, to separate or privilege the impact of one over the other. Reform of laws will change "the rule of private conduct," just as reform of the family will transform the state. Woll-stonecraft's perception of the cyclical, organic relationship between fa-milial and legal reform, which is always threatened by the forces of moral and political corrosion, finds its antecedents in the thought of Rousseau and Burke. Rousseau imagined the development of a patriar-chal, sex-roled, agriculturally self-sufficient family that could serve as the moral foundation of his ideal rural republic; yet he worried whether either such a republican family or state could withstand the viciousness of modern civilization and fully transcend the distorted models of so-cialization found in the bourgeois and aristocratic families of his time. Burke likewise feared that if revolutionary political and cultural change shifted the family from its safe, and intended, mooring within the di-vinely ordained hierarchies of the cosmos, it would cease to function as a aesthetic-affective basis for moral, social, and political development across a range of culturally specific governmental forms.

Also common to their respective conceptions of the family is their attentiveness to how the psychological experience of particular places shapes the emotional and ethical formation of citizens. In the *Social Contract*, Rousseau recounts the system of "rural" and "urban" tribes within which the civic identities of Roman citizens were formed. Rousseau argues that when rich urban citizens wished to be associated with the more virtuous and illustrious rural tribes, the tribes lost their not only their regional character but their moral character: "Tribes gen-erally no longer had a district or territory . . . so that the idea of the word *Tribe* thus shifted from the residential to the personal, or rather it be-came almost a chimera."[57] Corrupted by the infusion of rich urban elites, the rural tribes lost their constitutive membership of farmer-soldier-citizens and their attendant power to regenerate the moral and political virtue of the republic from the geographic periphery of the state. No longer was the rural tribe, located in a particular set of agri-cultural villages, "the nursery of those robust and valiant men who de-fended them (Rome) in time of war and fed them in time of peace."[58] Burke used similar arguments to lament the redrawing of geographic boundaries in revolutionary France in a way that subverted the people's emotional connections to the localities that served as the affective basis of a moderate form of patriotism in the ancien régime. Wollstonecraft likewise pointed out that a system of local day schools, wherein young students could walk from home to school and return home at night to be with their parents, would be the best way to reconcile the benefits of public education with private, familial education. Without the "exercise of youthful sympathies" within the forum of the family, people would miss an essential stage in their moral development, is the "recollection" of their "first affections and pursuits that gives ... to those that are afterwards more under the direction of reason."[59] She concludes that boarding schools are the moral equivalent of razing the family from the student's emotional landscape, and that although school vacations are not a viable substitute for residence at home, they are necessary for restoring a boarding student's sense of familial identity: "were (vacations) abolished, children would be entirely separated from their parents, and I question whether they would become better citizens by sacrificing the preparatory affections."[60] Here Wollstonecraft follows Rousseau and Burke in designating the family, alongside other small social units within its geographic locality (in her case, public coeducational day schools), as a "preparatory" environment in which the first affections and relationships of a child's life pave the way for his or her ability to perform the duties of citizenship.

A further commonality between Rousseau, Burke, and Wollstonecraft is their shared interest in considering the aesthetic, affective, ethical, and political import of the psychological experience of spatiality. It is not just particular places, but specific kinds of spaces, that enable human beings to consider the good of other human beings in their decision-making. For all three thinkers, there is an inverse relationship between the size of a social group or locale and its ability to generate the emotional attachments necessary for the habitual practice of the social virtues. Hence, Rousseau, Burke, and Wollstonecraft each celebrate smallness as an essential quality of effective forums for moral and civic education; the closer the inhabitants of a social unit are, the tighter their relationships become, the more intense their affections for one another grow, and the stronger their ability to extend these sympathies to human beings beyond their domestic circle, village, tribe, day school, class, or region turns out to be. Each of them recognize, however, the dangerous potential for small social groups to become self-absorbed to the point of emotional implosion, and hence consider the importance of extending and balancing the allegiances of human beings beyond the private family to a variety of social groups and the state itself, while maintaining the family as the foundational, formative space and set of relationships within which such communal thinking is initially made possible.

The Family, Liberal Democracy,
and the Legacy of the Enlightenment

Wollstonecraft, Burke, and Rousseau's common view of the family as a little platoon for the cultivation of the moral, social, and civic virtues remains one of the most important, yet largely ignored, legacies of Enlightenment political thought for the modern liberal tradition. Their belief in the fundamental role of the family as the schoolhouse for the civic virtues remains relevant for contemporary debates about the relationship between the family and the liberal state. Political scientists and theorists such as Robert Putnam (2000) and Peter Berkowitz (1999) have called attention to the pivotal role that nonstate institutions, such as families, churches, and voluntary community organizations, play in maintaining the moral health and political stability of modern liberal democracy.[61] Perhaps by looking back to the ideas of Rousseau, Burke, and Wollstonecraft, we can find a fruitful historical and theoretical framework in which we can further explore the political relevance of these nonstate institutions, and discover ways in which they can better serve as little platoons.

It is precisely because of the liberal state's insistence on separating church and state, public and private, and personal morality and public politics, and its intention to resist the indoctrination of its citizens in any single vision of the good life, that there is a greater need for nonstate institutions, such as families, churches, and other community groups, to take up the role of moral and civic education and provide the moral backbone for a regime that strives (however quixotically) to be as morally neutral as possible. The moral and political success of the liberal state depends on moral authorities external to itself, such as families and other small social groups. As William Galston (1991) and Stephen Macedo (1990) argue, these little platoons inculcate the moral, social, and civic virtues—such as tolerance, cooperation, and self-restraint—that are necessary for the smooth and peaceful operation of a liberal democratic society.[62] One of the inherent ironies of liberalism is that its pursuit of expanded individual freedom for its citizenry entails the formation of citizens who are capable of a moderate self-governance, respect for the rights of others, and performance of civic obligations alongside enjoyment of their legally guaranteed liberties. The nonpaternalistic state would eventually self-destruct without the educational assistance of families and other "parental" forms of socialization. Rousseau, Burke, and Wollstonecraft are three of the most important theorists of the crucial role the family plays in the formation of civic identity, and the presenta-tion of state stability, in modernity. Yet it is Wollstonecraft's ideal of the egalitarian family that has particularly shaped the development of the modern liberal democratic state as both a philosophical ideal and a political reality.

The middle Wollstonecraft's legacy to us today is the legal institu-tionalization of much of what she theorized and dreamed one day would come to be. The ideal of the egalitarian family is one of great gifts of Enlightenment political thought to modern liberalism. Leading women's rights advocates in the nineteenth and early twentieth centuries—such as Hannah Mather Crocker, Anna Wheeler, William Thompson, Robert Owen, Frances Wright, Flora Tristan, Sarah Grimké, Mathilda Anneke, Lucretia Mott, Susan B. Anthony, Elizabeth Cady Stanton, Charlotte Perkins Gilman, and Emma Goldman—used Wollstonecraft's philoso-phy of sex equality to ground their arguments and activities for reforms that aimed to remove the patriarchal hierarchies in the family, civil soci-ety, and the state that prevented the extension of full civil and political rights to oppressed groups such as women, blacks, and workers.[63] Their commitment to putting Wollstonecraft's philosophy into political prac-tice eventually made the ideal of the egalitarian family a legal norm of the liberal democratic state. As Wollstonecraft once wildly wished, many democratic countries now provide women the same political and property rights as men, protect children against the abuse and neglect of parents and other adults, guarantee girls the same education and social advantages as boys, and grant women the same right as men to divorce an abusive, adulterous, or absentee spouse. The laws of the modern lib-eral democratic state, as found in several north Atlantic nations, broadly facilitate the formation and practice of egalitarian relationships within the family, in a way that was unknown in Wollstonecraft's own time. There is still much work to be done, but Wollstonecraft would probably be pleasantly surprised by the progress made so far by many courageous women's rights advocates and activists who have invoked her arguments with the goal of putting her visionary ideas into political practice.

Charles Taylor (2004) has suggested that the ideal of the private, affectionate family is one of the fundamental micro "modern social imaginaries"—or "ways people imagine their social existence, how they fit together with others, how things go on between them and their fel-lows, the expectations that are normally met, and the deeper normative notions and images that underlie these expectations"—that shape and give meaning to human life in contemporary Western societies.[64] Taylor credits Rousseau's *Julie* as one of the premier texts that helped shape the development of the Western ideal of the private, affectionate family in the eighteenth century, and notes Wollstonecraft's "innovative" contribution to assessing the value of the nuclear family in a "critical democratic-egalitarian light." By crediting Wollstonecraft as a leader in the "long march" toward democratic inclusion, Taylor implies that Wollstonecraft's ideal of the egalitarian family and its role in making democratic politics possible in modernity can be seen as one of the most significant micro "modern social imaginaries" of the Western tradition, albeit one that has taken a long time to rise to prominence in our culture.[65]

To some degree, Wollstonecraft's philosophical design of an influential model of the egalitarian family means that she eclipses Rousseau and Burke in terms of her relevance to contemporary debates about the family's relationship to liberal democracy. Yet there are certainly fascinating parallels to be drawn between the animated, and often strident, public debates on the family in recent decades, and Rousseau, Burke, and Wollstonecraft's heated contributions to the feuds about the family in the Enlightenment. While some contemporary familial issues, such as same-sex marriage, had no political salience in their time, Rousseau, Burke, and Wollstonecraft exhibited a passionate concern with the family as a political entity that seems to also characterize the competing sides of today's public debates on the family and how it should be legally constituted. Although it is important to note, for the sake of historical and philosophical precision, that Wollstonecraft herself did not defend an ideal of same-sex marriage, it is certainly a valid application of her ideas to creatively extend her arguments to contemporary debates about how to make marriage a truly egalitarian social institution that is open to all adult couples who wish to enter its bonds, and thus supports, rather than exists in tension with, the values of the liberal democratic state.

Rousseau, Burke, and Wollstonecraft drew attention to the intersections between familial and political systems in the same way that our highly charged political debates on the family do today. While the dictum "the personal is political" was popularized by second-wave feminists in the late twentieth century, it could be said to have its philosophical antecedents in the late eighteenth century, perhaps especially in the writings of Rousseau, Burke, and Wollstonecraft on the political function of the family. As Taylor (2004) has noted, the development of a notion of a "private" sphere of family life, affectivity, and intimacy was inextricably tied to the rise of a notion of a "public" sphere of commerce, politics, and intellectual discourse in Europe and North America in the eighteenth century and beyond.[66] Although thinkers like Rousseau, Burke, and Wollstonecraft helped create the Western cultural understanding of the family as a private space, they did not conceive the family so much as a retreat from the public and the political, but as a resting-place in which the affective and ethical dimensions of public life were cultivated, and where the preconditions for politics were laid down.

Rousseau, Burke, and Wollstonecraft do not only help us to perceive the enduring, yet contested, political and philosophical relevance of the family to modernity, but also present us with the opportunity to consider how their concern with the family is an essential, yet often overlooked, part of Enlightenment political thought. Although they are sometimes one-dimensionally rendered as Romantic or anti-Enlightenment thinkers, Rousseau, Burke, and Wollstonecraft can alternatively be seen as illustrating the complexity of late Enlightenment thought. Through their meditations on the relationship between the family and the state, they teach us that the affections of humanity are as morally and politically significant as their capacity for rationality, social groups do not have to compromise, but ideally enable, the experience of individual freedom, and attention to the particularities of human experience paves the way for the realization of common goals and standards both within and across nations. Even as they challenge the postmodern caricature of eighteenth-century philosophy as hyperrationalistic, individualistic, and culture-blind, what keeps them in tune with the major refrain of Enlightenment political thought is their common perception of the pervasiveness of despotism and the moral duty to fight its spread through both ideas and actions.

Rousseau did not only observe that "man is born free, but everywhere is in chains": he claimed to offer a theory of republican government that, if implemented, would finally make these chains "legitimate."[67] Burke did not simply weep over the abuses of power he saw unfolding in America, Ireland, England, France, and India: he worked as a Member of Parliament, and a world-renowned author, to change the way that tyranny was perceived and confronted by humanity. Wollstonecraft shared Rousseau and Burke's expansive sympathies for the downtrodden of the world, and their conception of the family as the pivotal place in which such compassion is shaped. Yet by showing how their patriarchal, sex-roled ideals of the family were in fact agents of the most invidious form of despotism, Wollstonecraft cleverly turned Rousseau and Burke's arguments against tyranny and their anxieties about the family against them. By presenting the ideal of the egalitarian family, the abolition of all forms of slavery, and the extension of full civil and political rights to women and other disempowered groups as preconditions for the practice of authentic republican government, Wollstonecraft established herself as arguably the most prominent and philosophically consistent defender of the ideal of political equality during the Enlightenment. By publishing her controversial views in a groundbreaking book—the *Rights of Woman*—that has been internationally received, avidly read, publicly discussed, handed down, and reprinted through several generations of women's rights advocates and activists, she ensured her paradoxical place in posterity as perhaps the most significant, yet still largely unsung, theorist of the relationship between familial structures, political equality, and human freedom in the modern Western tradition.

Notes

Notes to Introduction

1. Naomi Tadmor argues that the term "family" was used to signify three main concepts in eighteenth-century English texts: (1) the household-family, or all the persons living in a single household, (2) the lineage-family, or people related by notions of pedigree, ancestry, and descent, and (3) the kin-ship-family, or people related by birth, marriage, or adoption. Although Rousseau, Burke, and Wollstonecraft's writings provide copious examples of the use of all three of Tadmor's concepts of the family, they often used the term "family" to mean one's closely related kin, especially as bound by marriage or birth, who live in the same home. Lawrence Stone defines the family in this way in his study of the family in early modern England: "those members of the same kin who live together under one roof." Lawrence Stone, *The Family, Sex and Marriage in England, 1500–1800* (London: Weidenfeld and Nelson, 1977), 21; Naomi Tadmor, *Family and Friends in Eighteenth-Century England: Household, Kinship, and Patronage* (Cambridge: Cambridge University Press, 2001), 18–25, 73–74, 103–107.

2. Mary Wollstonecraft, *A Vindication of the Rights of Woman*, in *A Vindication of the Rights of Men and A Vindication of the Rights of Woman*, ed. Sylvana Tomaselli (Cambridge: Cambridge University Press, 1995), 117, 292 (hereafter cited as *Rights of Woman* and *Rights of Men*).

3. I use the term "patriarchal" as it was commonly employed by seventeenth- and eighteenth-century political theorists—both by its critics like John Locke and its advocates like Robert Filmer—to describe a set of social relationships in which men were understood and empowered as the superiors, rulers, and public representatives of women and children throughout the spheres of family, civil society, and the state. I use the term "egalitarian" to describe the theory or practice of social relationships that minimize or nearly eliminate patriarchal rule by men over women and children, and authoritarian

215

rule by parents over children. I sometimes use the term "more egalitarian" rather than "egalitarian" in this study because even the most radical political theorists of the time—such as Locke and Wollstonecraft—stop short of conceptualizing or defending a completely egalitarian family form. And yet, in comparison to her predecessors Rousseau and Burke, and understood within the context of the eighteenth century, Wollstonecraft's ideal of the family is aptly described as egalitarian. By the term "sex-role differentiation," I mean the theory and practice of defining women's social roles primarily within the family as daughters, wives, mothers, and caretakers of the domestic sphere, yet defining men's social roles as bridging the realms of family, civil society, and the state as heads of household, breadwinners, and subjects or citizens. I use the term "sex" rather than "gender" in this study for the sake of historical and philosophical interpretive precision. "Sex" was the term used by Enlightenment thinkers to describe both the biological and cultural aspects of the identities of men and women. No strict notion of gender—or the cultural basis of sex identities—was salient in their time; even Wollstonecraft, a scathing critic of how traditional feminine culture systematically corrupts the sexual character of women, understood certain biological sex differences, such as women's capacities for childbirth and lactation and men's overall greater physical strength, as fundamental to the respective "biological-cultural" identities of women and men. For a classic analysis of the concept and practice of patriarchy and sex-role differentiation in the Enlightenment and beyond, see Carole Pateman's *The Sexual Contract* (Stanford: Stanford University Press, 1988). For scholars who employ the term "egalitarian," with similar caveats, to describe certain positions in eighteenth- and nineteenth-century political thought, see Charles Taylor's *Modern Social Imaginaries* (Durham: Duke University Press, 2004), 147, and Eve Tavor Bannet's *The Domestic Revolution: Enlightenment Feminisms and the Novel* (Baltimore: Johns Hopkins University Press, 2000), 1–21.

4. Philippe Ariès, *Centuries of Childhood: A Social History of Family Life*, tr. Robert Baldick (New York: Vintage, 1962); Roderick Phillips, *Family Breakdown in Late Eighteenth-Century France: Divorces in Rouen, 1792–1803* (Oxford: Clarendon Press, 1980); Stone, *Family, Sex and Marriage in England*; Lawrence Stone, *Road to Divorce: England, 1530–1987* (Oxford: Oxford University Press, 1990); James Traer, *Marriage and the Family in Eighteenth-Century France* (Ithaca: Cornell University Press, 1980); Randolph Trumbach, *The Rise of the Egalitarian Family: Aristocratic Kinship and Domestic Relations in Eighteenth-Century England* (New York: Academic Press, 1978).

5. David Cressy, *Birth, Marriage and Death: Ritual, Religion and the Life-Cycle in Tudor and Stuart England* (Oxford: Oxford University Press, 1997); Ralph Houlbrooke, *The English Family, 1450–1700* (London: Longman, 1984); Ralph Houlbrooke, *Death, Religion and the Family in England, 1480–1750* (Oxford: Clarendon Press, 1998); Alan Macfarlane, *Marriage and*

Love in England: Modes of Reproduction, 1300–1840 (Oxford: Blackwell, 1986); R. B. Outhwaite, *Clandestine Marriage in England, 1500–1850* (London: Hambledon Press, 1995); Keith Wrightson, *English Society: 1580–1680* (New Brunswick, NJ: Rutgers University Press, 1982).

6. For leading studies of the patriarchalism of early modern social contract theory, see Pateman, *The Sexual Contract*; Mary Shanley, "Marriage Contract and Social Contract in Seventeenth-Century English Political Thought," *The Western Political Quarterly* 32:1 (1979), 79–91. For other notable exceptions to the trend of overlooking the place of the family in Enlightenment political thought, see Richard Allen Chapman, "Leviathan Writ Small: Thomas Hobbes on the Family," *The American Political Science Review* 69: 1 (1975), 76–90; Susan Moller Okin, "Women and the Making of the Sentimental Family," *Philosophy and Public Affairs* 11:1 (1982), 65–88; Jacqueline Pfeffer, "The family in John Locke's political thought," *Polity* 33:4 (2001): 593–618; Diana Schaub, *Erotic Liberalism: Women and Revolution in Montesquieu's Persian Letters* (Lanham, MD: Rowman and Littlefield, 1995), 1–18, 55–70, 91–108.

7. Sankar Muthu, *Enlightenment against Empire* (Princeton: Princeton University Press, 2003); Carole Pateman, *Participation and Democratic Theory* (Cambridge: Cambridge University Press, 1970); John Rawls, *A Theory of Justice* (Cambridge: Belknap Press, 1971).

8. Carol Blum, *Rousseau and the Republic of Virtue* (Ithaca: Cornell University Press, 1986); Lynn Hunt, *The Family Romance of the French Revolution* (Berkeley: University of California Press, 1992); Linda Kerber, *Women of the Republic: Intellect and Ideology in Revolutionary America* (Chapel Hill: University of North Carolina Press, 1980); Joan Landes, *Gender, Representation and Revolution in Eighteenth-Century France* (Ithaca: Cornell University Press, 2001); Joan Landes, *Women and the Public Sphere in the Age of the French Revolution* (Ithaca: Cornell University Press, 1988).

9. Virginia Sapiro, *A Vindication of Political Virtue: The Political Theory of Mary Wollstonecraft* (Chicago: University of Chicago Press, 1992); Gary Kelly, *Revolutionary Feminism: The Mind and Career of Mary Wollstonecraft* (New York: St. Martin's Press, 1992); David Bromwich, "Wollstonecraft as a Critic of Burke," *Political Theory* 23:4 (1995), 617–634; Wendy Gunther-Canada, *Rebel Writer: Mary Wollstonecraft and Enlightenment Politics* (DeKalb: Northern Illinois University Press, 2001); Barbara Taylor, *Mary Wollstonecraft and the Feminist Imagination* (Cambridge: Cambridge University Press, 2003).

10. Steven Blakemore, *Burke and the Fall of Language* (Hanover, NH: University Press of New England, 1988), 31–60; James Boulton, *The Language of Politics in the Age of Wilkes and Burke* (London: Routledge and Kegan Paul, 1963), 97–133; Linda Zerilli, *Signifying Woman: Culture and Chaos in Rousseau, Burke and Mill* (Ithaca: Cornell University Press, 1994), 60–94 (hereafter cited as Zerilli 1994a).

11. Jean Starobinski, *Jean-Jacques Rousseau: la transparence et l'obstacle* (Paris: Plon, 1957); Judith Shklar, *Men and Citizens: A Study of Rousseau's Social Theory* (London: Cambridge University Press, 1969); Allan Bloom, "Introduction," *Emile, or on Education* (New York: Basic Books, 1979), 3–29; Susan Okin, *Women in Western Political Thought* (Princeton: Princeton University Press, 1979; reprint 1992), 99–194; Joel Schwartz, *The Sexual Politics of Jean-Jacques Rousseau* (Chicago: University of Chicago Press, 1984); Penny Weiss, *Gendered Community: Rousseau, Sex and Politics* (New York: New York University Press, 1993); Mira Morgenstern, *Rousseau and the Politics of Ambiguity: Self, Culture and Society* (University Park: Penn State University Press, 1996); Nicole Fermon, *Domesticating Passions: Rousseau, Woman and Nation* (Hanover, NH: University Press of New England, 1997); Lori Jo Marso, *(Un)Manly Citizens: Jean-Jacques Rousseau's and Germaine de Staël's Subversive Women* (Baltimore: Johns Hopkins University Press, 1999); Elizabeth Rose Wingrove, *Rousseau's Republican Romance* (Princeton: Princeton University Press, 2000).

12. For discussions of the influence of Rousseau's philosophy on family life, women's social roles, and children's education in late eighteenth-, early nineteenth-century continental Europe, Britain, and America, see the following: Jean Bloch, *Rousseauism and Education in Eighteenth-Century France* (Oxford: Oxford University Press, 1995); Blum, 45, 47, 235–37; Edward Duffy, *Rousseau in England: The Context for Shelley's Critique of the Enlightenment* (Berkeley: University of California Press, 1979), 9–31; Hunt 1992, 156; Linda Kerber, "The Republican Mother: Women and the Enlightenment—An American Perspective," *American Quarterly* 28:2 (1976), 187–205; Paul Merrill Spurlin, *Rousseau in America, 1760–1809* (Alabama: University of Alabama Press, 1969). For Burke's most prominent assessments of Rousseau, see the *Reflections,* and *A Letter to a Member of the National Assembly* (1791), in *Further Reflections on the Revolution in France*, ed. Daniel Ritchie (Indianapolis: Liberty Fund Press, 1992), 27–72 (hereafter cited as *National Assembly*). For evidence of Burke's exposure to Wollstonecraft and her writings, see "To Unknown, 26 January 1791" and "Letter to Mrs. John Crewe, 11 August 1795" in *The Correspondence of Edmund Burke*, ed. Thomas Copeland (Chicago: University of Chicago Press, 1967 and 1969), Vol. VI, 214 and Vol. VIII, 304. For the bulk of Wollstonecraft's references to Rousseau and Burke, see the *Rights of Men* and the *Rights of Woman*.

13. Even Locke, whose *Two Treatises of Government* attacked Filmer's defense of patriarchy and briefly and subtly supported a new, more egalitarian understanding of marriage and the parent-child relationship a century earlier than Wollstonecraft's *Rights of Woman*, still clung to the age-old, patriarchal notion that the husband—as "the abler and the stronger"—should take the decision-making role when two spouses disagreed about a matter of common

interest. John Locke, *Two Treatises of Government*, ed. Peter Laslett (Cambridge: Cambridge University Press, 1988), 321; Shanley, 89–90.

14. For Rousseau's reaction to women's movement into the public sphere, see *Letter to d'Alembert on the Theatre*, in *Politics and the Arts: Letter to d'Alembert on the Theatre*, tr. Allan Bloom (Glencoe: Free Press, 1960). For Burke's speech against the repeal of the 1753 Marriage Act in the House of Commons in 1781, see his "Speech on a Bill for the Repeal of the Marriage Act" in *The Works of the Right Honorable Edmund Burke* (Boston: Little Brown, 1868), Vol. VII, 132–136 (hereafter cited as *Marriage Act*). For Wollstonecraft's reaction to the legalization of divorce in France in 1792, see her final, incomplete novel, *The Wrongs of Woman, or Maria* (1798) in *The Works of Mary Wollstonecraft*, eds. Marilyn Butler and Janet Todd (New York: New York University Press, 1989), Vol. 1, 81–184 (hereafter cited as *Wrongs of Woman*). For historical studies of these events and social phenomena, see Landes 1988, Landes 2001, Outhwaite, and Phillips.

15. For example, Wollstonecraft cited Locke, Gregory, Fordyce, Rousseau, Macaulay, and Burke in the *Rights of Men* and the *Rights of Woman*; Rousseau cited Fleury, Fénelon, Locke, Montesquieu, and Crousaz in *Emile* and the *Social Contract*; and Burke cited Locke in *A Philosophical Enquiry into the Origin of our Ideas of the Sublime and the Beautiful*, Montesquieu and Rousseau in the *Reflections,* and Wollstonecraft in "Letter to Mrs. John Crewe, 11 August 1795."

16. Ellen McNiven Hine, "The Woman Question in Early Eighteenth-Century French Literature," *Studies in Voltaire and the Eighteenth Century* CXVI (Banbury, UK: The Voltaire Foundation, 1973), 65–79.

17. See note 12.

18. Jean-Jacques Rousseau, *Emile, or on Education,* tr. Allan Bloom (New York: Basic Books, 1978), 363 (hereafter cited as *Emile*); Jean-Jacques Rousseau, *Oeuvres Complètes*, eds. Bernard Gagnebin and Marcel Raymond (Paris: Librairie Gallimard, 1959), Vol. 4, 700 (hereafter cited as *Oeuvres*).

19. Edmund Burke, *Reflections on the Revolution in France*, ed. Conor Cruise O'Brien (New York: Penguin, 1986), 135 (hereafter cited as *Reflections*).

20. Ibid., 315.

21. Luke Gibbons, *Edmund Burke and Ireland: Aesthetics, Politics and the Colonial Sublime* (Cambridge: Cambridge University Press, 2003); Stephen K. White, *Edmund Burke: Modernity, Politics and Aesthetics* (Thousand Oaks, CA: Sage Publications, 1994), 60–79.

22. Francis Canavan, *The Political Reason of Edmund Burke* (Durham, NC: Duke University Press, 1960), 57, 75, 105, 126; C. P. Courtney, *Montesquieu and Burke* (Oxford: Blackwell, 1963), 41–43, 57, 148, 159, 181; Zillah Eisenstein, *The Radical Future of Liberal Feminism* (New York: Longman, 1981), 55–112; Charles Parkin, *The Moral Basis of Burke's Political Thought*

(Cambridge: Cambridge University Press, 1956), 86; Daniel Ritchie, "Desire and Sympathy, Passion and Providence: The Moral Imagination of Burke and Rousseau," *Burke and the French Revolution,* ed. Steven Blakemore (Athens: University of Georgia Press, 1992), 120–143; Peter Stanlis, *Edmund Burke: The Enlightenment and Revolution* (New Brunswick, NJ: Transaction Publishers, 1991), 159–191.

23. Barbara Taylor, "The Religious Foundations of Mary Wollstonecraft's Feminism" in *The Cambridge Companion to Mary Wollstonecraft,* ed. Claudia Johnson (Cambridge: Cambridge University Press, 2002), 99–118; Taylor 2003, 95–142; Eileen M. Hunt, "The Family as Cave, Platoon and Prison: The Three Stages of Wollstonecraft's Philosophy of the Family," *The Review of Politics* 64:1 (2002), 81–119.

24. Bonnie Anderson, *Joyous Greetings: The First International Women's Movement, 1830–1860* (Oxford: Oxford University Press, 2000), 10, 14, 54–55, 83; Eileen Hunt Botting and Christine Carey, "Wollstonecraft's Philosophical Impact on Nineteenth-Century American Women's Rights Advocates," *American Journal of Political Science* 48:4 (2004), 707–722.

25. Muthu, 260–266.

Notes to Chapter One

1. Wollstonecraft, "To Everina Wollstonecraft, Dublin, March 24, 1787," in *The Collected Letters of Mary Wollstonecraft,* ed. Ralph Wardle (Ithaca: Cornell University Press, 1979), 145.

2. Wollstonecraft, "To Gilbert Imlay, Paris, September 22, 1794." Ibid., 263.

3. *National Assembly,* 54.

4. Morgenstern, 4–5; Arthur Melzer, *The Natural Goodness of Man: On the System of Rousseau's Thought* (Chicago: University of Chicago Press, 1990), 7–8.

5. *National Assembly,* 52–53.

6. *Rights of Woman,* 114.

7. Rousseau himself repeatedly insisted that his entire corpus of writings represented a system of thought, in works such as his 12 January 1762 *Letter to Malesherbes,* his 1763 *Letter to Beaumont,* and his 1772 manuscript *Rousseau: Judge of Jean-Jacques* (Melzer, 4). Although the status of Rousseau's "intent" is contested, especially in the wake of postmodern literary theory, I am among those scholars who continue to see interpretive value in taking an author's declaration of his or her own intent at face value and using it as *one* stepping-stone, among many, to understanding dimensions of his or her thought more clearly.

8. There is a scholarly consensus that these works (perhaps with the addition of Rousseau's first major political essay, the 1749 *Discourse on the Sciences and the Arts,* or *First Discourse*) represent the heart of his mature

political theory. Many of his later works (*The Confessions* [completed 1765, published posthumously in 1782], *Rousseau: Judge of Jean-Jacques* [completed in 1772], and *The Reveries of the Solitary Walker* [completed in 1778, published in 1782]) are autobiographical. Other than the first part of the *Confessions*, they were not circulated during his lifetime and thus did not share the same immediate popular impact as his earlier works on European social and political life. Although some scholars (such as Christopher Kelly in *Rousseau's Exemplary Life* [Ithaca: Cornell University Press, 1987]) have argued for political readings of his autobiographical works, I focus on the theoretical works that explicitly deal with the relationship between the family and the state. It is interesting to note that the bulk of his major political writings deal explicitly with this topic. I do not include the *Discourse on the Sciences and the Arts* in my study of the early works that provide a philosophical foundation for Rousseau's theory of the relationship between the family and the state because the essay does not explicitly address this issue. Rousseau's other major and explicitly political work, the unpublished manuscript *Considerations on the Government of Poland* (1772), is his second attempt, after *Corsica*, to try to advise a nation on how to implement his theory of republicanism in its particular historical situation. Because I ultimately emphasize the fascinating textual links, as well as the philosophical overlap, between five key texts from the early 1760s that deal with the relationship between the family and the state, I do not include *Poland* in this study. Unlike Corsica, Poland does not receive a mention in the *Social Contract*, and thus falls outside the boundaries of my argument. A careful reading of *Poland*, however, reveals that Rousseau remains true to the principles of the *Social Contract* when advising this nation how to implement a republican constitution in less than ideal circumstances. A broader study could have fruitfully included it.

     9. Maurice Cranston, *The Solitary Self: Jean-Jacques Rousseau in Exile and Adversity* (Chicago: University of Chicago Press, 1997), xi–xii; Robert Wokler, *Rousseau: A Very Short Introduction* (Oxford: Oxford University Press, 2001), 13.

     10. Wokler, 19.

     11. Alice W. Harvey, "Introduction" to Jean-Jacques Rousseau, *Emile and Sophie, or Solitary Beings*, tr. Alice W. Harvey, in *Finding a New Feminism*, ed. Pamela Grande Jensen (New York: Rowman and Littlefield, 1996), 194.

     12. Frederick Watkins, "Editor's Introduction," in Jean-Jacques Rousseau, *Political Writings*, tr. and ed. Frederick Watkins (London: Thomas Nelson and Sons, 1953), xxxvii.

     13. Jean-Jacques Rousseau, *Julie, or the New Heloise*, trs. Philip Stewart and Jean Vaché (Hanover, NH: University Press of New England, 1997), 460–479, 578 (hereafter cited as *Julie*); *Oeuvres*, Vol. 2, 561–586, 704–706. *Emile*, 459–467; *Oeuvres*, Vol. 4, 837–849. Rousseau, *Emile and Sophie, or Solitary Beings*, in *Finding a New Feminism*, 198 (hereafter cited as *Emile and*

Sophie); *Oeuvres*, Vol. 4, 881–882. Rousseau, *Of the Social Contract*, in *The Social Contract and other later political writings*, ed. and tr. Victor Gourevitch (Cambridge: Cambridge University Press, 1997; reprint 2003), 78 (hereafter cited as *Social Contract*); *Oeuvres*, Vol. 3, 391.

14. Shklar, 214; Bloom 1979, 3–29; Melzer, 280.

15. Okin 1979, 99–194; Pateman 1988, 7, 9, 53–54, 86, 96–102; Pateman, *The Disorder of Women* (Stanford: Stanford University Press, 1989), 6.

16. Schwartz, 99–194; Weiss, 11; Morgenstern, 181–234; Fermon, 49–121; Marso, 7; Wingrove, 3–23.

17. While Schwartz defends this conception of marriage and the family as promoting "interdependence" between the sexes, Weiss argues that although Rousseau's theory of gender relations is internally consistent with his broader political thought, it is, from a feminist standpoint, inegalitarian and oppressive toward women. See Morgenstern,188n.

18. While Bloom briefly notes that *Julie, Emile,* and the *Social Contract* together provide "Rousseau's positive statement about the highest possibilities of society and the way to live a good life within it," he ultimately takes this argument in a different direction than I do by emphasizing the disconnect between Rousseau's theory of the family and the state, rather than their substantive interconnection. "Introduction," *Emile*, 29.

19. Rousseau, *Constitutional Project for Corsica*, in *Political Writings*, 285 (hereafter cited as *Corsica*); *Oeuvres*, Vol. 3, 907. *Rustique* can be translated as either "rustic" or "rural." While rural and rustic have essentially the same meaning in English, rustic is more limited and arcane in its connotation and usage in contemporary English (pertaining more to food, architecture, and "setting"), while rural is a more expansive in its connotation and usage (pertaining more to geography, demography, economics, and culture broadly speaking). Following Watkins's translation, I use "rural" to best capture Rousseau's meaning.

20. *Social Contract*, 73–78; *Oeuvres*, Vol. 3, 386–391.

21. Ibid., 78; *Oeuvres*, Vol. 3, 391.

22. Ibid., 79; *Oeuvres*, Vol. 3, 392–393.

23. Ibid., 76; *Oeuvres*, Vol. 3, 389.

24. Ibid., 79; *Oeuvres*, Vol. 3, 392. *Corsica*, 284; *Oeuvres*, Vol. 3, 906.

25. *Social Contract*, 79; *Oeuvres*, Vol. 3, 392.

26. Ibid., 78; *Oeuvres*, Vol. 3, 391.

27. *Corsica,* 330; *Oeuvres*, Vol. 3, 935.

28. Geneva existed as an independent Calvinist republican city-state from 1536 to 1792. It had an affiliation with (though not full membership in) the Swiss Confederation. The Valais, a rural and mountainous region southeast of Geneva, existed as an independent republican state, with a combination of aristocratic and democratic political institutions, during Rousseau's time. It also had an affiliation with, but not full membership in, the Swiss Confedera-

tion. Both Geneva and the Valais became cantons in the Swiss Confederation in 1813. The Vaud region of Switzerland, under the patrician administration of the city or canton of Berne, entered the Swiss Confederation in 1513. The Vaud region, like the Valais, contained a mixture of aristocratic and democratic political institutions. Rousseau was born and raised in Geneva (1712–1722), and visited the Valais and Vaud regions of Switzerland before the composition of his major political works. See Charles Gilliard, *A History of Switzerland*, tr. D.L.B. Hartley (London: George Allen and Unwin, 1955), 33–52. For Rousseau's celebration of the small city of Corte as the best capital for the proposed republic of Corsica, see *Corsica*, 292–293; *Oeuvres*, Vol. 3, 912.

    29. *Emile*, 363; *Oeuvres*, Vol. 4, 700.

    30. See note 12 in the introduction.

    31. Locke, *Some Thoughts Concerning Education,* in *Some Thoughts Concerning Education and Of the Conduct of the Understanding*, eds. Ruth Grant and Nathan Tarcov (Indianapolis: Hackett, 1996), 7–161; Locke, *Two Treatises of Government*, 303–330.

    32. *Emile*, 360; *Oeuvres*, Vol. 4, 697.

    33. Penny Weiss and Anne Harper, "Rousseau's Political Defense of the Sex-Roled Family," *Hypatia* 5 (Fall 1990), 102.

    34. Okin 1979, 99–194; Pateman 1989, 6.

    35. Bloom 1979, 3–29; Schwartz, 10–73; Allan Bloom, *Love and Friendship* (New York: Simon and Schuster, 1993), 39–156; Weiss and Harper, 91–111; Weiss, 54–89.

    36. Shklar, 214.

    37. Rousseau, *Discourse on Political Economy,* in *The Social Contract and other later political writings*, 3 (hereafter cited as *Political Economy)*; *Oeuvres*, Vol. 3, 241.

    38. Ibid., 5; *Oeuvres*, Vol. 3, 244.

    39. *Political Economy*, 5; *Oeuvres*, Vol. 3, 244.

    40. Ibid., 6; *Oeuvres*, Vol. 3, 244.

    41. Ibid., 20; *Oeuvres*, Vol. 3, 259.

    42. Ibid., 21; *Oeuvres*, Vol. 3, 260.

    43. Ibid., 15–16; *Oeuvres*, Vol. 3, 254–255.

    44. Ibid.,15; *Oeuvres*, Vol. 3, 254.

    45. Ibid., 22; *Oeuvres,* Vol. 3, 262.

    46. Rousseau, *Discourse on the Origin of Inequality,* in *Jean-Jacques Rousseau: The Basic Political Writings,* tr. Donald Cress (Indianapolis: Hackett, 1987), 48 (hereafter cited as *Second Discourse)*; *Oeuvres*, Vol. 3, 146–147.

    47. Ibid., 48; *Oeuvres*, Vol. 3, 147.

    48. Ibid., 60; *Oeuvres*, Vol. 3, 164.

    49. Ibid., 62; *Oeuvres*, Vol. 3, 167.

    50. Ibid., 62–63; *Oeuvres*, Vol. 3, 168.

    51. Schwartz, 10–73.

52. *Second Discourse*, 56; *Oeuvres*, Vol. 3, 157–158.

53. Ibid.; *Oeuvres*, Vol. 3, 158.

54. Ibid., 31–32; *Oeuvres*, Vol. 3, 119–120.

55. *Letter to d'Alembert on the Theatre*, 12; *Oeuvres*, Vol. 5, 102.

56. Ibid.,101; *Oeuvres*, Vol. 5, 93.

57. Pateman 1989, 21.

58. *Letter to d'Alembert on the Theatre*, 61; *Oeuvres*, Vol. 5, 56.

59. There were at least seventy-two French editions of *Julie* published in Europe during the eighteenth century. William Kenrick's 1761 English translation of *Julie, Eloisa*, went through fifteen editions before 1812. Jo-Ann E. McEachern, *Bibliography of the Writings of Jean Jacques Rousseau to 1800: Volume I, Julie, ou la Nouvelle Héloïse* (Oxford: The Voltaire Foundation Taylor Institution, 1993), 769–775; Philip Stewart, "Introduction," *Julie*, x.

60. William Mead, "*La Nouvelle Héloïse* and the Public of 1761," *Yale French Studies* 28 (1961), *Jean-Jacques Rousseau*, 18.

61. *Julie*, 16–17; *Oeuvres*, Vol. 2, 23.

62. Ibid., 16; *Oeuvres*, Vol. 2, 22.

63. *National Assembly*, 52; *Wrongs of Woman*, 95–96.

64. *Julie*, Appendix Three, 629–630.

65. See Trumbach.

66. Montesquieu's *Lettres Persanes*, Sophia's *Woman Not Inferior to Man* and *Women's Superior Excellence to Man*, and Richardson's *Clarissa* (1747–1748) are four prominent examples.

67. *Julie*, 294; *Oeuvres*, Vol. 2, 357.

68. Ibid., 306; *Oeuvres*, Vol. 2, 372.

69. Ibid., 66; *Oeuvres*, Vol. 2, 81.

70. Ibid., 67; *Oeuvres*, Vol. 2, 81–82.

71. Wingrove, 4–6, 232–235.

72. *Julie*, 305–306; *Oeuvres*, Vol. 2, 371.

73. Fermon,122–159.

74. Shklar, 23.

75. *Julie*, 544; *Oeuvres*, Vol. 2, 662.

76. *Julie*, 460–479, 578; *Oeuvres*, Vol. 2, 561–586, 704–706.

77. *Emile*, 459–467; *Oeuvres*, Vol. 4, 837–849.

78. See note 12 of the introduction.

79. For allegorical or philosophical readings of the *Emile*, see Bloom 1979, 15; Bloom 1993, 49–50; Schwartz, 10–73.

80. *Emile*, 360; *Oeuvres*, Vol. 4, 697.

81. For a discussion of the late eighteenth-century and early nineteenth-century ideal of the "domestic woman" that Rousseau in large part helped to create, see Gary Kelly's *Women, Writing and Revolution, 1790–1827* (Oxford: Clarendon Press, 1993), 3–29.

82. *Emile*, 199; *Oeuvres*, Vol. 4, 476.

83. Ibid., 40; *Oeuvres*, Vol. 4, 249–250.

84. Ibid., 40; *Oeuvres*, Vol. 4, 249.

85. Ibid., 40; *Oeuvres*, Vol. 4, 249.

86. Ibid., 448; *Oeuvres*, Vol. 4, 823.

87. Ibid., 474; *Oeuvres*, Vol. 4, 859.

88. Ibid., 473; *Oeuvres*, Vol. 4, 858.

89. Ibid., 474; *Oeuvres*, Vol. 4, 860.

90. Ibid., 475; *Oeuvres*, Vol. 4, 860.

91. Ibid., 474; *Oeuvres*, Vol. 4, 859.

92. Ibid., 474; *Oeuvres*, Vol. 4, 859–860.

93. *Social Contract*, 67; *Oeuvres*, Vol. 3, 380.

94. Ibid., 92; *Oeuvres*, Vol. 3, 406.

95. Ibid., 94; *Oeuvres*, Vol. 3, 407.

96. *Social Contract*, 93; *Oeuvres*, Vol. 3, 406–407.

97. Ibid., 101; *Oeuvres*, Vol. 3, 416.

98. *Emile*, 363; *Oeuvres*, Vol. 4, 700.

99. *Social Contract*, 105; *Oeuvres*, Vol. 3, 419–420.

100. Ibid., 112; *Oeuvres*, Vol. 3, 427.

101. *Emile*, 365; *Oeuvres*, Vol. 4, 703.

102. *Social Contract*, 81; *Oeuvres*, Vol. 3, 394.

103. Blum, 204–215; Hunt 1992, 151–191; Kerber 1976, 187–205; Landes 1988, 64–89.

104. Okin 1979, 194.

105. Steven Johnston, *Encountering Tragedy: Rousseau and the Project of Democratic Order* (Ithaca: Cornell University Press, 1999), 3–24.

106. *Julie*, 610; *Oeuvres*, Vol. 2, 743.

107. Starobinski, 99–150.

108. *Emile and Sophie*, 211; *Oeuvres*, Vol. 4, 898.

109. Marso, 29–78.

110. *Corsica*, 281; *Oeuvres*, Vol. 3, 904.

111. Ibid.

112. Ibid., 282; *Oeuvres*, Vol. 3, 904.

113. Ibid., 282–283; *Oeuvres*, Vol. 3, 905.

114. *Social Contract*, 104; *Oeuvres*, Vol. 3, 419.

115. *Corsica*, 283; *Oeuvres*, Vol. 3, 905.

116. Ibid.

117. Ibid., 283; *Oeuvres*, Vol. 3, 905.

118. *Corsica*, 283; *Oeuvres*, Vol. 3, 905.

119. Ibid., 299; *Oeuvres*, Vol. 3, 917.

120. Ibid.

121. Ibid., 300; *Oeuvres*, Vol. 3, 918.

122. Ibid., 301; *Oeuvres*, Vol. 3, 919.

123. Ibid., 302; *Oeuvres*, Vol. 3, 919.

124. Ibid., 316; *Oeuvres,* Vol. 3, 930.

125. Ibid., 286; *Oeuvres,* Vol. 3, 907.

126. Watkins, xxxvii–xxxviii.

127. See note 12 in introduction.

128. Shklar, 214.

129. James Miller, *Rousseau: Dreamer of Democracy* (New Haven: Yale University Press, 1984), 102–104.

130. Anonymous, "A Letter from M. Rousseau of Geneva to M. d'Alembert of Paris" and "Emilius and Sophia," in *The Annual Register* (London: J. Dodsley, 1810), Vol. 2 (1759), 479–484 and Vol. 5 (1762), 227–239, especially 227 and 238.

131. Rousseau, *The Confessions of Jean-Jacques Rousseau,* tr. J. M. Cohen (London: Penguin, 1971), 333; *Oeuvres,* Vol. 1, 357.

Notes to Chapter Two

1. Hunt 1992, 124.

2. *Reflections,* 135.

3. Ibid.

4. Ibid.

5. John Mullan, *Sentiment and Sociability: The Language of Feeling in the Eighteenth Century* (Oxford: Clarendon Press, 1988), 24.

6. *Emile,* 363; *Oeuvres,* Vol. 4, 700.

7. Boulton, 97–133; Blakemore 1988, 31–60; Zerilli 1994a, 60–94.

8. Alfred Cobban, *Edmund Burke and the Revolt against the Eighteenth Century* (London: George Allen & Unwin, 1929; reprint, New York: AMS Press, 1978), 11–96; Parkin, 30–53; Canavan 1960, 54–81; White, 5.

9. Conor Cruise O'Brien, *The Great Melody: A Thematic Biography of Edmund Burke* (Chicago: University of Chicago Press, 1992); Uday Singh Mehta, *Liberalism and Empire: A Study in Nineteenth-Century British Liberal Thought* (Chicago: University of Chicago Press, 1999), 2–3; David Bromwich, "Introduction," in Edmund Burke, *On Empire, Liberty and Reform: Speeches and Letters,* ed. David Bromwich (New Haven: Yale University Press, 2000), 1–39; Gibbons, 1–17.

10. Burke, *Letter to the Sheriffs of Bristol, on the Affairs of America,* in *The Works of the Right Honorable Edmund Burke,* Vol. II, 212 (hereafter cited as *Sheriffs*).

11. Burke, *Speech on Moving his Resolutions for Conciliation with the Colonies,* in *The Works of the Right Honorable Edmund Burke,* Vol. II, 106.

12. *Sheriffs,* 203.

13. Ibid.

14. Ibid., 212.

15. O'Brien, 3–86.

16. Burke, *Speech at the Guildhall in Bristol, Previous to the Late Election in that City,* in *The Works of the Right Honorable Edmund Burke,* Vol. II, 395 (hereafter cited as *Guildhall*).

17. *Guildhall,* 396.

18. The complete repeal of the Irish penal code or popery laws would not occur until 1829.

19. *Guildhall,* 404.

20. Stone 1990, 346–353.

21. Burke, *Speech on April 29, 1771,* in *The Writings and Speeches of Edmund Burke,* ed. Paul Langford (Oxford: Clarendon Press, 1981), Vol. II, 357.

22. Ibid., 357.

23. Outhwaite, 123–144.

24. Shelia Lambert, ed., "A Bill (with the amendments) to Amend an Act, Made in the Twenty-sixth Year of the Reign of his Late Majesty King George the Second, instituted, 'An Act for the better preventing of "Clandestine Marriages,"'" *House of Commons Sessional Papers of the 18th Century* (Delaware: SR, Inc., 1975), Bills 1780–81, Vol. 33, 245–248.

25. *Marriage Act,* 132.

26. Ibid.

27. Ibid.

28. Ibid.

29. Ibid., 134.

30. Ibid.

31. Ibid., 135.

32. Ibid.

33. *National Assembly,* 51–54; *Marriage Act,* 135.

34. *Marriage Act,* 136.

35. *Reflections,*194–195.

36. Frederick G. Whelan, *Edmund Burke and India* (Pittsburgh: University of Pittsburgh Press, 1996), 38. Although I preserve Burke's own spellings in quotations from his works, in my commentary I use the modern spellings of Burke's versions of Indian names and titles suggested by Whelan in *Edmund Burke and India,* xiii.

37. Ibid., 155–156.

38. Ibid., 159–160.

39. Burke, *Speech in Opening the Impeachment of Warren Hastings,* in *The Works of the Right Honorable Edmund Burke,* Vols. IX–X, 83 (hereafter cited as *Speech in Opening*).

40. Burke, *Speech in General Reply,* in *The Works of the Right Honorable Edmund Burke,* Vol. XI, 422 (hereafter cited as *General Reply*).

41. *Speech in Opening,* 23.

42. Burke, *Speech on Mr. Fox's East India Bill,* in *The Works of the Right Honorable Edmund Burke,* Vol. II, 476–477 (hereafter cited as *East India Bill*).

43. Ibid., 485.

44. Ibid., 488.

45. *General Reply,* 146.

46. David Hume, "Of Polygamy and Divorces," *Essays, Literary, Moral, and Political* (London: Ward, Lock and Co., 1870), 109–111; Adam Smith, *Lectures on Jurisprudence,* eds. R. L. Meek, D. D. Raphael, and P. G. Stein (Oxford: Clarendon Press, 1978), 150–159.

47. *Rights of Woman,* 170.

48. *Speech in Opening,* 380.

49. Ibid.

50. Ibid., 87.

51. *Speech in Opening,* 89.

52. Ibid.

53. J.G.A. Pocock, "Editor's Introduction," *Reflections on the Revolution in France* (Indianapolis: Hackett, 1987), xxxi.

54. Thomas Paine, *The Rights of Man, Part I, Thomas Paine: Political Writings,* ed. Bruce Kuklick (Cambridge: Cambridge University Press, 1989), 71.

55. Boulton,112.

56. *Rights of Men,* 17.

57. Zerilli, 1994a, 86; Ronald Paulson, *Representations of Revolution (1789–1820)* (New Haven: Yale University Press, 1983), 71, 65.

58. *Reflections,* 163.

59. Ibid.

60. Ibid., 164.

61. Ibid.

62. Duffy, 54–105.

63. *National Assembly,* 45.

64. Ibid., 47.

65. Ibid.

66. Ibid.

67. Ibid., 48.

68. Ibid., 49.

69. Ibid.

70. Ibid.

71. *National Assembly,* 49.

72. Ibid., 51.

73. Burke read Rousseau's *Social Contract.* Although he claimed in a 1790 letter that the work "left very few traces upon (his) mind" and that he considered it "a performance of little or no merit," we know that he at least gleaned a basic knowledge of Rousseau's concept of the general will, since he trounces it in *A Letter to a Member of the National Assembly. The Correspondence of Edmund Burke,* Vol. 6, 80–81; *National Assembly,* 51.

74. Burke was most likely familiar with one of the many late eighteenth-century editions of William Kenrick's 1761 English translation of Rousseau's *Julie*, which was retitled as *Eloisa: Or, a Series of Original Letters Collected and Published by J.J. Rousseau. Julie*, x, 650.

75. *National Assembly*, 51.

76. Ibid.

77. Ibid., 52.

78. Ibid.

79. Ibid.

80. Ibid., 53.

81. Ibid.

82. Ibid.

83. Ibid., 54.

84. Ibid.

85. Ibid., 55.

86. *Reflections*, 284.

87. Phillips, 1.

88. Burke, *The First Letter on a Regicide Peace*, in *The Works of the Right Honorable Edmund Burke*, Vol. V, 311 (hereafter cited as *First Letter*).

89. Ibid., 312.

90. Ibid.

91. Ibid., 313.

92. Ibid.

93. Ibid., 314.

94. Ibid.

95. See Phillips and Traer.

96. *First Letter*, 315.

97. Ibid.

98. Ibid.

99. Ibid., 312.

100. Burke, *The Fourth Letter on a Regicide Peace*, in *The Works of the Right Honorable Edmund Burke*, Vol. VI, 104 (hereafter cited as *Fourth Letter*).

101. *Reflections*, 181.

102. Burke, *An Appeal from the New to the Old Whigs*, in *Further Reflections on the Revolution in France*, 150 (hereafter cited as *Old Whigs*).

103. Burke, *A Letter to a Noble Lord* in *Further Reflections on the Revolution in France*, 323 (hereafter cited as *Noble Lord*).

104. Ibid., 322.

105. *Fourth Letter*, 106–107.

106. *Noble Lord*, 300.

Notes to Chapter Three

1. Canavan 1960, 85; Cobban 1929, 19, 37–71, 254–255; O'Brien, xxv; Parkin, 109–138; J.G.A. Pocock, *Politics, Language, Time* (New York: Atheneum, 1971), 232; Peter Stanlis, *Burke and the Natural Law* (Ann Arbor: University of Michigan Press, 1958), 29–84; White, 2–5.

2. White, 5.

3. Gibbons, 83–120. *Second Discourse*, 54–55; *Oeuvres*, Vol. III, 155–156.

4. Burke, *A Philosophical Enquiry into the Origin of our Ideas of the Sublime and the Beautiful,* ed. Adam Philips (Oxford: Oxford University Press, 1990), 37 (hereafter cited as *Enquiry*).

5. Ibid., 38.

6. Ibid., 39.

7. Kerber 1976, 187.

8. Linda Zerilli, "No Thrust, No Swell, No Subject? A Critical Response to Stephen K. White.*" Political Theory,* Vol. 22, No. 2 (May 1994), 323–328 (hereafter referred to as Zerilli 1994b).

9. *Enquiry*, 39.

10. Ibid., 40.

11. Laura Mulvey, "Visual Pleasure and Narrative Cinema," *Screen* 16 (3), Autumn 1975, 6–18.

12. *Enquiry*, 101.

13. Ibid.

14. Ibid., 43.

15. Ibid.

16. *Speech in Opening,* 341.

17. Claudia Johnson, *Equivocal Beings: Politics, Gender and Sentimentality in the 1790's* (Chicago: University of Chicago Press, 1995); 3; Andrew McCann, *Cultural Politics in the 1790's* (New York: St. Martin's Press, 1999), 51.

18. McCann, 37.

19. *Reflections*, 167–168.

20. Ibid., 168.

21. Cobban 1929, 107–111.

22. *Enquiry,* 45.

23. Ibid.

24. Ibid.

25. Ibid.

26. *First Letter,* 310.

27. Ibid., 317–318.

28. *Social Contract*, 81; *Oeuvres*, Vol. 3, 394. Montesquieu, *The Spirit of the Laws*, trs. A. Cohler, B. Miller, H. Stone (Cambridge: Cambridge University Press, 1995), 464.

29. *First Letter*, 319.
30. Burke, *A Letter to the Empress of Russia, November 1, 1791,* in *The Works of the Right Honorable Edmund Burke*, Vol. VI, 118.
31. *Reflections,* 59.
32. Ibid., 60.
33. Ibid., 63.
34. Ibid., 62.
35. Ibid., 67.
36. *Reflections*, 66.
37. Ibid., 67.
38. *Noble Lord,* 322.
39. *Reflections,* 69.
40. Ibid., 68.
41. Ibid., 121.
42. *Noble Lord,* 321.
43. Burke, *Letter to William Eliot,* in *The Works of the Right Honorable Edmund Burke*, Vol. 5, 127.
44. Hunt 1992, 89–123.
45. *Reflections*, 315.
46. Ibid.,135.
47. *General Reply,* 423.
48. *Fourth Letter,* 67.
49. *Reflections*, 196.
50. *Old Whigs*, 169.
51. Parkin, 30–82.
52. *Old Whigs,*161.
53. *Reflections,*120.
54. Ibid.
55. Ibid., 108.
56. Ibid., 109.
57. Ibid., 117.
58. *Reflections,* 140.
59. Ibid., 141.
60. Ibid., 274.
61. Ibid., 119.
62. Ibid., 194.
63. Ibid.
64. Ibid., 277.
65. Francis Canavan, *The Political Economy of Edmund Burke* (New York: Fordham University Press, 1995), 4–5.
66. Isaac Kramnick, *The Rage of Edmund Burke: Portrait of an Ambivalent Conservative* (New York: Basic Books, 1977), 3–11.
67. Zerilli 1994b.

Notes to Chapter Four

1. *Reflections,* 315; *Rights of Woman,* 256.
2. Gunther-Canada 2001, 3–12; *Rights of Woman,* 167.
3. Johnson, 25–29; Moira Gatens, "The Oppressed State of My Sex: Wollstonecraft on Reason, Feeling and Equality," in *Feminist Interpretations and Political Theory,* eds. Carole Pateman and Mary Shanley (Pennsylvania: Penn State Press, 1991), 115.
4. Sapiro, 258.
5. Kelly 1992, 140–170; Jennifer Lorch, *Mary Wollstonecraft: The Making of a Radical Feminist* (New York: Berg, 1990), 102; Laurie Langbauer, "Motherhood and Women's Writing in Mary Wollstonecraft's Novels," in *Romanticism and Feminism,* ed. Anne Mellor (Bloomington: Indiana University Press,1988), 208–219; Eisenstein, 89–108; Daniel Engster, "Mary Wollstonecraft's Nurturing Liberalism: Between an Ethic of Justice and Care," *American Political Science Review* 95:3 (September 2001), 577–588.
6. Sapiro, 16, 67, 257–59.
7. Moira Ferguson and Janet Todd, *Mary Wollstonecraft* (Boston: Twayne: 1984), 37, 53, 54, 72; Mary Poovey, *The Proper Lady and the Woman Writer* (Chicago: University of Chicago Press, 1984), 48.
8. Sapiro, xix–xxii.
9. Patricia Michaelson, "Religious Bases of Eighteenth-Century Feminism: Mary Wollstonecraft and the Quakers," *Women's Studies* 22:3 (1993), 288; G. J. Barker-Benfield, "Mary Wollstonecraft: Eighteenth-Century Commonwealthwoman," *Journal of the History of Ideas* 50:1 (1989), 97, 108; Melissa Butler, "Wollstonecraft versus Rousseau: Natural Religion and the Sex of Virtue and Reason," *Man, God, Nature and the Enlightenment,* ed. Donald Mell, Jr. (East Lansing, MI: Colleagues Press, 1988), 65–73.
10. Emma Rauschenbusch-Clough, *A Study of Mary Wollstonecraft and the Rights of Woman* (London: Longmans, Green and Co, 1898), 46–66; Elizabeth Pennell, *Mary Wollstonecraft* (Boston: Roberts Brothers, 1884; reprint, 1888), 352.
11. Hunt 2002, 81–119.
12. Taylor, "For the Love of God: Religion and the Erotic Imagination in Wollstonecraft's Feminism," in *Mary Wollstonecraft and 200 Years of Feminisms,* ed. Elaine Yeo (London: Rivers Oram Press, 1997), 15–35; Taylor 2003, 95–142. She focuses on the "Rational Dissenting Christian" basis of the bulk of Wollstonecraft's writings in Taylor 2002, 99–118.
13. About fifty biographies of Wollstonecraft have been written so far.
14. William Godwin, *Memoirs of the Author of A Vindication of the Rights of Woman* (London: Joseph Johnson, 1798); Pennell; Ralph Wardle, *Mary Wollstonecraft: A Critical Biography* (Lawrence: University of Kansas Press, 1951); Eleanor Flexner, *Mary Wollstonecraft: A Biography* (New York:

Coward, McCann & Geohegan, 1972); Claire Tomalin, *The Life and Death of Mary Wollstonecraft* (London: Weidenfeld and Nelson, 1974); Janet Todd and Marilyn Butler, "Introduction," *The Works of Mary Wollstonecraft*, Vol. I, 7–30; Lorch; Janet Todd, *Mary Wollstonecraft: A Revolutionary Life* (New York: Columbia University Press, 2001); Lyndall Gordon, *Vindication: A Life of Mary Wollstonecraft* (New York: HarperCollins, 2005).

15. Taylor 2003, 103, 108–109, 127.

16. See *The Book of Common Prayer*, "Articles of Religion" (London: His Majesty's Printer, 1731), 1–3.

17. Augustine, *City of God*, trs. G. Walsh, D. Zema, G. Monahan, D. Honan (New York: Image Books, 1958). Augustine is cited in *The Book of Common Prayer*'s "Articles of Religion," 3.

18. Taylor 2003, 111.

19. Ibid., 110.

20. Wollstonecraft, *The Cave of Fancy*, in *The Works of Mary Wollstonecraft*, Vol. 1, 192.

21. Ibid., 196.

22. Ibid., 198.

23. Ibid., 206.

24. Ibid.

25. *The Book of Common Prayer*, "Articles of Religion," 2.

26. Wollstonecraft, *Mary, a Fiction*, in *The Works of Mary Wollstonecraft*, Vol. 1, 8 (hereafter cited as *Mary*).

27. Ibid., 22.

28. *Mary*, 55.

29. Ibid., 30.

30. *Rights of Men*, 23.

31. *Mary*, 42.

32. Ibid., 11.

33. Ibid., 16.

34. Ibid., 17; *The Book of Common Prayer*, "Articles of Religion," 1–3.

35. *Mary*, 27.

36. Ibid., 29.

37. Ibid., 36.

38. Ibid., 50–51.

39. Ibid., 52.

40. Ibid., 73.

41. Ibid., 62.

42. Wollstonecraft, *Thoughts on the Education of Daughters*, in *The Works of Mary Wollstonecraft*, Vol. 4, 41 (hereafter cited as *Thoughts*).

43. See John 8:12–13; Luke 8:16–18; Mark 4:21–26; Matthew 25:1–13.

44. Wollstonecraft, *Original Stories from Real Life*, in *The Works of Mary Wollstonecraft*, Vol. 4, 360 (hereafter cited as *Stories*).

45. Ibid., 338.
46. Moira Ferguson and Janet Todd, *Mary Wollstonecraft* (Boston: Twayne, 1984), 21–22; Poovey, 55.
47. *Thoughts*, 31.
48. *Thoughts*, 11.
49. Ibid., 34.
50. Ibid., 22.
51. Ibid., 42.
52. Ibid., 41.
53. Ibid., 47.
54. Ibid., 40.
55. Ibid., 24.
56. Ibid., 43.
57. Ibid., 44.
58. Ibid.
59. *Stories*, 361.
60. Orm Mitchell, "Blake's Subversive Illustrations to Wollstonecraft's Stories," *Mosaic* 17:4 (1984), 17–34.
61. *Stories*, 405.
62. Flexner, 96.
63. *Rights of Woman*, 84.
64. Ibid., 94, 111.
65. Ibid., 236.
66. Rauschenbusch-Clough, 46–66.
67. James Hoecker, *Joseph Priestley and the Idea of Progress* (New York: Garland Publishing, Inc., 1987), 28–67.
68. D. O. Thomas, *The Honest Mind: The Thought and Work of Richard Price* (Oxford: Clarendon Press, 1997), 19–40.
69. Hoecker, 122–169.
70. *Rights of Men*, 40.
71. Ibid., 31.
72. Ibid., 40.
73. Ibid., 7.
74. Ibid., 54.
75. Ibid., 18.
76. Ibid.
77. Ibid., 40.
78. Ibid., 12.
79. Ibid., 26.
80. Ibid., 55.
81. *Rights of Woman*, 81.
82. *Rights of Men*, 55.
83. Ibid., 56.

84. Daniel Robinson, "Theodicy versus Feminist Strategy in Mary Wollstonecraft's Fiction," *Eighteenth-Century Fiction* 9:2 (1997), 183–202.

85. *Rights of Men*, 55.

86. Ibid., 61.

87. Ibid., 16.

88. Ibid.

89. *Rights of Men*, 57.

90. Ibid., 34.

91. Ibid., 7.

92. Ibid., 13.

93. Ibid.

94. Ibid.

95. Ibid., 64.

96. *Rights of Woman*, 263.

97. Ibid., 95.

98. Ibid., 235.

99. Ibid., 240.

100. Ibid., 275.

101. Ibid., 99–101.

102. Ibid., 247.

103. Ibid., 245.

104. Wollstonecraft, *Letter on the Present Character of the French Nation*, in *The Works of Mary Wollstonecraft*, Vol. 6, 445.

105. Wollstonecraft, *A Historical and Moral View of the Origin and Progress of the French Revolution*, in *The Works of Mary Wollstonecraft*, Vol. 6, 159.

106. Wollstonecraft, *Letters Written during a Short Residence in Sweden, Norway and Denmark* (Lincoln: University of Nebraska Press, 1976), 197 (hereafter cited as *Letters Written*).

107. Ibid., 198.

108. Ibid., 102.

109. *Letters Written*, 179–180.

110. Taylor 2003, 127.

111. *Letters Written*, 125–126.

112. Ibid., 80.

113. Rauschenbusch-Clough, 66.

114. *Wrongs of Woman*, 146.

115. Ibid., 88.

116. Ibid., 153–154.

117. Ibid., 154.

118. Ibid., 134.

119. Ibid., 167.

120. McCann, 165; Johnson, 69.

121. Todd 1992, vii; Langbauer, 208–219.

122. William Godwin, ed., *Lessons*, in *The Works of Mary Wollstonecraft*, Vol. 4, 468; Gordon, *Vindication*, 353–354.

123. Wollstonecraft, *Lessons*, 470.

124. Wollstonecraft, *Letters on the Management of Infants*, in *The Works of Mary Wollstonecraft*, Vol. 4, 459.

125. Ibid.

Notes to Chapter Five

1. *Rights of Woman*, 89.

2. Ibid.

3. *Rights of Men*, 14.

4. Ibid., 45.

5. *National Assembly*, 48.

6. Duffy, 42–53.

7. Ritchie; Stanlis 1991, 159–191; Courtney, 41–43, 57, 148, 159, 181; Canavan, 1960, 57, 75, 105, 126; Parkin, 86.

8. Annie Osborn, *Rousseau and Burke: A Study of the Idea of Liberty in Eighteenth Century Thought* (London: Oxford University Press, 1940); David Cameron, *The Social Thought of Rousseau and Burke* (London: Weidenfeld and Nicholson, 1973); Cobban 1929; Alfred Cobban, *Rousseau and the Modern State* (London: Random House, 1964).

9. See also Johnson, 32–33.

10. See also Kelly 1992, 84–102, and Bromwich 1995.

11. *Rights of Men*, 8–9.

12. Ibid., 15.

13. Ibid., 23.

14. Ibid., 21–23.

15. Ibid., 22.

16. Ibid., 23.

17. Ibid., 21.

18. Ibid., 9.

19. Ibid., 22.

20. Ibid., 60.

21. Ibid., 61.

22. Ibid., 60.

23. *Rights of Woman*, 138.

24. *Rights of Woman*, 91.

25. Ibid., 113.

26. *Enquiry*, 37–39.

27. *Rights of Men*, 47.

28. Ibid., 48.

29. Ibid., 23.
30. Ibid., 25.
31. Ibid.
32. *Rights of Woman*, 117 and 267–268.
33. Ibid., 109.
34. Ibid., 267.
35. Ibid., 110.
36. Ibid., 113.
37. Ibid., 122.
38. Ibid., 113 and 135. *Rights of Men*, 48.
39. *Rights of Woman*, 95.
40. Ibid., 99.
41. Ibid., 170.
42. Ibid., 117.
43. Ibid., 136.
44. *Emile*, 363; *Oeuvres*, Vol. IV, 700.
45. *Reflections*, 135.
46. *Rights of Woman*, 256.
47. *Rights of Woman*, 149.
48. Ibid., 22.
49. Ibid.
50. Ibid., 242.
51. Ibid., 249.
52. Ibid., 243.
53. Ibid., 244.
54. Ibid.
55. Ibid., 243.
56. Ibid., 274–275.
57. *Social Contract*, 129; *Oeuvres*, Vol. 3, 446.
58. Ibid.
59. *Rights of Woman*, 256.
60. Ibid., 257.
61. Robert Putnam, *Bowling Alone* (New York: Simon & Schuster, 2000); Peter Berkowitz, *Virtue and the Making of Modern Liberalism* (Princeton: Princeton University Press, 1999).
62. Stephen Macedo, *Liberal Virtues* (New York: Oxford University Press, 1990); William Galston, *Liberal Purposes* (Cambridge: Cambridge University Press, 1991).
63. Anderson, 10, 14, 54–55, 83; Botting and Carey.
64. Taylor 2004, 23, 101.
65. Ibid., 147.
66. Ibid., 104–107.
67. *Social Contract*, 41; *Oeuvres*, Vol. 3, 351.

Bibliography

Anderson, Bonnie. *Joyous Greetings: The First International Women's Movement, 1830–1860* (Oxford: Oxford University Press, 2000).

Ariès, Phillipe. *Centuries of Childhood: A Social History of Family Life,* tr. Robert Baldick (New York: Vintage, 1962).

Augustine. *City of God,* trs. Gerald Walsh, Demetrius Zema, Grace Monahan, and Daniel Honan (New York: Image Books, 1958).

Bannet, Eve Tavor. *The Domestic Revolution: Enlightenment Feminisms and the Novel* (Baltimore: Johns Hopkins University Press, 2000).

Barker-Benfield, G. J. "Mary Wollstonecraft: Eighteenth-Century Commonwealthwoman," *Journal of the History of Ideas* 50:1 (1989), 95–115.

Berkowitz, Peter. *Virtue and the Making of Modern Liberalism* (Princeton: Princeton University Press, 1999).

Blakemore, Steven. *Burke and the Fall of Language* (Hanover, NH: University Press of New England, 1988).

Bloch, Jean. *Rousseauism and Education in Eighteenth-Century France* (Oxford: Oxford University Press, 1995).

Bloom, Allan. "Introduction," in *Emile, or on Education,* ed. and tr. Allan Bloom (New York: Basic Books, 1979), 3–29.

———. *Love and Friendship* (New York: Simon and Schuster, 1993).

Blum, Carol. *Rousseau and the Republic of Virtue* (Ithaca: Cornell University Press, 1986).

Botting, Eileen Hunt, and Carey, Christine. "Wollstonecraft's Philosophical Impact on Nineteenth-Century American Women's Rights Advocates," *American Journal of Political Science* 48:4 (October 2004), 707–722.

Boulton, James. *The Language of Politics in the Age of Wilkes and Burke* (London: Routledge and Kegan Paul, 1963).

Bromwich, David. "Introduction," in Edmund Burke, *On Empire, Liberty and Reform: Speeches and Letters,* ed. David Bromwich (New Haven: Yale University Press, 2000), 1–39.

239

———— "Wollstonecraft as a Critic of Burke," *Political Theory* 23:4 (1995), 617–634.

Burke, Edmund. *The Correspondence of Edmund Burke*, ed. Thomas Copeland (Cambridge: Cambridge University Press, 1958–1978).

————. *Further Reflections on the Revolution in France*, ed. Daniel Ritchie (Indianapolis: Liberty Fund Press, 1992).

— *An Appeal from the New to the Old Whigs*, 73–201.

— *A Letter to a Member of the National Assembly*, 27–72.

— *A Letter to a Noble Lord*, 277–326.

————. "A Letter from M. Rousseau of Geneva to M. d'Alembert of Paris" and "Emilius and Sophia," in *The Annual Register* (London: J. Dodsley, 1810), Vol. 2 (1759), 479–484 and Vol. 5 (1762), 227–239.

————. *A Philosophical Enquiry into the Origin of our Ideas of the Sublime and the Beautiful*, ed. Adam Philips (Oxford: Oxford University Press, 1990).

————. *Reflections on the Revolution in France*, ed. Conor Cruise O'Brien (London: Penguin, 1986).

————. *Speech on April 29, 1771*, in *The Writings and Speeches of Edmund Burke*, ed. Paul Langford (Oxford: Clarendon, 1981), Vol. II, 357–359.

————. *The Works of the Right Honorable Edmund Burke* (Boston: Little Brown, 1868), Vols. I–XII.

— *Fourth Letter on the Proposals for Peace with the Regicide Directory of France*, Vol. VI, 3–112.

— *A Letter to the Empress of Russia*, Vol. VI, 113–119.

— *A Letter to the Sheriffs of the City of Bristol, on the Affairs of America*, Vol. II, 187–245.

— *Letter to William Eliot*, Vol. 5, 107–129.

— *Speech at the Guildhall in Bristol, Previous to the Late Election in that City*, Vol. II, 367–424.

— *Speech in General Reply*, Vol. XI, 157–445.

— *Speech in Opening the Impeachment of Warren Hastings*, Vols. IX–X, 329–493, 3–145.

— *Speech on a Bill for the Repeal of the Marriage Act*, Vol. VII, 131–142.

— *Speech on Moving his Resolutions for Conciliation with America*, Vol. II, 99–186.

— *Speech on Mr. Fox's East India Bill*, Vol. II, 433–542.

— *Three Letters on the Proposals for Peace with the Regicide Directory of France, Vol. V, 233–508*, Vol. VI, 9–112.

Butler, Marilyn, and Todd, Janet. "Introduction," in *The Works of Mary Wollstonecraft* (New York: New York University Press, 1989), 7–28.

Butler, Melissa. "Wollstonecraft versus Rousseau: Natural Religion and the Sex of Virtue and Reason," in *Man, God, Nature and the Enlightenment,* ed. Donald Mell, Jr. (East Lansing, MI: Colleagues Press, 1988), 65–73.

Cameron, David. *The Social Thought of Rousseau and Burke* (London: Weidenfeld and Nicholson, 1973).

Canavan, Francis. *The Political Economy of Edmund Burke* (New York: Fordham University Press, 1995).

————. *The Political Reason of Edmund Burke* (Durham: Duke University Press, 1960).

Chapman, Richard Allen. "Leviathan Writ Small: Thomas Hobbes on the Family," *The American Political Science Review* 69:1 (1975), 76–90.

Cobban, Alfred. *Edmund Burke and the Revolt against the Eighteenth Century* (London: George Allen and Unwin, 1929; reprint, New York: AMS Press, 1978).

————. *Rousseau and the Modern State* (London: Random House, 1964).

Courtney, C. P. *Montesquieu and Burke* (Oxford: Blackwell, 1963).

Cranston, Maurice. *The Solitary Self: Jean-Jacques Rousseau in Exile and Adversity* (Chicago: University of Chicago Press, 1997).

Cressy, David. *Birth, Marriage and Death: Ritual and the Life-Cycle in Tudor and Stuart England* (Oxford: Oxford University Press, 1997).

Duffy, Edward. *Rousseau in England: The Context for Shelley's Critique of the Enlightenment* (Berkeley: University of California Press, 1979).

Eisenstein, Zillah. *The Radical Future of Liberal Feminism* (New York: Longman, 1981).

Engster, Daniel. "Mary Wollstonecraft's Nurturing Liberalism: Between an Ethic of Justice and Care," *American Political Science Review* 95:3 (September 2001), 577–588.

Ferguson, Moira, and Todd, Janet. *Mary Wollstonecraft* (Boston: Twayne, 1984).

Fermon, Nicole. *Domesticating Passions: Rousseau, Woman and Nation* (Hanover, NH: University Press of New England, 1997).

Flexner, Eleanor. *Mary Wollstonecraft: A Biography* (New York: Coward, McCann & Geohegan, 1972).

Galston, William. *Liberal Purposes* (Cambridge: Cambridge University Press, 1991).

Gatens, Moira. "The Oppressed State of My Sex: Wollstonecraft on Reason, Feeling and Equality," in *Feminist Interpretations and Political Theory,* eds. Carole Pateman and Mary Shanley (University Park: Penn State Press, 1991), 112–127.

Gibbons, Luke. *Edmund Burke and Ireland: Aesthetics, Politics and the Colonial Sublime* (Cambridge: Cambridge University Press, 2003).

Gilliard, Charles. *A History of Switzerland*, tr. D.L.B. Hartley (London: George Allen and Unwin, 1955).

Godwin, William. *Memoirs of the Author of A Vindication of the Rights of Woman* (London: Joseph Johnson, 1798).

Gordon, Lyndall. *Vindication: A Life of Mary Wollstonecraft* (New York: HarperCollins, 2005).

Gunther-Canada, Wendy. *Rebel Writer: Mary Wollstonecraft and Enlightenment Politics* (De Kalb: Northern Illinois University Press, 2001).

Hine, Ellen McNiven. "The Woman Question in Early Eighteenth-Century French Literature," *Studies in Voltaire and the Eighteenth Century* CXVI (Banbury, UK: The Voltaire Foundation, 1973), 65–79.

Hoecker, James. *Joseph Priestley and the Idea of Progress* (New York: Garland Publishing, Inc., 1987).

Houlbrooke, Ralph. *Death, Religion and the Family in England, 1480–1750* (Oxford: Clarendon Press, 1998).

———. *The English Family, 1450–1700* (London: Longman, 1984).

Hume, David. *Essays, Literary, Moral and Political* (London: Ward, Lock and Co., 1870).

Hunt, Eileen M. "The Family as Cave, Platoon, and Prison: The Three Stages of Wollstonecraft's Philosophy of the Family," *The Review of Politics* 64:1 (2002), 81–119.

Hunt, Lynn. *The Family Romance of the French Revolution* (Berkeley: University of California Press, 1992).

Johnson, Claudia. *Equivocal Beings: Politics, Gender and Sentimentality in the 1790s* (Chicago: University of Chicago Press, 1995).

Johnston, Steven. *Encountering Tragedy: Rousseau and the Project of Democratic Order* (Ithaca: Cornell University Press, 1999).

Kelly, Christopher. *Rousseau's Exemplary Life* (Ithaca: Cornell University Press, 1987).

Kelly, Gary. *Revolutionary Feminism: The Mind and Career of Mary Wollstonecraft* (London: Macmillan, 1992).

———. *Women, Writing and Revolution* (New York: Oxford University Press, 1993).

Kerber, Linda. "The Republican Mother: Women and the Enlightenment—An American Perspective," *American Quarterly* 28:2 (Summer 1976), 187–205.

———. *Women of the Republic: Intellect and Ideology in Revolutionary America* (Chapel Hill: University of North Carolina Press, 1980).

Kramnick, Isaac. *The Rage of Edmund Burke: Portrait of an Ambivalent Conservative* (New York: Basic Books, 1977).

Lambert, Shelia, ed. "A Bill (with the amendments) to Amend the Act, Made in the Twenty-Sixth Year of the Reign of his Late Majesty King

George the Second, instituted, 'An Act for the better preventing of "Clandestine Marriages."'" *House of Commons Sessional Papers of the 18ᵗʰ Century* (Wilmington, Delaware: Scholarly Resources, 1975), Bills 1780–81, Vol. 33, 245–248.

Landes, Joan. *Gender, Representation and Revolution in Eighteenth-Century France* (Ithaca: Cornell University Press, 2001).

———. *Women and the Public Sphere in the Age of the French Revolution* (Ithaca: Cornell University Press, 1988).

Langbauer, Laurie. "Motherhood and Women's Writing in Mary Wollstonecraft's Novels," in *Romanticism and Feminism*, ed. Anne Mellor (Bloomington: Indiana University Press, 1988), 208–219.

Locke, John. *Some Thoughts Concerning Education*, in *Some Thoughts Concerning Education and Of the Conduct of the Understanding*, eds. Ruth Grant and Nathan Tarcov (Indianapolis: Hackett, 1996).

———. *Two Treatises of Government*, ed. Peter Laslett (Cambridge: Cambridge University Press, 1991).

Lorch, Jennifer. *Mary Wollstonecraft: The Making of a Radical Feminist* (New York: Berg, 1990).

Macedo, Stephen. *Liberal Virtues* (New York: Oxford University Press, 1990).

Macfarlane, Alan. *Marriage and Love in England: Modes of Reproduction, 1300–1840* (Oxford: Blackwell, 1986).

Marso, Lori Jo. *(Un)Manly Citizens: Jean-Jacques Rousseau and Germaine de Staël's Subversive Women* (Baltimore: The Johns Hopkins University Press, 1999).

McCann, Andrew. *Cultural Politics in the 1790s* (New York: St. Martin's Press, 1999).

McEachern, Jo-Ann E. *Bibliography of the Writings of Jean Jacques Rousseau to 1800: Volume I, Julie, ou la Nouvelle Héloïse* (Oxford: The Voltaire Foundation Taylor Institution, 1993).

———. Mead, William. "*La Nouvelle Héloïse* and the Public of 1761," *Yale French Studies* 28 (1961), *Jean-Jacques Rousseau*, 13–19.

Mehta, Uday Singh. *Liberalism and Empire* (Chicago: University of Chicago Press, 1999).

Melzer, Arthur. *The Natural Goodness of Man: On the System of Rousseau's Thought* (Chicago: University of Chicago Press, 1990).

Michaelson, Patricia. "Religious Bases of Eighteenth-Century Feminism: Mary Wollstonecraft and the Quakers," *Women's Studies* 22:3 (1993), 281–295.

Miller, James. *Rousseau: Dreamer of Democracy* (New Haven: Yale University Press, 1984).

Mitchell, Orm. "Blake's Subversive Illustrations to Wollstonecraft's Stories," *Mosaic* 17 (1984), 17–34.

Montesquieu, Charles Louis de Secondat. *The Spirit of the Laws*, trs. Anne Cohler, Basia Miller, and Harold Stone (Cambridge: Cambridge University Press, 1995).

Morgenstern, Mira. *Rousseau and the Politics of Ambiguity* (University Park: Pennsylvania State University Press, 1996).

Mullan, John. *Sentiment and Sociability: The Language of Feeling in the Eighteenth Century* (Oxford: Clarendon Press, 1988).

Multiple Authors. *The Book of Common Prayer* (London: His Majesty's Printer, 1731).

Mulvey, Laura. "Visual Pleasure and Narrative Cinema," *Screen 16* (3), Autumn 1975, 6–18.

Muthu, Sankar. *Enlightenment against Empire* (Princeton: Princeton University Press, 2003).

O'Brien, Conor Cruise. *The Great Melody: A Thematic Biography of Edmund Burke* (Chicago: University of Chicago Press, 1992).

Okin, Susan. "Women and the Making of the Sentimental Family,"*Philosophy and Public Affairs* 11:1 (1982), 65–88.

———. *Women in Western Political Thought* (Princeton: Princeton University Press, 1979; reprint 1992), 99–194.

Osborne, Annie. *Rousseau and Burke: A Study of the Idea of Liberty in Eighteenth-Century Thought* (London: Oxford University Press, 1940).

Outhwaite, R. B. *Clandestine Marriage in England, 1500–1850* (London: Hambeldon Press, 1995).

Paine, Thomas. *The Rights of Man, Part I,* in *Thomas Paine: Political Writings*, ed. Bruce Kuklick (Cambridge: Cambridge University Press, 1989).

Parkin, Charles. *The Moral Basis of Burke's Political Thought* (Cambridge: Cambridge University Press, 1956).

Pateman, Carole. *Participation and Democratic Theory* (Cambridge: Cambridge University Press, 1970).

———. *The Disorder of Women* (Stanford: Stanford University Press, 1989).

———. *The Sexual Contract* (Stanford: Stanford University Press, 1988).

Paulson, Ronald. *Representations of Revolution (1789–1820)* (New Haven: Yale University Press, 1983).

Pennell, Elizabeth. *Mary Wollstonecraft Godwin* (Boston: Roberts Brothers, 1884; reprint, 1888).

Pfeffer, Jacqueline. "The Family in John Locke's Political Thought," *Polity* 33:4 (2001), 593–618.

Phillips, Roderick. *Family Breakdown in Late Eighteenth-Century France: Divorces in Rouen, 1792–1803* (Oxford: Clarendon Press, 1980).

Pocock, J.G.A. "Introduction," in Edmund Burke, *Reflections on the Revolution in France*, ed. J.G.A. Pocock (Cambridge: Hackett, 1987), vii–lvi.

————. *Politics, Language, Time* (New York: Atheneum, 1971).

Poovey, Mary. *The Proper Lady and the Woman Writer* (Chicago: University of Chicago Press, 1984).

Putnam, Robert. *Bowling Alone* (New York: Simon and Schuster, 2000).

Rauschenbusch-Clough, Emma. *A Study of Mary Wollstonecraft and the Rights of Woman* (London: Longmans, Green and Co., 1898).

Rawls, John. *A Theory of Justice* (Cambridge: Belknap Press, 1971).

Ritchie, Daniel. "Desire and Sympathy, Passion and Providence: The Moral Imaginations of Burke and Rousseau," in *Burke and the French Revolution*, ed. Steven Blakemore (Athens: University of Georgia Press, 1992), 120–143.

Robinson, Daniel. "Theodicy versus Feminist Strategy in Mary Wollstonecraft's Fiction," *Eighteenth-Century Fiction* 9 (1997), 183–202.

Rousseau, Jean-Jacques. *The Basic Political Writings of Jean-Jacques Rousseau*, tr. Donald Cress (Indianapolis: Hackett, 1987).
— *Discourse on the Origin and the Foundations of Inequality among Men, 33–109.*
— *Letter to the Republic of Geneva, 25–32.*

————. *The Confessions of Jean-Jacques Rousseau*, tr. J. M. Cohen (London: Penguin, 1971).

————. *Constitutional Project for Corsica*, in *Political Writings*, tr. and ed. Frederick Watkins (London: Thomas Nelson and Sons, 1953), 277–330.

————. *Emile and Sophie, or Solitary Beings*, tr. Alice W. Harvey, in *Finding a New Feminism*, ed. Pamela Jensen (New York: Rowman and Littlefield, 1996), 193–235.

————. *Emile, or on Education*, tr. Allan Bloom (New York: Basic Books, 1979).

————. *Julie, or the New Heloise*, trs. Philip Stewart and Jean Vaché (Hanover, NH: University Press of New England, 1997).

————. *Letter to d'Alembert on the Theatre*, tr. Allan Bloom, in *Politics and the Arts: Letter to d'Alembert on the Theatre* (Glencoe: Free Press, 1960).

————. *Oeuvres Complètes*, eds. Bernard Gagnebin and Marcel Raymond (Paris: Librairie Gallimard, 1959), vols. 1–5.

————. *The Social Contract and other later political writings*, ed. and tr. Victor Gourevitch (Cambridge: Cambridge University Press, 1997; reprint 2003).
— *Discourse on Political Economy, 3–38.*
— *Of the Social Contract, 39–152.*

Sapiro, Virginia. *A Vindication of Political Virtue: The Political Theory of Mary Wollstonecraft* (Chicago: University of Chicago Press, 1992).

Schaub, Diana. *Erotic Liberalism: Women and Revolution in Montesquieu's Persian Letters* (Lanham, MD: Rowman and Littlefield, 1995).

Schwartz, Joel. *The Sexual Politics of Jean-Jacques Rousseau* (Chicago: University of Chicago Press, 1984).

Shanley, Mary. "Marriage Contract and Social Contract in Seventeenth-Century English Political Thought," *The Western Political Quarterly* 32:1 (1979), 79–91.

Shklar, Judith. *Men and Citizens: A Study of Rousseau's Social Theory* (Cambridge: Cambridge University Press, 1969).

Smith, Adam. *Lectures on Jurisprudence*, eds. R. L. Meek, D. D. Raphael, and P. G. Stein (Oxford: Clarendon Press, 1978).

Spurlin, Paul Merrill. *Rousseau in America, 1760–1809* (Tuscaloosa: University of Alabama Press, 1969).

Stanlis, Peter. *Burke and the Natural Law* (Ann Arbor: University of Michigan Press, 1958).

———. *Edmund Burke: The Enlightenment and Revolution* (Brunswick, NJ: Transaction, 1991).

Starobinski, Jean. *Jean-Jacques Rousseau: la transparence et l'obstacle* (Paris: Plon, 1957).

Stewart, Philip. "Introduction," in Jean-Jacques Rousseau, *Julie, or the New Heloise*, trs. Philip Stewart and Jean Vaché (Hanover, NH: University Press of New England, 1997), ix–xxi.

Stone, Lawrence. *Road to Divorce: England, 1530–1987* (Oxford: Oxford University Press, 1990).

———. *The Family, Sex and Marriage in England, 1500–1800* (London: Weidenfeld and Nelson, 1977).

Tadmor, Naomi. *Family and Friends in Eighteenth-Century England: Household, Kinship and Patronage* (Cambridge: Cambridge University Press, 2001).

Taylor, Barbara. "For the Love of God: Religion and the Erotic Imagination in Wollstonecraft's Feminism" in *Mary Wollstonecraft and 200 Years of Feminisms*, ed. Elaine Yeo (London: Rivers Oram Press, 1997), 15–35.

———. *Mary Wollstonecraft and the Feminist Imagination* (Cambridge: Cambridge University Press, 2003).

———. "The Religious Foundations of Mary Wollstonecraft's Feminism," *The Cambridge Companion to Mary Wollstonecraft*, ed. Claudia Johnson (Cambridge: Cambridge University Press, 2002), 99–118.

Taylor, Charles. *Modern Social Imaginaries* (Durham: Duke University Press, 2004).

Thomas, D. O. *The Honest Mind: The Thought and Work of Richard Price* (Oxford: Clarendon Press, 1997).

Todd, Janet. "Introduction," in *Mary, Maria and Matilda* (New York: New York University Press, 1991), xii–xxiii.

———. *Mary Wollstonecraft: A Revolutionary Life* (New York: Columbia University Press, 2001).

Tomalin, Claire. *The Life and Death of Mary Wollstonecraft* (London: Weidenfeld and Nelson, 1974).

Traer, James. *Marriage and the Family in Eighteenth-Century France* (Ithaca: Cornell University Press, 1980).

Trumbach, Randolph. *The Rise of the Egalitarian Family: Aristocratic Kinship and Domestic Relations in Eighteenth-Century England* (New York: Academic Press, 1978).

Wardle, Ralph. *Mary Wollstonecraft: A Critical Biography* (Lawrence: University of Kansas Press, 1951).

Watkins, Frederick. "Editor's Introduction," in Jean-Jacques Rousseau, *Political Writings*, tr. and ed. Frederick Watkins (London: Thomas Nelson and Sons, 1953), ix–xxxviii.

Weiss, Penny. *Gendered Community: Rousseau, Sex and Politics* (New York: New York University Press, 1993).

Weiss, Penny, and Harper, Anne. "Rousseau's Political Defense of the Sex-Roled Family," *Hypatia* 5 (Fall 1990), 99–111.

Whelan, Frederick G. *Edmund Burke and India* (Pittsburgh: University of Pittsburgh Press, 1996).

White, Stephen K. *Edmund Burke: Modernity, Politics and Aesthetics* (Thousand Oaks, CA: Sage, 1994).

Wingrove, Elizabeth Rose. *Rousseau's Republican Romance* (Princeton: Princeton University Press, 2000).

Wokler, Robert. *Rousseau: A Very Short Introduction* (Oxford: Oxford University Press, 2001).

Wollstonecraft, Mary. *The Collected Letters of Mary Wollstonecraft*, ed. Ralph Wardle (Ithaca: Cornell University Press, 1979).

———. *Letters Written during a Short Residence in Sweden, Norway and Denmark*, ed. Carol Poston (Lincoln: University of Nebraska Press, 1976).

———. *A Vindication of the Rights of Men and A Vindication of the Rights of Woman*, ed. Sylvana Tomaselli (Cambridge: Cambridge University Press, 1995).

———. *The Works of Mary Wollstonecraft*, eds. Marilyn Butler and Janet Todd (New York: New York University Press, 1989), Vols. I–VI.

— *The Cave of Fancy*, Vol. I, 191–206.

— *A Historical and Moral View of the Origin and Progress of the French Revolution*, Vol. VI, 15–235.

— *Lessons*, Vol. IV, 467–474.

— *Letter on the Present Character of the French Nation*, Vol. VI, 443–446.

— *Letters on the Management of Infants*, Vol. IV, 459.

— *Mary, a Fiction*, Vol. I, 5–73.

— *Original Stories from Real Life*, Vol. IV, 359–450.

— *Thoughts on the Education of Daughters*, Vol. IV, 5–49.

— *The Wrongs of Woman, or Maria*, Vol. I, 81–184.

Wrightson, Keith. *English Society: 1580–1680* (New Brunswick, NJ: Rutgers University Press, 1982).

Zerilli, Linda. "No Thrust, No Swell, No Subject? A Critical Response to Stephen K. White," *Political Theory* 22 (May 1994), 323–328.

———. *Signifying Woman: Culture and Chaos in Rousseau, Burke and Mill* (Ithaca: Cornell University Press, 1994).

Index